W9-CBP-025

BABYLONIANS

PEOPLES OF THE PAST

BABYLONIANS

H.W.F. SAGGS

University of California Press
Berkeley · Los Angeles

To my mother,
wife
and daughters,
in gratitude

University of California Press
Berkeley and Los Angeles, California

Published by arrangement with British Museum Press

First paperback printing 2000

ISBN 0-520-20222-8

Set in Goudy Old Style by Create Publishing Services
Printed in Great Britain by The Bath Press, Bath

9 8 7 6 5 4 3 2 1

Contents

Preface

IN THE 1840s the first major British archaeologist of Mesopotamia, Henry Austen Layard, was able to say, with little exaggeration, that twenty years earlier 'a case [in the British Museum] scarcely three feet square enclosed all that remained, not only of the great city, Nineveh, but of Babylon itself.' By the end of the nineteenth century the pioneer work of Layard and his successors and of French colleagues, soon followed by German and American scholars, had brought to the museums of Europe and the United States a great richness of data on the civilisation of ancient Mesopotamia back to the third millennium BC, with hundreds of thousands of clay tablets inscribed in two languages – one previously unsuspected – which had been dead for respectively two thousand and four thousand years.

During the twentieth century, collaboration by archaeologists from many nations has greatly increased the range of archaeological evidence, while work by linguists has gradually unlocked the secrets of the tablets, until today the historical record for some periods of ancient Mesopotamia is substantially better than for some centuries of Europe in the Christian era. Gaps and uncertainties do indeed remain, hopefully to be resolved by later discoveries, but it is now possible to offer a picture of the development of Mesopotamian civilisation, one of the main sources of our own, from before the beginning of the third millennium BC. It is this picture – at some points necessarily in very broad terms, at others in more detail – which I have attempted to depict in this book. Much relates to material in the British Museum, which houses one of the world's finest assyriological collections.

I am glad to have the opportunity of expressing my thanks to the Authors' Foundation, administered by the Society of Authors, for a grant to enable me to visit Berlin for the purpose of seeing the important assyriological collection in the Vorderasiatisches Museum.

H. W. F. Saggs
Long Melford, Suffolk, August 1994

Chapter One

THE REDISCOVERY
OF BABYLONIA

BABYLON (ANCIENT BABIL) stands with Athens and Rome as a cultural ancestor of Western civilisation. It was founded in the third millennium on the Euphrates in what is now Iraq, and in the early second millennium became capital of the south of the country, which was henceforth called, as one of its names, 'the land of Babil', Babylonia. In the strict sense, therefore, it is anachronistic to speak of Babylonia or Babylonians before the early second millennium. However, most of the features which characterised the Babylonian way of life, such as writing and cities and written laws, had their origins during the late fourth and the third millennia, which makes a good case for the land being regarded as Babylonia and its people as proto-Babylonians from a much earlier date.

The term 'Iraq' has political and nationalist overtones which make it inappropriate in most contexts when speaking of ancient civilisation. An older and more relevant name for the region is Mesopotamia, a term of Greek origin, meaning 'between the rivers'.[1] The rivers in question are the Tigris and the Euphrates; both of them rise in the mountains of eastern Turkey, to flow roughly south or south-east for respectively 2033 and 2720 km (1263 and 1690 miles) before joining with the Karun from south-west Iran to form the Shatt al-Arab, which empties into the Persian Gulf.

The Euphrates and Tigris provide south Mesopotamia with an easy communication system in a region bounded to the west by desert and to the east by mountains. To the north-west, towards present-day Aleppo, the Euphrates comes within little more than 160 km (100 miles) of the Mediterranean by an easy route which, except in high summer, is adequately watered throughout. The valleys of several tributaries further extend lines of communication; the most important are the two Zab rivers and the Diyala feeding into the Tigris, and the Habur into the Euphrates. Important also is the valley of the Karun river, which until the tenth century AD had a joint estuary with the Karkheh. From prehistoric times this river system and its valleys have given south-west Iran a close geographical and cultural link with south Mesopotamia, important in ancient history, and still reflected today in the name Arabistan, implying 'Arab land', used as an alternative designation for the province of south-west Iran which the Iranians call Khuzestan.

Mesopotamia has a natural northern boundary; this lies where the two rivers emerge from the foothills of the eastern Taurus, just north of an arc running from Urfa (ancient Harran) in Turkey to Mosul (ancient Nineveh) in Iraq. The land divides naturally into northern and southern sectors, which from the second millennium were known as Assyria and Babylonia. The region along the valley of the Karun and the southern section of the Karkheh was called Elam or Susiana. In this book we apply the names Assyria and Babylonia to all periods, regardless of an element of anachronism.

North and south Mesopotamia differ both in climate and in natural resources. The north has stone and various minerals, and much of it enjoys rainfall normally sufficient to grow crops of corn. Southern Mesopotamia, beginning at about Hit on the Euphrates and north of Baghdad on the Tigris, comprises the delta of the two rivers. Everywhere the soil is alluvial silt, stone is wholly lacking until well out into the western desert, and the rainfall, at less than 150 mm (6 in) per year, is inadequate to support permanent vegetation cover. However, because of the rivers the region is not totally arid. The river fringes are well watered and productive, with belts of willow and poplar and dense thickets of tall grass, rushes and tamarisk and other undergrowth. Between Nasariyah on the Euphrates and Amara on the Tigris there is a vast region of marsh, with beds of giant reeds, and lakes full of fish and water birds. Wherever canals are cut from the rivers for irrigation, vegetation can be lush. But such luxuriance is the exception, and today the greater part of the region is, unless irrigated, desert except for a brief carpet of verdure from spring storms. Yet it was here, in a region barely twice the size of Yorkshire and smaller than New Jersey, that civilisation began.

The ruins of most of the earliest cities lie in regions which are now markedly arid, and one may wonder how civilisation could begin in such adverse conditions. It fact, it did not; every ancient city of south Mesopotamia originally lay on a major channel or stream of the Euphrates, which has since shifted.

Shifting channels are a feature of the hydrology of the Euphrates. The river is slow moving, with a very shallow fall in its lower reaches. In consequence, the silt it brings down from the mountains tends to settle on its bed, constantly raising its level. During spring floods silt also builds up on the banks of the river, raising their level likewise. This process gradually raises the whole river, until it stands above the plain through which it flows. Sooner or later the river bursts its banks and floods out. Although a trickle may remain in the old course, the main flow finds a new lower bed, and the cycle begins again.

Finds of Palaeolithic stone tools in north Iraq proves the presence of humans there from about 100,000 BC, and small camps or settlements from about 9000 BC show the early stages of a change from total dependence on hunting and gathering, towards the domestication of animals and exploitation of cereal plants. We do not know when the first humans arrived in south Mesopotamia. Archaeology can trace farming settlements there only from the mid-sixth millennium, but it could have been the haunt of hunters, fishers and nomadic pastoralists many millennia earlier, without their leaving evidence traceable by present archaeological techniques.

Because of the behaviour of the Euphrates over the preceding millennia, the first human comers would have found a region much more inviting and less arid than now. Besides several major channels of the Euphrates (there were still at least three in the third millennium), there would have been many minor streams and ditches, and swamps like the present southern marshlands. Such conditions produced more vegetation than now, so that the region was not only highly favourable for hunting, fishing and cattle rearing, but also offered easy possibilities for any settlers who brought with them a tradition of growing grain crops; they had only to sow their grain on the dry levees of former river-banks, and it would produce crops with minimal further attention until harvest. As population increase called for bigger harvests, the settlers could easily increase the area of cornland by digging ditches to drain strips of wet land, and using those ditches – primitive canals – to bring water to further strips of land which were otherwise too dry. These were small beginnings, but they began the process which over the millennia gave the world such great ancient cities, known from the Bible, as Uruk (Erech of Genesis 10:10), Ur of the Chaldees and Babylon.

The Bible ensured that the memory of the civilisation of ancient Mesopotamia was never entirely lost; through it the names of Babylon, Nineveh and Ur of the Chaldees remain symbols as powerful as Athens and Rome. Classical writers also played their part. Herodotus in the fifth century BC paid a visit to Babylonia for material for his *Histories*,[2] and was followed in the next century by Alexander the Great. So great an impression did Babylon make upon Alexander, that he conceived the plan of adopting it as the capital of his world empire. He actually began rebuilding its great ziggurat (stepped tower), a monument of the type remembered in the Bible as the Tower of Babel, but had only reached the preparatory stage of dismantlement when he died.

This was the end of Babylon as a capital city. Alexander's successor Seleucus replaced it by a new foundation on the Tigris, and later conquerors followed his lead. But the memory of Babylon's site and greatness was never lost. A mound in the extreme north of the ruins always retained the name Babil, and several early Islamic geographers, such as the tenth-century Ibn Hawkal, described the remains of the city. Biblical associations gave Mesopotamia an interest for Europeans, so that some early pilgrims included it in their itineraries. The earliest to leave a written record of this was a Spanish Jew, Benjamin of Tudela, in the twelfth century. He visited the ruins of Babylon, estimating their circumference as thirty *myl*, equivalent to about 24 km (15 miles), which, if one includes areas of rubble beyond the ancient walls, is not far out. Benjamin saw the Tower of Babel in the massive ruins of the ziggurat of Borsippa (Birs Nimrud) on the other side of Hillah (see pl. 1).

The high Renaissance saw an increasing interest in the ancient world, and from the sixteenth century onwards a number of European travellers visited Mesopotamia, bringing back accounts of its antiquities. The first, so far as we know, to interest himself in the ancient writing of the region was an Italian, Pietro della Valle. In a letter in 1621 he gave copies of some of the signs, composed of groups of wedges, and in 1625 he was commenting on wedge-shaped inscriptions on bricks he had collected from ruins at a site identified centuries later as ancient Ur. There was a Latin-derived word 'cuneiform' which the science of Anatomy already used to express the sense 'wedge-shaped', and from 1700 this was adopted as the standard term in English for this kind of writing. Germans called it *Keilschrift* ('wedge-writing').

The first traveller to publish cuneiform inscriptions in a form which could serve as a basis for decipherment was a Dane, Carsten Niebuhr, in 1774–8. His inscriptions came not from Mesopotamia itself but from the site of ancient Persepolis in south-west Persia (now Iran). Although all the signs in these inscriptions were cuneiform, they were of three different kinds. Niebuhr recognised that these must represent three distinct writing systems, one of which, because of the small number of its signs, must be alphabetic.[3] A distinguished orientalist named Friedrich Münter, another Dane, agreed, and went on to argue that the second script, which had too many signs for an alphabet, must be syllabic, and that the third, with still more signs, must contain ideograms, that is, symbols representing complete words. Münter showed on historical grounds that the inscriptions probably derived from the Old Persian royal house of the Achaemenids (sixth to fourth centuries BC).

Hard on the heels of Münter's observations came a breakthrough in the decipherment of the alphabetic cuneiform script. The credit for this lay with a young German grammar-school master, Georg Friedrich Grotefend, of Göttingen. Grotefend, following Münter's assumption about the historical setting of these inscriptions, worked on the correct hypothesis that the alphabetic script had been used to write Old Persian, a language already known. By 1802 he was able to assign accurate values to eleven signs, and to recognise certain words and personal names.

Completion of what Grotefend had begun took several decades, with scholars of various nations playing honourable parts. The major figure in the final step was an Englishman, Henry Creswicke Rawlinson, whose professional circumstances gave him the advantage of access to texts unavailable to others. Rawlinson, an excellent linguist, was an intelligence officer in the East India Company in India, and in 1835 was posted as a military adviser to Persia. There he spent his spare time copying ancient rock inscriptions. In 1837, working on two short inscriptions he had copied near Hamadan, he noticed that they were virtually identical except for two groups of signs in each, of which the second group in one inscription corresponded to the first group in the other. He correctly deduced that these groups were royal Achaemenid names, and that the duplicated group represented the current king in one inscription and the father of the current king in the other. This enabled him to identify three royal names, as Grotefend had earlier done, and in part to solve the alphabet. But to advance beyond the point Grotefend had reached required longer texts. These were available. By far the longest of the trilingual inscriptions was high up on a cliff face at Bisitun (sometimes called Behistun), near Kermanshah, and these Rawlinson now copied. At the end of 1843 he was appointed British Resident and Consul in Baghdad, but continued his researches. By 1845 he had completed the decipherment of the Old

Persian alphabetic script, and in 1847 was able to publish a complete translation of the Persian of the Bisitun inscription, with commentary and alphabet.

With one version of a major trilingual translated, there was now hope of breaking the two other cuneiform scripts. One of the scripts, with 111 signs, proved to be a syllabic system for writing Elamite, an ancient language of south-west Iran. Relatively few texts are extant in this system, and its decipherment is not relevant for Babylonian history. The script of greatest importance was the third, which Rawlinson referred to, not inaccurately in the context in which he was researching, as 'the Babylonian writing'. The very large number of signs in this system made it clear that it must have contained ideograms as well as syllograms. We now know that it was used from the mid-third millennium to the time of Christ to write the Semitic language today called Akkadian,[4] of which the two principal dialects were Babylonian and Assyrian.

Rawlinson now set himself to decipher this script. By the autumn of 1846 he could make out the sense (with about fifty per cent accuracy) of the cuneiform on bricks of Nebuchadnezzar from Babylon. He was fortunate in that from the end of 1845 he had large amounts of new inscriptions at his disposal from the very productive excavations which had just begun at Nimrud in Assyria (see p. 13). Yet the basic key remained the long trilingual inscription at Bisitun, and in summer 1847 Rawlinson was there again, making at some risk to life and limb a more accurate copy of the Babylonian version.

Rawlinson was not alone; scholars in Europe were also working on the decipherment. One of the most able was an Irish orientalist, Edward Hincks. In some respects he was ahead of Rawlinson, who as late as 1850 still thought that the Babylonian script might contain alphabetic elements.[5] It was also Hincks who first recognised that the cuneiform script must have been invented for a non-Semitic language. Another scholar who made some important contributions was the linguist and ethnologist Edwin Norris, assistant secretary – later librarian – of the Royal Asiatic Society, who saw Rawlinson's edition of the Bisitun inscription through the press and later published the first Assyrian Dictionary. Others who contributed included Jules Oppert in France, and W. H. Fox Talbot, famous in another field as a pioneer of photography.

By the early 1850s all these scholars were claiming an approximate understanding of relevant texts. To test these claims, the Royal Asiatic Society in 1857 requested Rawlinson, Hincks and Oppert to translate independently a text which Fox Talbot had already dealt with. When the results of the four scholars were compared, the large measure of agreement proved that 'Babylonian' cuneiform had indeed been deciphered.

The earliest excavations

Some early travellers had brought back mementoes from Mesopotamia, but nothing meriting the name of archaeology took place there until the nineteenth century. The first to attempt a dig was a certain Claudius James Rich. Rich was a brilliant young Englishman with a flair for oriental languages, who in 1808, when still not twenty-four, had been appointed by the East India Company as its Resident in Baghdad, a post of considerable commercial and political consequence. In 1811 he spent ten days in the ruins of Babylon, surveying the whole site and making excavations. He paid a second visit in 1817, and on each occasion published a memoir. A poem by Byron reflects the stir these publications made in England, when it speaks of

> ... Some infidels, who don't
> Because they can't, find out the very spot
> Of that same Babel, or because they won't
> (Though Claudius Rich, esquire, some bricks has got,
> And written lately two memoirs upon't).

Rich died of cholera in 1820, and his finds from Babylon, together with antiquities he had collected at Nineveh, went to the British Museum, where they formed the most important ancient Mesopotamian collection yet known in Europe (see fig. 1).

In the twenty years after Rich's death, a number of travellers explored south Mesopotamian sites, including Babylon, but there was no excavation of importance. Serious archaeology in Mesopotamia began in the early 1840s. Although the main impetus was antiquarian curiosity, the course of events was coloured by political rivalry between France and Great Britain. Until the Suez canal was opened in 1869, the main route to India, other than the long sea voyage round Africa, passed through Mesopotamia, then part of the Ottoman Empire, making it important to European powers. Great Britain had dominant commercial and political influence in Baghdad and Basra, and in 1842, to counterbalance this, the French Government opened a consulate in Mosul. They appointed to it Paul-Emile Botta, a physician and botanist[6] with considerable experience in Arab countries.

There was an understanding that Botta should use the opportunity of his appoint-

1 *One of the Babylonian finds of C. J. Rich, donated to the British Museum after his death, to form the nucleus of its present major assyriological collection.*

ment to make archaeological researches. Across the Tigris from Mosul is the huge mound of Kuyunjik, which we now know was ancient Nineveh. Botta began by opening trenches here, but because he was not digging deeply enough he found nothing more than a few bricks and fragments of alabaster with cuneiform inscriptions. Early in 1843 he heard of the finding of sculptured slabs at Khorsabad, 22 km (14 miles) to the north-east, and transferred his attention there. Almost at once he found important bas-reliefs and inscriptions. The French Government promptly gave him financial and diplomatic support, which enabled him to continue, despite the local opposition which his spectacular success had stirred up.

Henry Austen Layard now comes on the scene (see fig. 2). A young Englishman interested in foreign travel, he had, after qualifying as an attorney in 1839, set out overland with the intention of practising in Ceylon. But en route he became fascinated with the peoples of the Orient and its ancient monuments, and got no further than Persia. Finally in 1842 he decided to return home, and had travelled as far as Constantinople (Istanbul) when circumstances brought him into contact with the British Ambassador there, Sir Stratford Canning. The astute Canning recognised the potential value of Layard's acumen and considerable first-hand knowledge of the Near and Middle East, and gave him employment as a private secretary, using him on unofficial fact-finding missions.

Layard had had the ambition to excavate in north Mesopotamia before Botta ever arrived in Mosul,[7] and now took the opportunity to engage Canning's interest. By autumn 1845 he had persuaded Canning to subsidise him privately for two months or so of excavation. As his primary site, Layard chose Nimrud, a mound 12 m (40 ft) high and some 24 ha (60 acres) in extent 32 km (20 miles) south of Mosul. Beginning work on 9 November, he had immediate success, finding cuneiform inscriptions, bas-reliefs, carved ivories and huge limestone winged bulls.

Like Botta, Layard encountered local obstruction, but Sir Stratford Canning dealt with this. He enjoyed considerable influence in the Ottoman capital, and in the summer of 1846 was able to transmit to Layard a vizirial letter, 'authorising the continuation of the excavations and the removal of such objects as might be discovered.' Layard had already been opening other large mounds in the district, and now, despite attempted interference from the French consul who had succeeded Botta, he undertook a brief exploratory dig at Kuyunjik.

Canning now arranged that the British Museum should take over responsibility for the excavations, with Layard as their agent, backed by official funds. With Hormuzd Rassam, a native Christian, as his assistant, he continued excavation at Nimrud, finding inter alia further important bas-reliefs, copper and iron armour, vases of alabaster and glass, and marble human-headed lions and other large sculptures.

Layard had already dispatched two loads of his smaller finds to London, and early in 1847 he organised the removal of two of the most spectacular large items, a colossal bull and lion, floating them down to Baghdad on rafts, from where they were taken by native boats to Basra, for transshipment to England.

2 *Sir Henry Austen Layard, father of assyriology.*

Layard also made a brief exploratory dig at another site which was to prove of the highest importance. This was Kalah Shergat, the site of Ashur, the ancient religious capital of Assyria. He still had some money remaining, so he now returned to Kuyunjik for a more extensive dig. Within a month he had explored nine chambers, finding a wealth of bas-reliefs, mainly scenes of war; there were also winged bulls 5 m (16 ft) high, and clay tablets with cuneiform inscriptions. After his departure, a close friend of his, Henry James Ross, a British merchant, kept the excavations going on a small scale.

Layard's finds, including bas-reliefs and the colossal stone lion and bull, were on display in the British Museum by August 1847. They created an enormous sensation, to which their biblical relevance – nothing less than the rediscovery of the Assyrians – made no small contribution. Layard himself, back in England from July 1847, was lionised, and his account of his excavations, published in the form of a travel journal, became a best-seller. He also published a volume of the principal cuneiform texts, and drawings of his principal finds. The University of Oxford recognised his achievements by awarding him the degree of DCL, and he was given an official appointment to an Anglo-Russian commission set up to delineate the frontiers between the Ottoman and Persian empires. However, on the advice of Sir Stratford Canning, he quickly resigned the latter, to become an attaché (unpaid) at the embassy in Constantinople.

Layard undertook a second expedition in 1848–51. This time his principal excavations were at Kuyunjik, although he also did some further work at Nimrud, and when circumstances permitted extended his efforts to other sites, including Babylon and Nippur in the south. His finds at Kuyunjik were spectacular; they included a group of ten colossal bulls which formed the grand entrance to a palace, as well as some fine bas-reliefs depicting battle scenes, among them the siege of biblical Lachish by Sennacherib (2 Kings 18:13–17). But the most important find was a major archive of cuneiform tablets. This was part of a library collected by Assyrian kings, chiefly Ashurbanipal in the seventh century BC; Layard's successor, Hormuzd Rassam, excavated the rest of it in 1853, and these tablets, now in the British Museum, remain one of the most important sources for cuneiform studies. Layard prophetically said of them: 'They furnish us with materials for the complete decipherment of the cuneiform character, for restoring the language and history of Assyria, and for inquiring into the customs, sciences, and ... literature, of its people.'[8]

After 1851 Layard abandoned archaeology for politics, leaving his former assistant, Hormuzd Rassam, to continue the work on behalf of the British Museum.

Excavations in Babylonia

The earliest major archaeology in Mesopotamia was exclusively in Assyria, although Rawlinson had made small-scale excavations in some southern sites in his quest for inscribed objects to assist in decipherment of cuneiform. Between 1849 and 1855 W. K. Loftus, a geologist attached to the Anglo-Russian Boundary Commission, examined and in some cases undertook limited excavation at several southern sites; among them were Nuffar (ancient Nippur), Muqayyar (ancient Ur), Abu Shahrain (ancient Eridu), Warka (ancient Uruk, Erech of Genesis 10:10), Tell Sifr and Senkereh, as well as Susa in Elam (south-west Iran). His most productive work was at Senkereh, where he unearthed important royal inscriptions and found inscribed bricks which enabled the site to be identified as ancient Larsa; according to some scholars, although the majority dissent, the latter was the Ellasar of Genesis 14:1. At Tell Sifr, since identified as ancient Kutalla, Loftus found a large collection of copper vessels and tools, and about a hundred cuneiform tablets.

The French government now began to show an interest in south Mesopotamia, and supported an expedition which in 1852 undertook several months of not very productive work at Babylon, with briefer periods at Birs Nimrud (ancient Borsippa) and Al-Ukhaimir (ancient Kish). With the encouragement of Rawlinson, J. E. Taylor, British consul at Basra, carried out two seasons of digging at Muqayyar (1854 and 1855), finding inscriptions which proved it to be the ruins of ancient Ur. Other southern sites which he briefly examined included Abu Shahrain (Eridu) and Tell Al-Lahm.

In 1855 Rawlinson returned to England, where he devoted himself to the translation and publication of cuneiform texts. This was the aspect of Mesopotamian studies which was now attracting most attention, and there was no further excavation of significance in south Mesopotamia for two decades. Archaeology resumed in 1877, when Ernest de Sarzec, French consul in Basra, began digging at a site at Tello (since identified as ancient Girsu), where Arabs had been finding statuary and cuneiform tablets. The results from his first two seasons of work were impressive, opening a new dimension in ancient Mesopotamian history. The style of the statuary and the script on cuneiform tablets showed them to be much earlier than those from sites hitherto excavated; de Sarzec had in fact pushed history back to the third millennium. Altogether de Sarzec undertook eleven campaigns, the last in 1900, in the course of which he excavated tens of thousands of clay tablets; illicit digging in his absence produced many more. Other French archaeologists continued his work at the site from 1903–9 and 1929–33.

The discovery of Sumerian

The tablets found by de Sarzec were of great importance. Not only were they significant for history, but also they were written almost exclusively in a language whose existence no one had suspected until 1850. The third form of cuneiform on the Bisitun inscriptions (see pp. 10 and 142) – at that time called Babylonian – had been deciphered on the correct assumption that the language was Semitic, but as early as 1850 the astute Hincks had recognised from the phonology that this writing system could not have been invented for a Semitic language. As the contents of the Kuyunjik library began to be deciphered, it became apparent that some whole texts, and portions of others, were written in an unknown language which was not of the Semitic group. Some of the Kuyunjik texts listed cuneiform signs with the 'Babylonian' pronunciation in one column and the pronunciation in the unknown language in another. Others gave grammatical forms in 'Babylonian', with equivalents in the unknown language. This made possible the first steps in the analysis of the mystery language.

From the second millennium onwards, one of the titles often applied to rulers of south Mesopotamia was 'king of Sumer and Akkad'. This suggested that Babylonia originally consisted of two parts designated by these names, whose peoples spoke different languages, one called Sumerian and the other Akkadian. In 1855 Hincks suggested (wrongly) that Akkadian was the name of the unknown language; by 1869 the French scholar Oppert had recognised that its correct name was Sumerian.

Doubts about the non-Semitic cuneiform language went beyond its name. A French scholar, Joseph Halévy, challenged its very existence, arguing that it was no more than a cryptographic system for writing Babylonian, used by the priests to give their texts a certain mystique. Accumulating evidence proved him wrong about Sumerian as a language, but behind his linguistic arguments were wider issues: in part he was opposing the idea that the creation of ancient Mesopotamian civilisation was due to a distinct race called Sumerians, and in this his views were not without substance (see p. 29).

The Old Testament and cuneiform studies

By 1870 the literal truth of the Bible was beginning to come under attack from the critical researches of Old Testament scholars, and the finding of cuneiform studies, with their confirmation of such biblical records as Sennacherib's attack on Jerusalem, were welcome to traditionalists as an ally against disbelief. A young bank note engraver, George Smith, was so interested in such links that he spent his spare time studying relevant material in the British Museum. This led to his being appointed an assistant to copy tablets for publication. He worked to such good effect that in 1872 he was able to announce to the Society of Biblical Archaeology an exciting discovery: he had found the counterpart of the biblical Flood story on a broken tablet. So great was national interest that the *Daily Telegraph* promptly put up the money for Smith to go out to Mesopotamia to seek the rest of the tablet. Remarkably he succeeded. By the end of the decade cuneiform studies were so well established in the consciousness of the English-speaking world that Gilbert and Sullivan's *Pirates of Penzance*, first produced in 1880, has the omniscient Major-General Stanley singing the topical line: 'I can write a washing bill in Babylonic cuneiform'.

Archaeology in the late nineteenth century

Between 1878 and 1882 Rassam was again in Mesopotamia, where he not only excavated simultaneously at several sites, but also where possible bought up tablets which had been excavated illicitly. Some later writers have vented their disapproval of such procedures, designating them as 'looting' or 'a scramble for antiques', but this is unduly harsh. Certainly important information was lost by the failure to keep adequate records of exact find-places, but Rassam was not the only offender, and early excavators cannot reasonably be blamed for not observing the standard of techniques only devised after their time.

In the late 1880s both Germany and the United States of America joined the field of Mesopotamian archaeology. A German team, headed by the architect R. Kolde-wey, undertook a season of excavation in 1887 at Surghul (ancient Nina) and Al-Hiba (ancient Lagash) north-east of Tello. Americans did some exploratory work in Babylonia in 1887, but it was not until 1889 that an American expedition began serious digging, choosing Nuffar (ancient Nippur) as their site. They made a major find of cuneiform tablets, but were attacked by Arabs shortly after and forced to leave. They returned for three further digs between 1890 and 1900, obtaining important data on Ekur, the great temple of Enlil, and on its ziggurat, and finding thousands more clay tablets. They also did some work at Bismaya (ancient Adab) and at Fara; the latter was ancient Shuruppak, in Babylonian tradition the Flood city.

Two major long-term excavations began at the end of the nineteenth century. In 1897 a mission, financed by the French government, began work at Susa, the capital of ancient Elam, where Loftus had earlier made soundings. Although this was outside Mesopotamia proper, close links from earliest times made it very relevant to ancient Mesopotamian civilisation. Among many inscribed objects found there was the stele bearing the important laws of King Hammurabi (see pp. 101ff.). The Susa expedition continued, with breaks, until 1939. In 1899 the German Oriental Society in Berlin (die deutsche Orient-Gesellschaft) began excavations at Babylon under Koldewey, and worked continuously until stopped by war in 1917. An assistant of Koldewey, W. Andrae, excavated at Ashur from 1903 to 1914. The French and German expeditions were models of scientific archaeology, and the German expeditions in particular developed techniques which still play a part in Mesopotamian archaeology today.

With the break-up of the Ottoman empire at the end of the First World War, Iraq became a state under a British Mandate. Archaeology resumed in 1919, when representatives of the British Museum undertook work at the sites of Ubaid, Eridu and Ur. This was followed in 1923 by a major joint expedition of the British Museum and the University Museum of the University of Pennsylvania under the direction of C. L. Woolley. This excavated mainly at Ur, with some subsidiary work at Ubaid, until 1934; there were important finds, of which the most spectacular were the Royal Tombs (see pp. 64–5). Ubaid, briefly excavated further by the Oriental Institute of the University of Chicago in 1937, proved to be a site of the earliest prehistorical culture of south Mesopotamia. Other important digs in south Mesopotamia between the two world wars included an expedition of Oxford University and the Field Museum of Chicago to Kish and subsidiary sites between 1922 and 1933; a French archaeological mission directed successively by H. de Genouillac and A. Parrot at Tello (ancient Girsu) and Senkereh (ancient Larsa) between 1929 and 1934; a German expedition from Berlin at Warka (ancient Uruk) 1928–39, and an expedition of the Oriental Institute of the University of Chicago at Asmar (ancient Eshnunna) and other sites in the Diyala valley 1930–4. Over the border in Syria, the French began excavating Tell

Hariri on the middle Euphrates at the end of 1933. This proved to be ancient Mari, a major outpost of Babylonian civilisation, which was to yield thousands of cuneiform tablets of the first half of the second millennium.

After a break during the Second World War, archaeological work in Iraq resumed very fruitfully, with other nations besides Great Britain, the United States, France and Germany now participating. One new collaborator was Iraq itself: the country had developed a flourishing Directorate-General of Antiquities, which regularly undertook digs and restoration work at ancient sites. Others who played an important part included scholars from (inter alia) Japan, Denmark, Italy, Spain, Belgium and USSR. Mesopotamian archaeology came to a halt, which one hopes will only be temporary, with the outbreak of the Gulf war in 1991.

Chapter Two

PREHISTORIC
BEGINNINGS

THE BIBLE HAS much to say about Babylon and the Babylonians. It witnesses to the wide spread of Babylonian trade, when it mentions a valuable Babylonian garment in Palestine before the Israelite settlement (Joshua 7:21). It tells of the Tower of Babel and of an embassy Merodach-baladan, a king of Babylon, sent to the king of Judah. There is much about King Nebuchadnezzar, from the account of his siege of Jerusalem to stories in Daniel of how God humbled him for his pride. It was to Babylonia that some of the people of Jerusalem were deported after its fall, and Psalm 137:1 mentions the Jews exiled there. The prophets denounce Babylon in the time of its glory, and Daniel tells of the carousals at the palace of King Belshazzar (actually regent) before the city fell to conquerors from Iran. Isaiah mocks at Babylon's idols, and foresees its impotent gods Bel (Marduk) and Nebo (Nabu) being carried off on pack-animals (46:1–2). Ezekiel, who at one time actually lived in Babylonia (1:1–4), denounces the Babylonian cult of Tammuz practised in Jerusalem (8:14), and gives an account of the Babylonian king using divination on campaign (21:21). And the Apocrypha has a lively tale, *Bel and the Dragon*, about the deceptions pagan priests practised in consuming the daily provisions supposedly eaten by their god. The classics, too, tell something of Babylon, from its Hanging Gardens and scraps of mythology and history to the shameful sexual practices alleged against its good name. But Babylon had been national capital for nearly a millennium before the earliest of these reports, and its antecedents went back to before 3000 BC.

There were agricultural settlements in south Mesopotamia from before 5000 BC, and the first cities and writing began there in the late fourth millennium. The first half of the third millennium (the Early Dynastic period, abbreviated ED) saw the development of city-states both in Mesopotamia and in Syria, the latter markedly under south Mesopotamian influence, and possibly founded as colonies. Shortly after 2400 BC Sargon of Agade conquered all these city-states to create the first empire (the Agade or Sargonic empire), which eventually controlled much of the Near East. At its collapse after about a century, the city-states reasserted themselves, until in the last century of the third millennium a second empire (the Third Dynasty of Ur, abbreviated III Ur) arose. This in turn collapsed under the pressure of nomads moving in from north Syria.

These nomads, ethnically Amorites, settled and formed kingdoms (Old Babylonian period). One of these kingdoms, Babylon, achieved national supremacy soon after 1800 BC, and gave the whole country the name Babylonia. When it collapsed at about 1600 BC, a Kassite dynasty, originally from east of Babylonia, took over. Quickly adopting Babylonian institutions, they ruled much of the country down to the middle of the twelfth century, when they were superseded by a native dynasty (Second Dynasty of Isin), which already controlled the south.

At about this time a new wave of nomadic immigration began, bringing considerable dislocation. This time the nomads were Aramaeans. Assyria further north began to meddle in Babylonia late in the second millennium. By the early ninth century we hear of Chaldeans (of uncertain origin) mainly in the south of the country, and from the last third of the eighth century the history of Babylonia was largely a struggle for domination between the Assyrians and the Chaldeans. When Assyria fell to a coalition of Chaldeans, Babylonians and Medes at the end of the seventh century, a strong new dynasty (the Neobabylonian or Chaldean dynasty), founded by the father of Nebuchadnezzar, succeeded to much of the former Assyrian empire, including Palestine. Native Babylonian rule finally came to an end when Cyrus the Persian took Babylon in 539 BC (Achaemenid period).

Such was the history of Babylonia in brief. Behind it were many major developments in human history, some well understood, some we are only now beginning to understand, and others which it remains for future discoveries to reveal.

Biblical and geological evidence

The Bible tells us that, as the descendants of Noah 'journeyed from the east, ... they found a plain in the land of Shinar; and they dwelt there' (Genesis 11:2). In Shinar they used bricks as their building material, and created cities and great temple towers (11:3–4). Genesis 10:10 identifies Shinar as the land where Babel (Babylon), Erech (Uruk) and Accad (Akkad) were, that is, the alluvial basin of the lower Tigris and Euphrates. Shinar was a form of Sumer, a name that the ancient inhabitants came to apply to the southernmost part of Mesopotamia.

Today the waters of the Euphrates and Tigris, joined by the Karun from south-west Iran, merge east of Nasariyah to form the Shatt al-Arab (see fig. 3), which enters the Persian Gulf about 160 km (100 miles) to the south-east. The site of ancient Ur, which is near Nasariyah, is thus today 210 km (130 miles) from the sea. But the head of the Persian Gulf may have been much nearer to Ur in prehistoric and early historic times. One would expect silt deposits in the Shatt al-Arab over the millennia to result in a continual build-up of land, pushing the head of the Persian Gulf further and further to the south-east. If this conclusion is correct, before 3000 BC the Gulf

3 *The Shatt al-Arab at the junction of the Euphrates and Tigris rivers. In local tradition this was the site of the Garden of Eden.*

shoreline would have been a long way north-west of its present position. Some third-millennium texts seem to confirm that this was so; for example, a text of a king of Ur, Ur-Nammu (2113–2096 BC), speaks of 'the shore of the sea' as though it was close to the principal temple of Ur.

This was the general view until 1952. But in that year two geologists, Lees and Falcon, upset traditional thinking. They published an article in which they argued that tectonic movement (shifting of the earth's crust) produces a constant sinking in south Mesopotamia, sufficient to counterbalance any rise in level due to silt deposits. Thus, they concluded, the position of the head of the Persian Gulf can have undergone no more than minor changes since prehistoric times. It was always much where it is now.

This hypothesis no longer stands. More recent geological research suggests that the older view, although over-simplistic, was basically sound.[1] The prehistory of the region, as currently understood, is as follows. At the height of the last Ice Age, c. 15,000 BC, the Persian Gulf was dry land. As the earth warmed up and the ice caps melted, sea level rose, until by 5000 BC or soon after the Persian Gulf stood up to 2.5 m (9 ft) above its present level. The head of the Gulf was then 160 km (100 miles) or so north-west of its present position, and south Mesopotamia was less arid than much of it is today. Afterwards a cooler and drier climate set in, bringing a drop in sea level. This, coupled with silt deposits, gradually caused the head of the Persian Gulf to move south-eastwards to its present position.

Early urban civilisation

Civilisation, in the sense of a way of life associated with cities and using writing, began in south Mesopotamia in the fourth millennium. But this was not the sudden single-handed achievement of a master race. Behind it lay many millennia of human advance. Already, 300,000 years ago, an early form of man was using fire, and fashioning tools and weapons. Our own form of man, Homo sapiens, emerged in Africa by 90,000 BC and by 30,000 BC had supplanted Neanderthal man throughout Europe.

Soon after, trading was taking place as far away as 400 km (250 miles) from the supply base, as the distribution of flint from an identifiable source in Poland shows. By 20,000 BC man had invented the needle, a tool which greatly facilitated the making of clothing for protection against the bitter cold of the last Ice Age. Man had also learnt many other skills: he could control the movement of herds of wild animals for more effective hunting; he knew how to store food; and he could build shelters and long-term camp sites. These last achievements prepared the way for further advances, since it was only a step from storing wild cereals to sowing and cultivating them, and it was an easy transition from semi-permanent camp sites to permanent villages.

These latter developments began after the end of the last Ice Age, from about 9000 BC, in an arc running from Palestine along the foothills of the Taurus to the foothills of the Zagros. What made it possible to adopt these measures was the presence of wild sheep and goats, and of wild wheat and barley and adequate rainfall. Genesis 2:16–3:23 reflects these beginnings, when it tells how mankind, after first living in a garden where food was to be had for the gathering, was driven out to an existence dependent on tillage of the soil.

Despite the new developments, hunting remained important for millennia. The creation of hunting camps was a factor which led people from the nuclear foothill areas to move out on to the plains, where they eventually established permanent villages in places with adequate rainfall or a perennial water source. Jericho was one striking early instance of the last factor, developing round a copious spring and becoming a fortified town as early as the eighth millennium. Another was Çatal Hüyük in the Taurus foothills, which by the late seventh millennium was a substantial town with major artistic achievements. There were probably other very early instances, as yet undiscovered. One likelihood is Erbil in north-east Iraq. This is an enormously high mound, obviously of extreme antiquity, in a place ideally situated for very early occupation, but it has never yet been excavated to virgin soil.

Archaeological terminology

Another early advance was pottery. The skill of baking clay to form terracotta was already known by 25,000 BC,[2] but it was not until about 8000 BC that it began to be applied to the making of pots for food storage. Henceforth pottery types form a useful marker of connections between settlements.

For archaeologists of the prehistoric period, pottery is important for relative dating, since pottery type was one aspect of the background of a settlement. Features which identify ancient pottery include the type of clay; the shape, function and thickness of vessels; whether the pots are handmade or thrown on a slow or fast wheel; whether or not they are decorated; what designs they bear and in what colours; how the pigment was applied; how heavily the pots were fired; and whether they were fired in oxidising or reducing conditions. Gradual modification of such features suggests a stable population; sudden replacement of old forms by new may well indicate a population change.

Archaeologists use the term 'assemblage' to cover the physical equipment characteristic of a particular prehistoric society. It includes such points as type of brick, architectural forms, materials used (e.g. stone or metals), presence or otherwise of cylinder seals, types of tool, whether or not the wheel was known, evidence on religion, methods of disposal of the dead, use of animals, foodstuffs, and presence or not of long-distance imports such as obsidian or lapis lazuli. The name of the pottery type, usually taken from the site at which it was first recognised, is commonly applied to the whole assemblage.

The earliest pottery yet known from north Mesopotamia comes from sites south of Jebel Sinjar. In the view of the excavator of Umm Dabaghiyah, the best known of these sites, it was not basically an agricultural settlement but an outpost for onager-hunters. However, the next earliest pottery type was certainly associated with agricultural settlements; this was a painted ware, not very widely dispersed, called Hassuna, after a site 30 km (20 miles) south of Mosul, with its earliest forms dated to about 6000 BC. Partly contemporary with later stages of Hassuna, and formerly taken as a later phase of it, is the painted pottery named Samarra, dated to around 5500 BC, with decoration more elaborate and aesthetically more pleasing than that of Hassuna. Some Samarran settlements lie south of the rainfall agriculture area, showing that they must have used primitive irrigation; traces of small canals have been recognised at one of the main sites with Samarran features, Choga Mami near Mandali on the border with Iran. The most important Samarran settlement yet known is Tell es-Sawwan, near the city of Samarra; this is the earliest site in Mesopotamia with a defensive wall.

From later in the sixth millennium comes a striking painted pottery known as Halaf ware (see pl. II). This was first recognised at Tell Halaf in the Habur valley in north Syria, but has since been found in north Mesopotamia and across the whole region from the Mediterranean across north Syria to beyond Diyarbakir in Anatolia. There are two possible explanations for this wide spread: trading contacts across the area, or the arrival of a new element of population. Favouring the latter is that Halaf pottery was associated with forms of building unlike anything that preceded; in addition, some Halaf villages were established not over Hassuna settlements, which preceded them, but on fresh sites nearby, suggesting discontinuity of population.

In south-west Iran, geographically linked by river plains with south Mesopotamia, there was an agricultural settlement at Ali Kosh soon after 6000 BC, but for south Mesopotamia proper there is as yet no evidence for any such settlement before about

5500 BC.[3] But all that the archaeological evidence proves for the period before 5500 BC is the absence of permanent villages, not the absence of humans. Nomadic pastoralists or groups who lived by fishing, fowling, and collecting edible plants could well have occupied south Mesopotamia long before permanent agricultural settlements arose, so it is not a necessary conclusion that the first settlements were due to recent immigrants. But to know about cereal cultivation they must have had some kind of link with agricultural communities elsewhere. It could have been with Choga Mami, since the earliest agriculturalists in south Mesopotamia used a six-row variety of barley also found there but distinct from the two-row variety cultivated further north.[4]

UBAID PERIOD

The earliest pottery type in south Mesopotamia is called Ubaid, after the site of that name near Ur. Archaeologists subdivide successive phases either into Early and Late Ubaid, or into Ubaid I to IV. Alternative terms for Ubaid I and II are Eridu and Hajji Muhammad, after the sites where finds of these periods were first identified. Eridu (Ubaid I) pottery appears to have been limited to a small area around its find-place, Abu Shahrain (ancient Eridu) 11 km (7 miles) south-west of Ur, but Hajji Muhammad (Ubaid II) pottery was found much more widely, from Kish in north Babylonia to the Arabian coast of the Persian Gulf. Late Ubaid pottery was distributed further still, from Arabia to Syria, with a related type of pottery in south-west Iran. Distribution so far afield can hardly have been due to colonisation, but points rather to widespread trading connections. Radiocarbon determinations suggest a date of about 5500 BC for early Ubaid, with the Late Ubaid period ending at or just before 4000 BC.

URUK AND JAMDAT NASR PERIODS

The next archaeological period is called Uruk, after the ancient name of Warka, biblical Erech. This huge site was meticulously excavated by German scholars, who identified eighteen levels. The latest level, I, was Early Dynastic (see below); the four earliest levels were Ubaid or transitional, and those in between were designated Uruk, sub-divided into early, middle and late phases. It is in Late Uruk (Uruk IV) that the earliest examples of true writing were found,[5] comprising clay tablets inscribed with pictographs (see figs 24–7). The first writing we can actually read, from early in the third millennium, was in Sumerian, but some scholars argue that the writing system was originally devised by people who spoke some other language. A slightly more developed form of writing is found in tablets from the site Jamdat Nasr and Uruk levels III–II. The Uruk IV and Jamdat Nasr cultural stages considered together are sometimes called Protoliterate. We take the date of the Jamdat Nasr period as approximately 3000 to 2900 BC; some scholars put it a century or two earlier.

EARLY DYNASTIC PERIOD

After the Jamdat Nasr period came a marked growth of city-states, characteristically governed by local dynasties. This is therefore the Early Dynastic (ED) period, conventionally divided into ED I (beginning c. 2900 BC), ED II (c. 2750 BC) and ED III (*c.* 2600 BC). The period ended with the accession, at a date we now generally take as 2371 BC, of Sargon of Agade, the first empire-builder (see pp. 66ff.).

THE FOURTH-MILLENNIUM ACHIEVEMENT

From about 3500 BC (the Late Uruk period) certain features make Uruk (biblical Erech) stand out from other settlements. The first was its sheer size; a recent survey estimates this as at least 120 ha (300 acres), perhaps as much as 200 ha (490 acres). Other striking features included: advanced irrigation techniques; monumental buildings, notably one called the 'White Temple', a structure on a high platform whose origin went back to the Ubaid period; sculpture; the increasing use of copper; the beginning of writing; cylinder seals; larger economic units; and the beginning of the organisation of labour.

There were other fourth-millennium settlements moving in the same direction as Uruk, and several of the features mentioned had antecedents elsewhere. The cylinder seal had its precursor in the stamp seal, attested at Buqras on the Euphrates in north Syria as early as 6000 BC. Uruk's achievement was to adapt the seal to a form suitable for rolling over clay tablets. The organisation of labour in industry found at Uruk in the late Uruk period was not an entirely new concept, since copper-smelting operations on this basis took place at Sheikh Hasan in Syria as early as the middle Uruk period.

Writing too had its antecedents. Sheikh Hasan is one of several sites which provide evidence of precursors of writing, in the form of hollow clay balls associated with small clay discs, spheres, cones and tetrahedrons, used in a primitive accounting system. Tell Brak in the Habur valley had baked pots marked with signs for numerals, and Habuba Kabira near Carchemish and other sites have yielded crude clay tablets which bear nothing but numbers (see fig. 5). What Uruk did was to take an old system of recording numbers of things and develop it into a simpler and more convenient form which became true writing (see pp. 46ff.).

Uruk's achievement was to bring together developments already under way in many places in the Euphrates valley. It was able to do this because of an exceptionally favourable ecology. Once irrigation had been mastered, the Euphrates gave the cities of south Mesopotamia an unlimited supply of water, which together with the very fertile soil and the unfailing sun ensured heavy harvests. The prosperity of early Uruk attracted immigration from surrounding smaller settlements, and this, with natural increase, resulted in a population large enough to support craft specialisation.

Chronology

The further back we go, the more difficult it is to fix absolute dates, and there is often a case for speaking only in terms of archaeological periods. However, dates, even if only approximate, can be helpful. In this book we mainly adhere for convenience to the well-established chronology used in the latest edition of *Cambridge Ancient History*, even though, as we point out below, this is probably inaccurate by approximately half a century for the early second and late third millennia.

5 Above *Cuneiform writing probably developed from an earlier recording system widespread in the ancient Near and Middle East. This archaic clay tablet bears numerals only, reflecting a stage intermediate between recording system and writing system.*

4 Left *Stone sculpture from Tell al-Ubaid, representing a priest of the ED III period.*

Many events in the first millennium can be accurately fixed. For this we have to thank Assyrian records. The Assyrians dated each year by an official who served as *limmu* (holder of a certain religious office). *Limmu* lists were kept, sometimes with important events in the year noted alongside. One of these records adds the information: 'In the month Siwan, the sun was eclipsed'. Modern astronomers can calculate that this solar eclipse took place in 763 BC, and from this the rest of the series of *limmu* entries provides accurate dates back to just before 1100 BC.

For earlier periods, there are two types of date list. One type covers whole dynasties, the other gives regnal years of particular kings. If one could fix the date of a single year of a single king, one could obtain exact dates over long periods. It is possible to obtain such a fixed point, from three sets of data: records of heliacal risings and settings[6] of the planet Venus; data on lengths of lunar months; and records of lunar eclipses.

THE PLANET VENUS
Copies remain of Babylonian records of risings and settings of Venus in the first half of the second millennium, and one entry is linked to the eighth year of Ammisaduqa, the

fourth successor of Hammurabi of Babylon. But there are problems. Firstly, the ancient copyist made mistakes; some figures cannot be reconciled with astronomical calculations. Secondly, movements of Venus are periodic, so that the records would be approximately compatible with those movements at repeated intervals. However, other evidence limits the range within which the observations must lie, so that only four dates come into consideration for the first year of Ammisaduqa: 1702 BC, 1646 BC, 1638 BC, and 1582 BC. Datings based on these dates are called respectively the Long Chronology, Middle Chronologies (the two middle dates), and the Short Chronology.

P. J. Huber, the mathematician who analysed the data most recently, concludes that it is the Long Chronology which fits the astronomical data from the Venus tablets most exactly. The Short is borderline, and the two Middle Chronologies fit very poorly. Mathematically there is a 99 per cent likelihood that the first year of Ammisaduqa was 1702 BC.[7]

LUNAR MONTHS

The Babylonians used a lunar calendar, in which the month began with the sighting of the new moon. The actual period between successive new moons is 29.53 days, but an observer necessarily sees the length of a lunar month as either 29 or 30 days. Mathematically it works out that 53 per cent of lunar months appear to have 30 days, against 47 per cent with 29 days. It is possible to calculate astronomically how many 30-day months any reign would have had on particular chronologies, and datings on economic tablets show how many there actually were. The predictions and the facts fit best on the Long Chronology.

LUNAR ECLIPSES

Lunar eclipses were recorded as omens of disaster. One such is connected with the murder of a king of III Ur, who must have been Shulgi. Another lunar eclipse was taken to predict the destruction of III Ur, at the end of the reign of its last king, Ibbi-Sin. The period between the death of Shulgi and the end of the III Ur empire was 42 years, so if we can find by calculation two lunar eclipses 42 years apart which fit the eclipses described in the omens, we can tie these eclipse records to absolute dates. There was such a pair, datable astronomically to 2095 BC and 2053 BC. The latter therefore, rather than the conventional date of 2006 BC, marks the end of the III Ur empire.

Further back in time, dating becomes increasingly doubtful. A document called the *Sumerian King List* (abbreviated SKL) purports to supply lengths of reigns and dynasties back to the beginning of the third millennium and before, but some of these figures are unreliable. A particular source of error is that the document represents all dynasties as strictly consecutive, whereas some certainly overlapped. Also, some of its figures are grossly exaggerated, running to hundreds or thousands of years for the earliest kings in the list.

RADIOCARBON ANALYSIS

Before 3000 BC, radiocarbon analysis is helpful. Briefly, this depends on the fact that neutrons in cosmic radiation strike nitrogen atoms in the upper atmosphere to produce a proportion of radioactive carbon atoms (^{14}C). These combine with oxygen atoms to become part of the carbon dioxide in the earth's atmosphere. Atmospheric carbon dioxide is absorbed by vegetation and goes into the food cycle. All living matter therefore contains a proportion of ^{14}C, which carbon exchange maintains at a constant value. When an animal or plant dies, the exchange ceases. Radiocarbon atoms lose their radioactivity at a rate which can be calculated; the time taken to lose half the initial radioactivity is called the half-life. For ^{14}C this was originally taken as 5570 years, but has been revised to 5730 years. Analysis of the residual radiocarbon in an ancient bone or piece of wood will therefore give a value for its age. This value is normally quoted with a stated margin of error, which may be up to three hundred years either way.

There are factors which can affect the reliability of radiocarbon datings (or 'determinations', as they are usually called). If the sample of material for analysis has been contaminated with more recent organic matter, the result will not be reliable. Any result based on the older value of 5570 years for the half-life will need to be recalibrated to produce a more correct dating. Also, the calculations assume that cosmic radiation during the last six thousand years has been constant; if there has been any significant change, this could introduce an error, which could then be corrected by dendrochronology if available.

Ethnic elements in earliest Mesopotamia

In the second half of the third millennium, south Mesopotamia was the centre of two successive empires. The first, founded shortly after 2400 BC, was based on a capital Akkad in the north of the country, and the rulers wrote their inscriptions largely in a Semitic language, today called Akkadian. The second, the III Ur empire, flourished in the final century of the millennium. Its capital was at Ur in the south, and its royal inscriptions were almost exclusively in Sumerian. After the collapse of the second empire, Sumerian was dead as a spoken language, and Akkadian took its place. Later texts often referred to Babylonia as 'Sumer and Akkad'.

This led earlier historians to interpret the third-millennium history of south Mesopotamia in racial, or, as one would say now, ethnic terms. The country was, they concluded, inhabited by two distinct peoples, Sumerians and Akkadians. These peoples were of different geographical origin, and were distinguished not only by language but also by religion, art, law and other social institutions. It was assumed that the two groups were engaged in a perennial struggle for control of the whole country, in which the Akkadians finally emerged victorious.

Fuller evidence makes an interpretation in terms of racial conflict untenable; and a racial approach to other aspects of third-millennium society is also dubious. However, the existence of two language groups is a fact, and presents questions which need an answer. Which language group was there first? Did one group come in by immigration or invasion after the land had been settled by the other? Does one of these groups deserve sole credit for the first steps towards ancient Mesopotamian civilisation; or could that have been the work of a third group which preceded both?

The last is at least a possibility. Some of the earliest cities of south Mesopotamia, and its rivers, have names which some scholars think cannot be explained as either Sumerian or Semitic in origin. There are also lexical elements – terms, for example, for 'farmer', 'smith', 'carpenter', and 'date' (the fruit) – of which the same could be said. This could mean that some third language group inhabited south Mesopotamia before speakers of Sumerian or Akkadian arrived. Those who hold this view refer to the unidentified tongue as the 'substratum language', or call the people concerned 'Proto-Euphrateans'. But since place-names and river names are highly persistent, any such language could have ceased to be spoken long before our first written evidence.

Akkadian was a language of the Semitic family, to which later Hebrew, Aramaic and Arabic also belong. It was widely used alongside Sumerian at the time of the empire founded by Sargon of Agade (2371 BC). The ratio of names in extant documents gives an idea of the balance of the two languages. It is not suggested that everyone's name was in his or her mother tongue, but it is not unreasonable to suppose some connection. If we find a predominance of a particular language in a large sample of personal names, we may conclude that this was the mother tongue of the majority of the group. On this basis, in the twenty-fourth century a majority of people in the south spoke Sumerian as their mother tongue, and a majority in the north Akkadian. We have no statistical evidence on how many were bilingual.

But there were people with a Semitic-speaking background in south Mesopotamia before the twenty-fourth century. A stone bowl from Ur in the first half of the twenty-fifth century BC with an Akkadian dedication proves this; the dedication was in honour of a king of Ur composed by his wife, so the wife certainly, and the king possibly, spoke a Semitic language. Still earlier evidence for this comes from tablets found at Tell Abu Salabikh, datable to about 2600 BC. Although all these tablets were written in Sumerian, many were produced by scribes with Semitic names; this must mean that many of these scribes came from an Akkadian-speaking background. The *Sumerian King List*, which received its final form just after 2000 BC, attests the presence of Semitic speakers earlier still; among the kings of the First Dynasty of Kish, which ruled in the twenty-eighth century, it includes at least five kings with names of Semitic origin. For Semitic-speaking families to have become sufficiently prominent in south Mesopotamia to produce rulers by about 2750 BC, there must have been Semitic-speaking elements there from 2800 BC at the latest.

Apart from Akkadian, the main Semitic languages spoken BC are all first encountered in a region bounded by the Euphrates to the east and north Syria to the north. There are no grounds for thinking that the geographical antecedents of Akkadian were different. The earliest Akkadian speakers in Mesopotamia must therefore have been immigrants from that region. But there are no data on the first migration of speakers of proto-Akkadian; whether this movement of people took place only a century or so before 2800 BC, or much earlier, we do not know.

Tablets of the Jamdat Nasr period, datable to about 3000 BC, were written in Sumerian, showing the presence in south Mesopotamia of speakers of that language from that date. To go back earlier, we have to examine the archaeological evidence.

Archaeology shows no marked break between the Late Uruk and the Jamdat Nasr periods, so there is unlikely to have been any major population change, suggesting that Sumerian speakers were already present in south Mesopotamia in the second half of the fourth millennium.

Earlier than this there is conflicting evidence. Archaeological evidence shows no sudden break between Late Ubaid and Early Uruk, favouring the conclusion that Sumerian speakers had been there since Ubaid times. Site surveys, however, suggest a major decline in population in south-west Iran after the Middle Uruk period, at a time when the population density in southernmost Mesopotamia was increasing. This could be explained by immigration into south Mesopotamia from south-west Iran, marking the entry of a Sumerian-speaking strain, which later became dominant. Some Sumerian traditions hint that the earliest Sumerian speakers had close links with Iran (see p. 32). But even if the original Sumerian speakers did have roots in Iran, the majority of later Sumerian speakers could well have been descendants of speakers of the old substratum language, who had gradually adopted Sumerian as their mother tongue.

At some time in the fourth millennium, therefore, Sumerian speakers and Akkadian speakers were distinct ethnic groups. But it is very dubious to assume without proof that this was still true for the second half of the third millennium, and that there were two distinct social systems, religions, legal systems, forms of art and the like.

Third-millennium Sumerian texts make a distinction between two terms, *ki-en-gi* and *ki-uri*, which eventually came to denote the southern and northern parts of Babylonia, and to be rendered into Akkadian as Sumer and Akkad. This was formerly taken as proof that the ancient people themselves thought in terms of two distinct ethnic groups. But *ki-uri* did not come into use as a designation for northern Babylonia until the end of the third millennium, and originally denoted the district around Ur, with *ki-en-gi* probably the district around Nippur. Since both districts used Sumerian, the terms originally cannot have signified a distinction between two ethnic groups. In fact there is no third-millennium text which suggests that the inhabitants of south Mesopotamia thought of themselves as two population groups, Sumerians and Akkadians, distinct from one another. They were quite ready to remark on ethnic differences if they considered them relevant, as we see from the comments they made upon the curious customs of the nomadic Amurru (see p. 92). But no third-millennium text gives any indication that it was of consequence whether a person was Sumerian-speaking or Akkadian-speaking.

This is not to suggest total uniformity throughout south Mesopotamia in religion, laws and other social customs. Differences there were, but these had no direct linkage with either genetic factors or language; their origin lay in environment and history. Terrain as a dividing factor was more significant than language, since it affected such basic matters as land use and food production, and through them, law and religion. Obviously the basis of food supply in an area of marshlands was fishing and fowling; in regions of grassland it was mainly cattle-rearing; and in other ecologies it was date-orchards or the growing of corn. Such ecological differences would inevitably be reflected in dissimilarities both in land-tenure customs and in the nature of the principal deities.

Until the last quarter of the third millennium, the Sumerian language was predominant in the south of the country and Akkadian in the north. Since there were significant ecological variations between the north and south of south Mesopotamia, some societal differences did coincide with a different language background. But there was no causal link. The 'Sumerians', to whom some books ascribe the sole credit for the civilisation which developed in third-millennium Mesopotamia, were in reality a blend of peoples, speaking at least two and perhaps more languages, who had long since ceased to be distinct ethnic groups. It is misleading to use the terms 'Sumerians' and 'Akkadians' in the sense of clearly differentiated ethnic groups; the only proper use for these terms is as shorthand for 'speakers of Sumerian' and 'speakers of Akkadian'. The civilisation which bloomed in the third millennium was a joint achievement of peoples who, within the constraints of their local ecology, all shared the same basic concepts and the same way of life.

Early tradition in myths and epics

The early people of Mesopotamia did not think in terms of history. They saw their institutions and way of life not as developments from more primitive forms but rather as something which the gods had decreed in the beginning and which had existed unchanged for ever. With no concept of social progress, they had no incentive to make a conscious record of life in the thousand years before 2500 BC, when some of the most momentous advances in human society were taking place.

They did, however, leave behind myths and epics (see pp. 151–2) which reflect conditions of very early times, the myths rather earlier than the epics. Some of the myths involve a land called Tilmun, thought of as a kind of Paradise, where there was neither sickness nor death. Although after 2200 BC this name denoted Bahrein and Failaka and perhaps nearby parts of the Arabian side of the Persian Gulf, in the early third millennium it seems to have meant somewhere in south Iran. Another allusion to Iran comes in an epic in which the people of Uruk were trading donkey loads of grain with a land Aratta beyond seven mountain ranges, in exchange for semi-precious stones. Since the mountains can only have been the Zagros, Aratta must have been in Iran. The two peoples clearly worshipped the same goddess Inanna, shared the same culture, and apparently understood the same language. Are these perhaps hints that the earliest Sumerian speakers had a homeland further east before they settled in south Mesopotamia?

One epic shows Gilgamesh, a heroic ruler of Uruk, felling trees in a mysterious mountain forest guarded by a demonic ogre (see pp. 110–11). By the first millennium

6 Above left *Attendant carrying fish, from the Standard of Ur.*

7 Above right *Statuette of a bearded man of high rank, from the mid third millennium.*

the forest was thought of as on the Amanus, but originally it was on the flanks of the Zagros, and the story reflects the beginning of deforestation there. Other traditions speak of an early hero, either Gilgamesh or a predecessor Enmerkar (see p. 78), building the walls of Uruk, which reflects the beginning of the general building of fortification walls for cities. In another epic about Gilgamesh, Uruk is threatened by the powerful king of Kish, upstream on the Euphrates. Gilgamesh wanted to resist, but first had to consult an assembly of the Elders of the city and the warriors; this indicates that although by the second half of the third millennium kings had almost absolute power, in the Early Dynastic II period, to which Gilgamesh belonged, rulers, however prestigious, governed only by consent.

Myths reflect a still earlier stage of democratic decision-making. In them, although some members of the pantheon are recognised as senior, divine beings take decisions by discussion among the whole body, in which goddesses are as important as gods. This mirrors on the divine level a stage of human society when women had full equality with men in decisions about community affairs. These myths tie up with an even earlier stage of society reflected in prehistoric religion, when the predominant supernatural being was not a god but a Mother-goddess, represented in innumerable examples from the Old Stone Age onwards.

Myths also contain reflections of technological developments. One of them tells how the great god Ninurta overthrew a monster Asag, and turned it into stone; Asag's offspring were also personified stones, and the king of all these beings was denoted by a term read *šammu* in Akkadian. As a substance, *šammu* was a type of stone capable of piercing and polishing other stones. Technologists have demonstrated that it must have meant a form of emery, and the myth reflects the beginning of the use of this material for grinding, polishing and cutting. The introduction of emery as a tool for grinding and cutting was linked to a marked shift from soft stones to hard stones such as lapis lazuli and haematite for cylinder seals after the Jamdat Nasr period.[8]

Religious concepts in the early third millennium

Before texts become available, knowledge of religion depends almost exclusively upon art. Examples of religious art from the Upper Palaeolithic period show that at that time there were three areas of particular concern: success in the hunt, fecundity in the species hunted, and human fertility. Central to the last were figurines of women shown as heavily pregnant or grossly fat; examples continue right down to the Halaf period (see fig. 8). The Neolithic revolution (after 10,000 BC) brought new emphases. In particular, the old figurine of a pregnant woman began to develop into a Mother-goddess or Great Mother, the supreme supernatural being, who personified the power which prehistoric people recognised behind birth, motherhood and fertility. Corresponding male deities did not develop until much later.

Except for the Mother-goddess, prehistoric people did not see supernatural powers in human form. Rather, they recognised supernatural powers (*numina*, singular *numen*) in natural phenomena. Typical examples are the sky, the wind, water, the sun, the moon, thunderstorms, and wild animals (see figs 9, 43).

There is a good example of this in the far south of Mesopotamia, where the oldest settlements were in regions of marsh and lagoon. There the settlers saw a *numen* in the sweet waters, upon which all life manifestly depended. If they dug into the ground, they quickly came upon water, giving the idea of a great ocean of fresh water beneath the earth. This they called *abzu*, not at first a personal being but a *numen* which could either give life or, by flooding, destroy it. Later the idea developed that behind *abzu* there was a god in human form, who controlled it.

At the end of the fourth millennium cities began to develop in south Mesopotamia, and with this came a more complex way of life. Although fertility always remained a primary concern in Babylonian religion, there were now additional needs, and changes in the way people saw the supernatural powers. *Numina* gradually gave way to anthropomorphic deities (see fig. 10). A settlement had always needed the protection of supernatural powers in order to flourish, so as these powers took anthropomorphic form, every city had its own tutelary god or goddess. People now came to believe that city-states were aboriginal creations of their gods, and that the gods had decreed all aspects of human society from the beginning. Therefore, because within the developing city-states there were various institutions, and officials responsible for directing different functions, there must have been a corresponding pattern in the divine world. Consequently the great gods, and the deities of the cities, were thought of as having their own courts, with consorts and families, and extensive staffs ranging from viziers down to hairdressers. Every human activity and craft was believed to be the responsibility of some deity. By this process a huge pantheon developed, so that by the time of the earliest god lists, from Fara (c. 2600 BC), it totalled nearly four thousand named deities, organised on the analogy of human society.

Although almost all supernatural powers became conceived as deities in human form, one can frequently see traces of earlier non-human forms, especially in the third millennium. Thus, Enki, the god of Eridu and of the watery deep, had a Sumerian title

8 Left *The earliest representations of supernatural power in human form were figurines associated with the fertility of women. This example is from Chagar Bazar in north Mesopotamia.*

9 Below *Bulls had religious significance as the embodiment of divine power and as fertility symbols. This clay bull figurine comes from the Ubaid period, before 4000 BC.*

10 Top *The goddess Ishtar, identified by a star and standing on a lion, reflects earlier theriomorphic concepts of deity. From an Assyrian seal, c. 700 BC.*

11 Above *Mountain storms in north Iraq are often associated with great swathes of black cloud, suggesting a gigantic bird of prey with outspread wings. This led to the representation of the supernatural power behind the storm as the bird-monster Imdugud (Sumerian for 'heavy cloud'). The god Ninurta later absorbed these characteristics.*

Dara-abzu, which literally meant 'Ibex of the *abzu*', reflecting the concept of him as a beast in the marshes with his horns protruding above the water as reeds. In a text of the late third millennium, the ruler Gudea of Lagash describes how he saw the god Ninurta in a dream; he had wings like a bird-monster (see fig. 11) and his lower part was the Flood. In art, the Sun-god is shown with rays streaming from him, the Storm-god stands on a bull (his earlier non-anthropomorphic representation), and a Vegetation-god holds a bunch of dates and has plants growing from the shoulders and head (see pl. III). Gula, goddess of healing, is represented by a dog and Ishtar by a lion (see fig. 10). The name of the goddess Ninsuna means 'Queen (or Owner) of the wild cows', but there are indications that in an earlier stage she was envisaged in cow form, and that her name was originally Nin-Sun, 'Lady Wild Cow'.

At the head of the national pantheon were Enlil, originally meaning 'Lord Wind', and An (Akkadian form Anu), meaning 'Sky'. Enlil was the patron deity of Nippur in central Sumer. He was credited with cosmic creation, which he achieved by separating heaven from earth. He invented the pickaxe, indispensable for primitive agriculture, and used this tool to create mankind, who sprouted from the ground broken up by his axe. In mythology he held the 'Tablet of Destinies', by which the fate of every living being was decreed. An (Anu) had a special relationship with kingship, and was also the creator. The duplication of Enlil and Anu as creator went back to the fact that each of these gods had originally headed a local pantheon. Some theogonies surmounted the theological contradiction by making An the father of Enlil.

A third god, Enki (Semitic Ea), came to stand alongside An and Enlil in the first rank. His name is variously interpreted to mean either 'Lord Earth' or 'Controller of the soil'. It was he who controlled the *abzu*, the sweet waters beneath the earth which were the source of life. From him also mankind obtained their knowledge of the crafts needed for civilised life. Some local pantheons show traces of other rankings. There are indications of a local pantheon in which Enki was chief god; and Sippar, whose city deity was the Sun-god Shamash, has yielded texts which place Shamash first in seniority, with Ea second and Enlil third.

All the great gods had spouses, but one goddess had supreme powers in the pantheon in her own right and not as the wife of a great god. Since her major concern was fertility, she was clearly a survival of the ancient Great Mother. Of the many names and forms she bore, the two commonest were Ninhursag and Inanna (earlier spelling Innin), representing two different forms of the Great Mother. Ninhursag appears to be the goddess in a form which antedated agriculture and the city-state, whereas many of Inanna's features suggest an origin in an agricultural economy (see fig. 18).

Other prominent deities included the Sun-god (see fig. 12) and the Moon-god. Since the Sun-god, Utu in Sumerian and Shamash in Akkadian, could look down on the earth as he daily crossed the heavens in his chariot, no human action was hidden from him and he became God of Justice. The Moon-god, Nanna or Sin, controlled the calendar. The son of Enlil, Ninurta, was in origin a god of the storms which drenched the mountains and made the rivers flood. Another name for him was Ningirsu. There was also a Plague-god, whose prominence reflected the fear of epidemic disease in ancient cities. He was known by various names, reflecting independent origin in different places, but his commonest name was Nergal.

The Underworld was a separate domain, originally ruled by a great goddess, Ereshkigal. She was sister and rival of Inanna, a connection which expressed the polarity of Death against Life. As changes in human society reduced the status of women, this became reflected in a myth which told how Nergal became king of the Underworld and took Ereshkigal as his consort.

12 *Mythology saw the Sun-god as rising from behind the eastern mountains, escorted by attendants, as on this cylinder seal impression.*

Trade

South Mesopotamia lacks raw materials. There is no stone for quarrying, no metal ores, and no timber other than date-palm, poplar and willow, none of them suitable for major buildings. Everything needed for a technologically more advanced life therefore had to be obtained by trade.

We have already noticed epics which touch upon trade during the first half of the third millennium. *Enmerkar and the Lord of Aratta* tells of donkey caravans of corn sent across the Zagros mountains to Aratta in Iran in exchange for semi-precious stones, and the *Epic of Gilgamesh* has the hero making a dangerous journey to fell timber in a mountain forest which must have been in the Zagros. In the first half of the third millennium there must also have been trading connection with places as far away as north Afghanistan, which was the nearest source of lapis lazuli, of which considerable use was made for cylinder seals and religious art in south Mesopotamia. Also large quantities of unworked lapis lazuli as well as artefacts were found at Ebla in north Syria, together with carnelian, which came from India. Further evidence of long-distance trade is given by the widespread occurrence in the middle of the millennium of bronze made from an alloy of tin and copper, since the only available source of the tin was deposits in Afghanistan[9] and the copper probably came from Oman. Sargon of Agade was certainly trading by sea with Oman in the twenty-fourth century (see p. 68).

The Flood: archaeological and literary data

The biblical story of the Flood has its counterpart (and perhaps its origin) in Mesopotamian tradition. Since major floods have always been a threat to south

Mesopotamia the question arises: was the Mesopotamian tradition simply a mytho-logical expression of a constant anxiety, or was it based on the memory of some particular flood of unparalleled magnitude? If the latter, what was the date of the Flood?

Mesopotamian records offer some clues on when the Flood was believed to have occurred. According to the *Epic of Gilgamesh*, Gilgamesh went to consult Uta-napishtim, the sole survivor from the Flood, to discover how he obtained eternal life (see pp. 111–12). Behind the Gilgamesh traditions was a real person, who lived at about 2700 BC, and the epic represents Uta-napishtim's exploits as remote in time from Gilgamesh, implying an interval of at least two centuries. This makes 2900 BC the latest date for Uta-napishtim's Flood. SKL places the Flood before the First Dynasty of Kish, which would be compatible with this.

At several south Mesopotamian sites excavators came upon layers of apparently water-laid silt, prima facie indicating a major flood. One such, found by Sir Leonard Woolley at Ur in 1928–29, lay immediately above the final phase of the Ubaid level, indicating a date not later than 3500 BC, too early to fit the *Gilgamesh* tradition; it has been suggested that this layer was not water-laid silt but wind-blown sand, but this has not been substantiated. At Kish three or four different flood layers were identified, the earliest from the beginning of the ED period, at about 2900 BC. There is also evidence from Fara, the site of Shuruppak, the city with which the *Epic of Gilgamesh* links Uta-napishtim. Here there was a layer of alluvial sterile clay and sand, datable to the beginning of the ED period, which could correspond with the earliest flood stratum at Kish.

On balance, the archaeological evidence seems to point to a flood of particular severity at about 2900 BC, which might be the basis of literary themes about a world-wide Flood, attested first in Mesopotamia and then in other parts of the ancient Near East.

Others have seen the origin of the Flood story in an event far earlier, the end of the last Ice Age, when the level of the Persian Gulf rose by several metres (see p. 22). But the time-scale of both the rise and retreat of the waters of the Gulf was far, far too long to be compatible with tradition.

Chapter Three

EARLY CITIES

THE EARLIEST SETTLEMENTS in southernmost Babylonia were small villages in areas rendered habitable by the proximity of swamps, lakes or small streams, fed from the Euphrates. Even today it is possible to survive in the southern marshes of Iraq by fishing and collecting edible plants, so people may have lived there before the use of agriculture and irrigation. It was only after these resources began to be exploited, giving abundant yields of grain and a fast increase in population, that some villages began to grow to city size. This growth was aided by movement into the most successful settlements of people from less prosperous villages nearby and perhaps of nomadic populations. The city which enjoyed the most considerable expansion was Uruk, which by ED I probably had a population of between forty and fifty thousand. Other cities were also developing, among them Ur, Lagash, Nippur, Kish and probably Shuruppak (see fig. 14). Such cities constituted the centres of wider political units, city-states, some of which contained more than one city; the city-state of Lagash, for example, had at least three cities: Lagash itself, Girsu and Nina.

Early building and architecture

In the marshlands of south Iraq there is a species of giant reed which grows to 3.5 m (12 ft) or more. Tied into tight bundles, they make a good substitute for pillars, and are still used by marsh Arabs as the framework for buildings ranging from simple huts to large ornate guest houses (see pl. IV). Some of the earliest buildings in south Mesopotamia were of this type; they are represented in a religious context in early art (see fig. 19) and on cylinder seals (see fig. 17), and traces of ancient reed huts have been found at several prehistoric sites. The symbol of the great goddess Inanna (see figs 16, 18, 19), used before 3000 BC, is usually interpreted as a bundle of these reeds bound together to make a decorated doorway pillar. There are also texts which mention reed buildings. In one version of the Flood story the benevolent god Ea

13 Left *The delicate drawing of the gazelle on this plaque of the ED III period, alongside cuneiform, calls into question a suggestion sometimes made that the change from pictographs to impressed cuneiform came about as a result of problems in drawing on clay.*

14 Below *Shuruppak was prominent in ancient Mesopotamian tradition as the city of the great Flood. This piece of relief from Shuruppak, ED IIIa period (2600–2500 BC), shows a boating scene.*

15 *Left Naked men bringing offerings in honour of the great goddess Innin (Inanna), on an alabaster vase of about 3000 BC from Uruk (see figs 18, 32).*

16 *Below Symbols (ring-topped standards) of the great goddess Inanna on the left of this cylinder seal impression of the Uruk IV period (just before 3000 BC) (see also figs 18, 19).*

17 *Early cylinder seals, like this of the Jamdat Nasr period, represent structures of reed construction, evidence for the reed hut as one of the earliest types of secular or religious building in south Mesopotamia.*

18 *Symbols (pair of ring-topped standards) of the goddess Innin (Inanna) on the top register of the alabaster vase from Uruk (see figs 15, 32).*

secretly warned the Flood hero Uta-napishtim of the forthcoming catastrophe by addressing a message to the place where he was sleeping, beginning: 'O reed hut, listen! O wall, give ear!' Obviously, Uta-napishtim's abode was a reed hut. There were also religious rituals which had to be performed in a reed hut, and although the extant texts are only from the second millennium or later, they reflect the usage of much earlier times.

Apart from reed structures, the first building material for south Mesopotamia was a small rectangular mud-brick. These were laid flat in horizontal courses, sometimes waterproofed with bitumen which occurs as an outcrop at various places in Iraq. By the end of the ED I period, these had been superseded by a larger plano-convex brick, usually of mud, sometimes baked – laid on edge in a herring-bone pattern. In more prestigious buildings stone might be used. Buildings were flat-roofed, with palm-trunks for rafters, infilled with palm branches and covered with clay. Structures within third-millennium buildings included arches, vaults, buttresses, ceremonial entrances, pillars, stairs, drainage systems and sometimes lavatories. Doors swung on a peg set in a hollow in a block of stone; the door-hinge was unknown throughout Babylonian civilisation.

TEMPLES

In ancient thought, man was created to serve the gods, and without the presence and goodwill of its god or goddess no settlement could prosper. The deity therefore needed his or her own dwelling place, and basically a temple was the house of a god. Temples were the earliest monumental buildings. As early as 9000 BC, before humans began to make permanent houses for themselves, there was a stone-built shrine at Jericho. In south Mesopotamia the oldest known religious building was a chapel built on virgin sand in the earliest occupation level at Eridu, datable to the half millennium before 5000 BC. It was a small structure, not more than 3.5 m (12 ft) long, with a niche at one

19 A religious scene from Uruk, end of the fourth millennium. The sloping ring-topped standards on each side of the hut approached by the sheep were the origin of the later cuneiform symbol for the goddess Inanna.

end where the god's image or symbol stood, and in front of it an offering-table. In later levels the temples became larger and more elaborate.

The earliest shrines had a priest to attend to the god's needs, and a share in the community land for the priest's support. As cities developed, the shrines grew with them. Before the middle of the third millennium, they had become imposing temples, with courtyards, multiple chapels and warehouses, and were by then thought of as having been founded by the gods themselves in primeval times. The modest plots of land, originally provided for the support of shrines, had grown into great temple estates; and the single priest had evolved into a large staff of cultic officials (see fig. 21), administrators and workers, both slave and free.

In its basic form, a temple began as a rectangular chamber with a niche for the divine statue or symbol in one of the short sides. Entry was originally by a door in one of the long sides, but later it became more usual to have the entrance in the short side facing the altar. A brick altar stood in front of the niche which housed the deity's image or symbol, and further from the niche were other brick tables for offerings. Around the walls were brick benches to accommodate statues. In some sanctuaries there is evidence of wall-paintings. In most cases a temple quickly grew by the addition of series of chambers on both long sides, and subsidiary shrines to associated deities might be added to the main shrine. Alternation of buttresses and recesses would break the plainness of outside walls, and decoration might be added by inserting finger-sized baked clay cones horizontally into mud-plaster on the walls. With their ends painted black, red or white, patterns of these cones gave a pleasing mosaic effect (see pl. v). The space outside the main entrance would be enclosed to produce a courtyard, and in some cases, as at Khafajeh in the Diyala region in the ED III period, there was an oval enclosing wall around the whole complex.

Closely associated with temples were ziggurats (see fig. 20). These were stepped towers, in their final form up to seven stages high. They are best known from the III Ur period onward, but had earlier precursors. (Some scholars would dispute the last statement.) At Warka, as early as the Jamdat Nasr period, there was a temple on a platform 12 m (40 ft) high, reached by a stairway, and this may reasonably be taken as

20 Above *The ziggurat of Nimrud (the ancient Assyrian capital Calah) remains as a prominent landmark in north Iraq.*

22 Above *Example of early writing. The origin of some of the pictographs (such as the head and palm tree at lower left) is still evident. At an early date the direction of writing altered so that signs originally vertical appeared horizontal.*

21 Above left *Priests often combined responsibility for the cult with administrative activities. This statue represents a priest of the III Ur period (c. 2100–2000 BC).*

the prototype of the ziggurat. Temple platforms of ED date have also been found at Kish and elsewhere. But the most convincing evidence for the existence of true ziggurats well before the end of the third millennium is the representation on seals of ED date of what can hardly be other than multi-staged towers. The ziggurat always had a small shrine on its summit, which some take to have been a resting-place for the deity on his or her way from heaven down to the main temple at ground level.

Beginning and development of writing

Writing is first attested in southern Mesopotamia in the half millennium before 3000 BC. The earliest examples so far found are on clay tablets from the site Warka, which represents ancient Uruk, biblical Erech. A few tablets bear no more than marks representing numerals, but most comprise both pictographs and numeral signs, scratched on lumps of clay (see figs 24–7). Some of the earliest tablets took the shape of flattened round buns, and had obviously been moulded between the palms of the hands; in some cases one can still see the impression of the skin pattern. Other tablets were shaped like a miniature square cushion. The writing tool was obviously some pointed implement, probably a sharpened reed, since subsequently the stylus was always called a reed. The earliest writing from Uruk was notes to remind the writer of details rather than a full explicit record; it represented no grammatical elements, and it was not until after 2500 BC that signs came to be written strictly in the order in which they needed to be read.

There are indications of antecedents of writing well before true writing appeared at Uruk. These, found at sites from Jericho to Iran, take the form of small clay tokens,

23 Clay tokens, *the antecedents of true writing.*

24 Above Clay tablet from Uruk IV
period, inscribed with pictographs
and numerals. The pictograph at the
top and bottom right developed
into the cuneiform sign for grain.

25 Left Very early writing, with
pictographs.

26 Below left Very early writing
on a clay tablet, about 3000 BC.
The sign in the lower centre, a
head and stylised bread, developed
into the cuneiform sign meaning to
eat. In the absence of grammatical
elements, the language is
uncertain.

27 Below Very early writing, with
pictographs and numerals.

typically an inch or less across, taking the form of spheres, discs, cones, bicones, tetrahedrons and other shapes, sometimes with incised marks (see fig. 23). From the mid-fourth millennium such tokens are sometimes found inside or in association with hollow clay balls (*bullae*); there are examples from sites in south-west Iran, north Mesopotamia and north Syria. Sometimes the bullae bear impressed marks corresponding in number and form to the tokens inside. These must have been some sort of recording or accounting system to accompany or check the movement of goods or animals.

This accounting system became true writing when tokens representing objects were converted into signs incised on clay tablets. This stage seems to be reflected by certain signs in the earliest Uruk writing system; these have no obvious pictorial basis, but show similarities to some designs on tokens. For example, the earliest form of the sign for 'sheep' used on clay tablets was a cross inside a circle, and it is difficult to see how this can have arisen directly from a picture of a sheep. But one of the tokens of an earlier period took the form of a disc with an incised cross. We do not know for certain what the latter meant, but it is not unreasonable to take the sign for 'sheep' on clay tablets as a two-dimensional representation of it. From such beginnings, writing rapidly developed as pictographs were invented to supplement the older token symbols.

The scholar who published the archaic Uruk tablets was professor Adam Falkenstein of Heidelberg. He calculated that they contained about nine hundred pictographs, and estimated that further pictographs not yet found might bring the total number originally in use up to about two thousand. Later researchers have concluded that some pictographs in the archaic Uruk tablets are only variants, so that Falkenstein's estimates should be halved.

No one can yet read these earliest examples of writing with any assurance; it is not even certain what language they represented. However, about thirty per cent of the signs can be identified with later cuneiform signs which can be read, and this gives a clue to the probable contents. They seem to be almost exclusively lists of commodities and livestock and the like. By the Jamdat Nasr period, up to half of the pictographs can be read, and although understanding of the tablets is still only slight at this stage, it is sufficient to establish that by this time the language was Sumerian.

Cylinder seals

Another development of the Uruk period was the cylinder seal, a cylindrical piece of hard material with an incised design. This replaced the earlier stamp seal and remained a characteristic feature of Babylonia down to the Achaemenid period. Both stamp and cylinder seals had an economic function, but a cylinder seal had the advantage over a stamp seal of enabling a design to be rolled over a much larger area in one operation.

Typically a cylinder seal was about the size of a thumb, although it could be anything from less than half to more than twice that size. Most commonly it was about

28 Above left *Stamp and cylinder seals.*

29 Above right *An early form of cylinder seal, with one end representing a ram.*

one and a half times as high as broad, although there are exceptions, with some squat, others tall and slender, and some with concave sides (see fig. 28). In the earliest period the commonest material was a soft stone such as marble or limestone. After technical problems of cutting and piercing hard stones had been overcome (see p. 34), hard stones such as haematite, obsidian and lapis lazuli increasingly came into use. Other materials sometimes found include shell, gold or silver, sometimes over a bitumen core, faience or frit, and occasionally, in peripheral areas, baked clay. Seal-cutting must have become an independent skilled craft very early, although there is no direct evidence for seal-cutters' workshops until after the middle of the second millennium. There was a considerable range of designs, which might be cut with a chisel, a bow-drill or a rotating wheel. Cylinder seals almost always have some means of suspending them. In the earliest examples this might be a perforated lug at one end; in some early examples (see fig. 29) it took the form of a ram or other animal. Later, perforation through the long axis became general.

Particular periods and areas had their own characteristic types of design for cylinder seals, with a range of different patterns or scenes. Particular types of design seem to have identified the social status of the seal-owner. Thus, in burials at Ur, one finds two contrasting subjects on cylinder seals – scenes representing a banquet and scenes of contest. The banquet scenes are most commonly found on cylinder seals of valuable lapis lazuli (see fig. 31), in association with gold objects, while the contest scenes

commonly occur on seals of much less expensive shell, and are associated with copper objects. Officials changed their seals as they climbed the administrative ladder.

Early technology

Until the end of the ED period we are, except for hints from myths and epics, almost totally dependent upon archaeology for information on how people lived, since there are very few relevant texts.

One important invention of the Uruk period was the potter's wheel; one of these, 90 cm (3 ft) in diameter and made of baked clay, was found at Ur. Another was the plough, which greatly increased agricultural productivity; its existence in the Uruk period is proved by a pictogram. A later development from this was an attachment by which seed was sown direct into the ploughed furrow (see fig. 30).

The Uruk period saw the beginning of industrialisation. Archaeology revealed an installation at Uruk which comprised shelving trenches, with indications of exposure to a high temperature, associated with banks of fire-pits. The number of fire-pits suggests that this was a metal foundry in which up to forty workers were engaged. Pottery of uniform type also occurs widely, pointing to mass production in units considerably larger than a single worker could have operated. One of the early pictographic texts contains signs which some scholars see as cataloguing different classes of worker. Evidence of kilns, and an abundance of copper implements, point to an efficient metal technology. The copper had to be obtained from abroad, probably from the far end of the Persian Gulf, and this, together with the presence of lapis lazuli from Afghanistan, proves long-distance trade.

Social organisation

Most of our knowledge about early social organisation is gleaned from myths and epics, eked out by comparative material from primitive societies elsewhere. The general picture we get is of a gradual change from what has been called 'primitive democracy' to a society with an increasing degree of stratification in respect of wealth and power. In the earliest settlements, all land was community land, with rights shared out between the extended families who made up the community. Myths indicate that decisions affecting the community were made in an assembly of all men and women, who co-operated in tasks associated with their land rights and shared what was produced.

The rise of cities brought major modifications. As an administrative structure developed, certain individuals came to exercise particular authority, and the hereditary principle tended to vest this authority in particular families. By the ED II period

30 Opposite above *One important invention of Mesopotamia was the seeder-plough. This monument, from the seventh century* BC, *shows such an implement, invented much earlier.*

31 Opposite below *In the early dynastic period a favourite design on cylinder seals was a banquet scene, as here.*

(after 2750 BC), to which Gilgamesh belonged, there was a powerful ruler at the top of the social structure. He was not yet, however, all-powerful, since in important state decisions such as going to war he had to consult an assembly of heads of families and warriors. But women no longer participated in the consultation process. The citizens' assembly retained a degree of authority in some matters to the end of the third millennium and even later.

By the ED III period (about 2600 BC), land had ceased to be distributed throughout the entire citizenship, so that some people now had no land rights. This was in part because later immigrants could not expect to enjoy parity with the earliest settlers; but the main factor was that much of the land had come into the ownership either of the temple estates, or of what was often called 'the palace', that is, the organisation headed by the city ruler. The interests of the temples and the palace could clash, but they were interlinked, and there are instances of a man from the temple administration becoming city ruler, while at some periods and places members of the city ruler's family largely controlled the temple administrations. The temple or the palace could and often did enlarge its estates by creating new irrigation canals to make hitherto uncultivated land available for agriculture, but some of their land must earlier have been community land. Until the twenty-fourth century we have no explicit data on how city rulers managed to increase their land holdings at the expense of land-owning families, but their powers undoubtedly gave them advantages in economic transactions with land-owning families.

In the earliest settlements the priest must have received a share of land, which members of the community would cultivate for him to allow him to devote himself full-time to the needs of the god. Temple estates began to develop as worshippers donated to the temple an increasing share of the community's resources, in the form of land and labour, to ensure the continued goodwill of the deity, upon whom the community's welfare depended.

It was formerly believed that such developments had virtually put an end to community or private ownership of land by the middle of the third millennium. But it is now recognised, on the basis of land sale texts, that a significant amount of land – perhaps between a quarter and a half of all cultivated land – remained with extended families and outside the state sector throughout the third millennium. Alongside this, however, there were those outside who had no land rights at all. Some of these were poor dependent people with restricted rights, and others were slaves. The inequality of wealth between the different classes is reflected archaeologically in marked differences in the size of houses.

City rulers

Three titles were in use in the third millennium to designate the ruler of a Sumerian city-state: *en*, *lugal*, and *ensi*. The oldest title was *en*. This originally meant the human spouse (male or female) of the city deity, who participated as bridegroom or bride of the deity in the Sacred Marriage. He or she lived in a special building or chamber called the *giparu*, which housed the bed for the sacred marriage. The Sacred Marriage

32 *Alabaster vase from Uruk, 105 cm (41 in) high, about 3000 BC. The three friezes together represent a cult procession (see fig. 15). The procession is headed at the top of the vase by a man approaching a woman in a cloak, who is either the goddess Innin (Inanna) or a priestess representing her (see fig. 18). The man is her bridegroom in the Sacred Marriage.*

was an annual ritual in which the *en*, of the opposite sex to the city-deity, had sexual relations with a priestess or priest representing the goddess or god, to ensure fertility and abundance for the city. Gilgamesh was an *en* in the ED II period (from *c.* 2750 BC). Aspects of the rite are represented on contemporary seals and an Uruk period vase (see figs 15, 32), and it was still practised near the end of the third millennium, giving the man who was king supremacy in the religious as well as the secular sphere. Eventually this title came to denote 'lord' generally.

The term *lugal* was composed of Sumerian *lú* 'man' and *gal* 'great', thus literally 'great man'. It developed the meaning 'owner', and became applied to the man whom the assembly chose to lead them in war. He would normally be a young man of outstanding qualities from a rich land-owning family, whose dependants could serve as a nuclear army. Such a man was well placed to increase his power and make it permanent, so that the term eventually came to mean 'king', as the Akkadian translation shows.

Ensi was originally the term for the official who organised the collective agricultural work of a settlement – its irrigation, sowing, harvesting, and the like. It came to be commonly used for a minor city ruler not powerful enough to be called a king, or a governor ruling on behalf of an overlord.

THE CITY-RULER AS PROTECTOR

The lower a person was in the economic scale, the more vulnerable he or she was to oppression. A slave had to accept this, but a free citizen would feel that he or she had an ultimate hope for protection in the city-state ruler. Rulers came to be praised for their care for citizens. Thus in a composition of the III Ur period a subject proclaims: 'Say to the king . . . thus says your servant: "My king takes care of me, I am a son of the city of Ur. Because my king is a god, he will not allow anyone to despoil my paternal estate." '

Economic problems could arise by temple or state officials using extortion, or by the rich exacting unjust terms when a poor person needed to sell something. From soon after the middle of the third millennium some rulers were making deliberate attempts to rectify such abuses, although it is questionable to what extent such measures produced any lasting benefits. No doubt one factor in any such measures was an attempt to secure the support of a particular class or group, but we may also credit such rulers with a perception that some activities were unjust and contrary to the will of the gods.

The first example of a conscious attempt to alter some aspects of the social order comes in a text of Uru-inim-gina, ruler of the city-state of Lagash for seven years just after 2380 BC. Written in Sumerian, this is not a decree but part of a larger text reporting the king's activities. The part relevant here lists measures he had taken to alter the situation as it had been 'in former times'. The text is difficult to understand in detail, but certain things are clear. Such classes as boatmen, farmers and herdsmen were relieved of certain obligations, and some official posts were abolished. Burial fees payable to priests were halved, and usurped property was returned to the temples. And there is the specific claim that Uru-inim-gina accepted it as a responsibility to Ningirsu (chief deity of the city-state) that he would not hand over the widow and orphan to the powerful.

Kings later in the third millennium or at the beginning of the second showed a corresponding concern for the protection of the economically weak. In the final century of the millennium we have the first code of laws, from the Ur III Dynasty, formerly attributed to Ur-Nammu (2113–2096 BC), but now recognised as the work of his son Shulgi (see p. 102). These laws, referring to the economic measures the king had introduced, also give protection to widows, orphans and the poor (see p. 88). Lipit-Ishtar (1934–1924 BC) speaks in his laws of the emancipation of formerly free citizens who had fallen into slavery. A hymn of the same period refers to a king who reduced to four days a month the corvée service to which a poor freeman was liable.

Social stratification and slavery

State ownership of large tracts of land left many people without land rights, and this was a major factor in social stratification. In the conditions of ancient south Meso-potamia, people who enjoyed no rights over land could survive only by accepting dependence upon those who owned the primary means of production. Some could maintain themselves in specialised occupations – well-known examples include scribes, merchants, builders, jewellers, weavers, cylinder seal cutters, carpenters and sackmakers – but for others the only resort was to serve as a pool of labour, mainly on temple or palace land. In some circumstances they might hire out their labour as free men, but in others they might become dependants of temple or state and less than free. Thus it came about that there were three orders or estates in the society of ancient Babylonia: free citizens, slaves, and an intermediate group who were not slaves but yet did not enjoy full citizen rights. Some scholars use the term 'serf' for people in this last class; it is here proposed to call them villeins.

The Laws of Hammurabi (see p. 101ff.) make an explicit distinction between these three estates. At a number of places they contrast the rights and duties of the free citizen (*awilum*, Sumerogram LÚ), the villein (*muškenum*, Sumerogram MAS.EN.GAG), and the slave (*wardum*, feminine *amtum*, Sumerograms ARAD, GÉME).

SLAVES

A king could call himself a slave in relation to his god, or a subject, even if actually a free man, could call himself the slave of the king. But such usages did not affect the essential legal difference between a free man and a slave. Slaves were legally owned by another person, or by an organisation, and could be sold, inherited, exchanged or, as frequently happened in dedications to a temple, given away.

Slave ownership certainly went back to the early third millennium, and some scholars see it as already attested in the second half of the fourth millennium, on the basis of signs in the archaic texts from Uruk, which they take to refer to male and female slaves in hundreds.[1] But translations of the archaic Uruk texts are at best informed guesses, so too much should not be built on this. The original source of slaves was raids abroad. The ideogram for 'female slave' [⧖] makes this clear; it was a combination of [▽], the symbol for 'woman', with [▴▴], the symbol for 'mountain', and originally meant 'woman from the mountain'. In early times male prisoners of war were often killed, but if not they might be held in neckstocks (see fig. 39) until sufficiently subdued. Sometimes they were blinded to render them more tractable. In many cases prisoners of war were eventually donated to a temple, although others, particularly women, might become slaves of private citizens. However, prisoners of war were not always reduced to slavery; at some periods they and their descendants might rank as villeins. Except for those who became slaves as prisoners of war, most slaves were people born to parents of the slave class.

Slaves frequently attempted to run away, and sales of slaves often gave the buyer an indemnity against this for the first hundred days. Potential runaways could be fettered or confined in a special building of the temple. To help a slave escape was a serious offence; the Laws of Eshnunna prescribed a fine for anyone who concealed a fugitive slave, and Hammurabi's laws made death the penalty for assisting a slave to escape. To protect the owners against loss, slaves were normally marked in some way, sometimes by a characteristic hairdo; Hammurabi's laws prescribe that a barber who wilfully cut this away should lose his hand. Alternatively slaves might be branded with a hot iron like cattle. In such cases the owner's mark, or for a temple slave the god's symbol, was burnt on the slave's hand or wrist. There was no compassion for age or gender, and in the New Babylonian period we meet a six-year-old slave girl whose wrist was marked with the name of her two owners.

Slaves could be bought and sold within the country, but there was virtually no international slave trade. In later periods at least, a slave might be apprenticed to learn a trade, such as baking, shoemaking, weaving, or building, and by the New Babylonian period there were many slaves who were craftsmen. Slaves received the same rations as free workers. For both slaves and villeins these were normally in the form of barley or flour (about two litres per man per day, less for a woman), beer, oil or fat. They would also receive footwear and cloth, or as an alternative to the last, wool with which they could weave their own garments. At special occasions such as festivals, they might additionally receive fish, dates, meat, fruit and dairy products (see fig. 33).

Slaves had no legal protection against harsh usage. To injure or kill a slave was an offence, but it was an offence not against the slave but against his or her owner, who received pecuniary compensation. There seems to have been nothing to prevent an owner from grossly ill-using or even killing his or her slave if he or she so wished. In the worst circumstances private slavery could be far harsher than temple slavery, and a case is recorded in which it was alleged that a woman in private slavery had escaped and put a false temple mark on her hand. However, there were circumstances in which the rights of a person of the *awilum* class over a slave were restricted. If, for instance, the wife of an *awilum* provided her husband with a slave-girl for the purpose of bearing children and the girl bore sons, her mistress lost the right to sell her.

Slaves owned by an individual or family were predominantly used for work in

33 *Cow husbandry was an important feature of the ancient Mesopotamian economy. The top section of this frieze from Tell al-Ubaid, ED III period (c. 2600 BC), shows a dairy scene. The figures are of limestone, mounted on a slab of slate, 22 cm (nearly 9 in) high.*

private households. But the economy of Babylonia was never dependent upon slavery, and many families owned no slaves at all. Slaves did not at any time play a big role in agriculture, perhaps because of the difficulty of controlling groups of slaves in such circumstances. The head of the household or other male members of the family took it as a matter of course that female slaves were available sexually, and in consequence many slave children had blood ties with the free family. According to the Laws of Hammurabi, if the head of the family had children by a slave-girl and formally adopted them, they became free citizens and shared in inheritance of the father's property. If the head of the family did not adopt such children, they remained slaves for the time being and had no inheritance rights, but after the death of the father they and their mother received their freedom.[2]

Slaves were not necessarily at a disadvantage economically. At some periods they could own houses, herds and slaves of their own, rent land, lend the ancient equivalent of money, join in business ventures with free men, and even have a free man arrested for debt. A temple slave could attain a high position in the temple administration. In theory a slave could be manumitted, but judging by the paucity of documents attesting such cases, this was exceptional. A slave could not buy his freedom, since in the last resort all that he owned belonged to his master. Even a wealthy slave could be sold, when the price he fetched would reflect the value of the assets he controlled.

How far slaves were normally considered to have the right to a family life remains in doubt; certainly slave families were sometimes broken up, young children being sold without their parents, or mother and children without the father. On the other hand, we meet cases of slaves stably married with children, and one of Hammurabi's laws provides for a slave contracting marriage with a free woman: 'If a slave of a palace or a slave of a subject has married a woman of the free class, and she has borne sons, the slave's owner may not claim the woman's sons for slavery.'[3] But although the slave's sons were not slaves, he himself did not become free. If the slave died, his wife retained her dowry, if she had brought one, and the rest of the joint property was divided between the slave's owner and the wife, whose half went to her sons.

VILLEINS

The term *muškenum* occurs several times in Hammurabi's laws, occasionally with a broader sense than 'villein'. For example, we find 'slave of the palace' contrasted with 'slave of a *muškenum*', with no mention of 'slave of a free citizen'; since free citizens could undoubtedly own slaves, *muškenum* in such instances must mean 'subject (of the king)'. However, usually it refers to a category of people who enjoyed more rights than a *wardum* (slave) but less than an *awilum* (free citizen). An offence against a *muškenum* incurred a lesser penalty than one against an *awilum*; thus, if a man caused the death of the pregnant daughter of an *awilum*, his own daughter was put to death, but if the woman was the daughter of a *muškenum*, the penalty was half a mina of silver. On the other hand, when a person became liable to a financial penalty, it was higher for an *awilum* than for a *muškenum*; thus, in case of divorce, a *muškenum* paid only one-third of the *awilum* rate.

In some contexts *muškenum* was used not of a specific social class but in the sense of 'poor man', 'destitute person'. In that sense it has come down into modern Arabic as *miskîn*, 'poor', and has been taken over into Italian (*meschino*) and French (*mesquin*) with the same meaning.

The nucleus of the villein class comprised descendants of earlier free citizens who had lost some of their rights in consequence of economic adversity. Others were in origin foreign immigrants, prisoners of war who had not become slaves, fugitives from some other city-state, and society's rejects, such as widows and orphans. Often their economic circumstances were no better than those of slaves.

Villeins substantially outnumbered slaves. They normally engaged in agricultural work or animal husbandry on temple estates or royal lands; women might serve as weavers. The legal rights of villeins varied at different periods; by the Old Babylonian period an injury to a *muškenum* incurred a penalty of half that of an injury to a free citizen. Unlike a slave, a villein could without question have a wife and children. Whereas a slave could be sold, a villein could not. Neither slaves nor villeins were free to uproot themselves and move away; a slave was limited to the land of the household to which he belonged, a villein to the royal or temple estate where he worked.

CITIZENS

This category includes both those who had hereditary land rights and those with none. Those without land often became either artisans or hired labourers; the latter are first mentioned in texts in the III Ur period, but they must have been a feature of agricultural practice earlier. By Old Babylonian times they are found working both on privately owned land and on land in the state sector, and several clauses of Hammurabi's laws legislate for them.

Owners of private land might work it in person with their families, with the assistance of hired labour if necessary. The temples and the palace had extensive administrative and economic networks, and it was usual for both to allocate parcels of land to their administrators and officers as prebends. Normally, if an official had a son able to perform the relevant service, his father's allocation of land would in due course pass to him, although the land remained state property and could not in principle be sold. However, during periods of state weakness families who had held land over a long period might begin to claim it as hereditary property.

In some circumstances a person of free birth might be reduced to slavery. This could happen, for example, with convicted criminals and their families. If a farmer had through negligence caused the loss of his neighbour's crops by flooding, and could not repay the damage, his goods were forfeit and he could be sold into slavery. Another case, set out in detail in the Laws of Hammurabi, concerned a wife convicted of certain offences against her husband:

> If the wife of a free man ... has set her mind on leaving, and
> misappropriates something or squanders her household property and
> treats her husband badly, and they convict her, if her husband says he
> will divorce her, he may do so; ... if he says he will not divorce her, her
> husband may marry another woman, and the [convicted] woman shall
> live in her husband's house as a slave.[4]

Another legal text (not in Hammurabi's laws) says that a father whose adopted son has denied him may put a slave-mark on him. Exceptionally, particularly in the later period, children might be sold into slavery in times of famine to keep them alive.

A free man might surrender his wife, son, or daughter into servitude for debt, but this was limited to a maximum period of three years, and Hammurabi's laws do not use the word for 'slavery' in this connection.

The first dynasties

The people of ancient Mesopotamia believed that the gods had decreed all the institutions of their society, chosen the sites of cities and ordained that the land should be ruled by a succession of dynasties. Such beliefs became enshrined in traditions, which scholars collected. Towards the end of the third millennium these were edited in the compilation known as the *Sumerian King List* (see p. 28), which recorded all dynasties or supposed dynasties back to when kingship was first 'lowered from heaven'. However, the compilers were not scientific historians, and worked on two unsound presuppositions. They supposed, firstly, that every dynasty ruled the whole of what became Babylonia, and secondly, that dynasties were all consecutive, with no overlaps.

SKL says that kingship, when first lowered from heaven, lighted in Eridu – the most southerly Sumerian city – where two kings reigned for 64,800 years. It then passed successively to Bad-tibira, Larak, Sippar, and Shuruppak, with no reign less than 18,600 years. Then came the Flood and swept everything away. When kingship was let down from heaven again, it lighted first on Kish in the north of the country, with a line of kings whose reigns were in no case more than 1560 years. With the twenty-second king of this dynasty, En-me-bara-ge-si, tradition and history meet. Despite being credited with a reign of nine hundred years, this king was a real person. We know this from a piece of an alabaster vase in the Baghdad Museum which bears a form of his name in archaic script.

SKL names En-me-bara-ge-si's son and successor as Agga, who appears in a Sumerian epic as a contemporary and rival of the hero Gilgamesh of Uruk. There is a problem here. SKL places the dynasty to which Gilgamesh belonged in succession to the First Dynasty of Kish, and if we took its figures at face value, there would be a gap of some two thousand years between Agga and Gilgamesh. Some dynasties which SKL regarded as consecutive must have been contemporary.

SKL provides further links between tradition and history with its next post-Flood dynastic centre, Ur. For the First Dynasty of this city it names five kings; there are contemporary inscriptions for three of these.

The compilers of SKL clearly had access to reliable traditions about early dynasties, despite their mistaken belief that every dynasty ruled the whole of south Meso-potamia. Some early dynasts were indeed accepted as paramount ruler over much of the country, and perhaps in one or two cases over all of it, but no one before Sargon of Agade in the twenty-fourth century was able to maintain a permanent claim to kingship over the whole of south Mesopotamia.

Modern scholars refer to the period between Jamdat Nasr and Sargon as the Early Dynastic, which they subdivide into phases I, II, and III to reflect societal changes and developments. ED III is sometimes further subdivided into IIIa and IIIb. Absolute datings are disputable, but we assume the following:

ED I	2900–2750 BC
ED II	2750–2600 BC
ED IIIa	2600–2500 BC
ED IIIb	2500–2371 BC

Successive phases of ED are distinguished mainly by archaeological features, in-cluding changes in pottery style and types of vessel, subjects of cylinder seals and techniques of cutting them, types of bricks, metal working techniques, architecture, and stages of writing. There were also social changes which came with the growth of cities.

Increasing populations and the opening up of more land for agriculture gave a

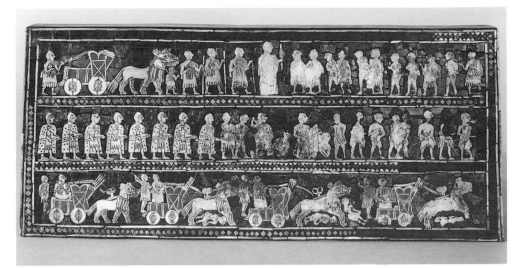

34 *War scene showing chariots and soldiers, from the Standard of Ur, found in a Royal Tomb of Ur.*

situation in which conflict could break out over disputed territory or competition for water rights in a shared canal. By the ED II period, rulers could organise bodies of fighting men running into thousands and equip them with weaponry, so war between city-states became a feature of life. The threat of attack led to the building of city walls as a defence system. Tradition has it that the walls of Uruk were built by Gilgamesh; an epic recounts how he was able to withstand attack by the powerful King Agga of Kish. Some kings of south Mesopotamian city-states made raids right outside the country, in quest of such raw materials as large timber. A Sumerian dedication on a vase from about 2570 BC describes a ruler of Kish as 'conqueror of Hamazi', an unidentified place somewhere in the hills 320 km (200 miles) to the north.[5] Mesilim, king of Kish (c. 2600 BC), was able to extend his hegemony 190 km (120 miles) to the south-east as far as Umma and Lagash, so that when those two city-states were in dispute over land and water rights, it was he who arbitrated a settlement and set up a boundary marker.

Inscriptions over a century after Mesilim's arbitration give a detailed account of the course of the long-standing Lagash-Umma conflict.[6] The territory of the two states abutted in an area called 'edge of the *edin*'[7], meaning the open plains between cities. Obviously the two cities had expanded their cultivated lands until they met in what had once been open country. The solution originally agreed was that Umma should cultivate the disputed area, and pay Lagash part of the yield of grain as rent. But this solution soon broke down. Rulers of Lagash from about 2500 BC onwards recorded the sequel. The first to do this was Urnanshe (see fig. 36), but it is his grandson and second successor, Eanatum,[8] who gives the fullest details of the dispute. He left three inscriptions, of which the longest is preserved on the monument called 'Stele of the Vultures' (see fig. 35). Eanatum claims that during the reign of his father, Akurgal, the ruler of Umma had broken the rental agreement, invaded the territory, and smashed

35 Left *Part of the 'Stele of the Vultures', a monument set up by Eanatum of Lagash to commemorate his victory over the rival city-state of Umma.*

36 Opposite above *It was a work of piety for ancient Mesopotamian kings to participate in temple-building. This shows Urnanshe, ruler of Lagash (late twenty-sixth century), carrying a basket of bricks on his head.*

the boundary monument set up by Mesilim. Ningirsu, city-god of Lagash, appeared to Eanatum in a dream and commanded him to act, promising that the citizens of Umma would rise against their ruler. In obedience to Ningirsu, Eanatum attacked Umma, and, although wounded by an arrow, regained control of the disputed territory. He then compelled the ruler of Umma to swear oaths by six great gods that in future Umma would respect the territory of Lagash and not divert any of its irrigation channels.

Eanatum's two successors both faced further boundary infringements. The second of them, his nephew Enmetena, took firm action. After accusing the ruler of Umma not only of diverting irrigation channels but also of owing a huge quantity of barley as arrears of rent and interest due under the original settlement, Enmetena attacked and defeated him. The discredited ruler escaped to Umma, only to be assassinated and replaced by a nephew.

Some seventy years later we find the current ruler of Lagash, Uru-inim-gina (c. 2380 BC), recording that Umma had again attacked his city, plundering its temples of precious metals and lapis lazuli. By now Umma was the dominant power, and its ruler Lugalzagesi was aiming at control of all south Mesopotamia; his advance was brought to an end only by the rise of Sargon of Agade.

37 Below *Religious scenes on the Standard of Ur, showing seated people and a procession of animals and men.*

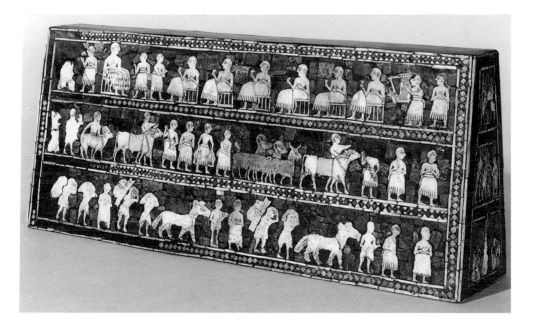

38 *Third-millennium Mesopotamia already had board games. This is an example of a gaming board and counters, from before the middle of the third millennium, found at Ur.*

Royal tombs of Ur

After the First World War C. L. Woolley (later knighted as Sir Leonard) directed a major dig at Ur. In 1927 he began to excavate an ancient cemetery, which proved to be dated to the first half of the third millennium and to contain some two thousand burials. In the great majority of the burials, the corpse had been wrapped in matting or put into a coffin of reeds, wood or clay, and laid in a grave from 120–360 cm (4–12 ft) deep. The bodies had no particular orientation, but lay on one side in the attitude of sleep. Accompanying the body there were often beads, ear-rings, a knife, a pin to fasten the shroud, and perhaps a cylinder seal, and away from the matting or coffin there would be grave offerings in the form of weapons, tools, and vessels which had contained food and drink.

Such was the standard type of burial; but Woolley found sixteen burials of a very different kind, now dated to the ED IIIa period (2600–2500 BC). These were interred much more deeply in tombs of solid stone or stone and brick; the tombs were of one to four chambers, and very rich in equipment and ornaments of gold, silver and lapis lazuli. No two tombs were identical in their equipment, but among the more striking finds were a helmet of beaten gold in the form of a wig (see pl. VIII), and bowls, chisels, a saw and lamps, all of gold. There was also a gold dagger with a hilt of lapis lazuli (see pl. VI), golden tweezers, axe-heads of electrum and a bull's head in gold (see pl. VII), constituting part of a lyre. There were lions' heads in silver, silver tables, containers of silver or alabaster, and a great wealth of necklaces and other personal adornment in precious metals and lapis lazuli (see figs 37, 38).

As Woolley interpreted the archaeological evidence, the first stage in these burials was to dig a pit more than 9 m (30 ft) deep, and 12 × 9 m (40 × 30 ft) at its base, with access by a sloping shaft in one side. In this pit the tomb was constructed.

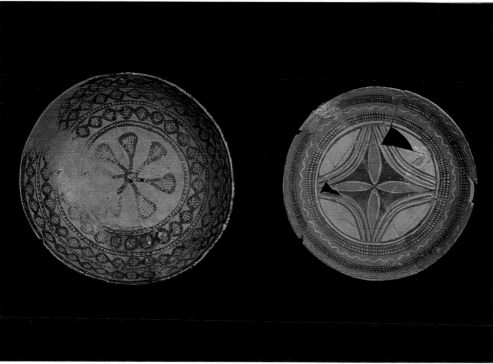

PLATE I Top *The ziggurat of Birs Nimrud (ancient Borsippa) in 1956. Some regard this as the original of the Tower of Babel.*

PLATE II Above *Decorated bowls of the prehistoric (fifth-millennium) Halaf culture.*

PLATE III Above *Basalt representation of a vegetation deity, from Lagash, ED III period.*

PLATE IV Opposite above *A reed house of Arabs in the marshes of south Iraq. Some of the earliest temples in ancient south Mesopotamia were of similar structure.*

PLATE V Opposite below *In the late fourth millennium, temple columns and walls were decorated with designs formed by inserting clay cones with coloured ends. The example shown here is from Uruk.*

PLATE **VI** Above left *Gold dagger and sheath, found in one of the Royal Tombs of Ur.*

PLATE **VII** Above right *Golden bull's head from the Royal Tombs of Ur, part of a lyre.*

PLATE **VIII** Below *Golden helmet from the Royal Tombs of Ur.*

PLATE IX *The ziggurat of Aqarquf (ancient Dur-Kurigalzu), built by the Kassites near the Tigris as part of a defence system against attack from the east.*

PLATE X *Reconstruction of the Ishtar Gate in Babylon.*

PLATE **XI** Above *Reconstruction of a section of Nebuchadnezzar's Processional Way in Babylon.*

PLATE **XII** Overleaf *The so-called 'Ram in the Thicket', from the Royal Tombs of Ur, was actually part of a Sumerian motif showing two goats, one on each side of a sacred tree.*

An astonishing feature of these burials was that each had associated human sacrifices, numbering from three to seventy-four victims. In most cases the victims had died at the time of the main burial. Where the tomb consisted of only one chamber, the sacrifices took place in the pit. Rows of bodies lay there, predominantly female, wearing golden ear-rings, silver combs, necklaces of lapis lazuli and gold, and ornate head-dresses of lapis lazuli, carnelian and golden leaves. In multi-chambered tombs, the principal burial, decked out in rich array, would be placed in the main chamber in a wooden coffin or on a bier, with some of the subsidiary dead, presumably personal attendants, in other chambers nearby. Music must have been a feature of the rituals, since lyres were found; in one tomb these were placed on the bodies of female attendants who had already died. There were also bodies of soldiers carrying daggers and spears, some partly of gold or silver.

In the sloping entrance passage, Woolley found the remains of the wagons which had been used to transfer the principal burial and the furniture to the tomb. The draught oxen had been slaughtered and had fallen on top of their grooms, who had obviously died earlier. According to Woolley, none of the bodies showed any sign of violence or disorder, and he concluded, on the basis of a small cup accompanying each body, that all the victims had died by self-administered poison. Technically this was self-immolation rather than human sacrifice.

The richness of the contents of the tombs led Woolley to conclude that they were royal. This assumption receives a degree of support from names inscribed on some of the objects, a few of which can be linked to kings of Ur of the Early Dynastic period. No burial, however, is directly identified with a royal name, and in one case the name of a known king occurs in the burial chamber of a female corpse. It is therefore possible that the royal names did not identify the persons buried but were there because royal persons had made dedications at some ritual vital to Ur.

There are some alternative suggestions about the nature of these tombs. One is that the principal burials were persons who had served as substitute kings and queens when evil omens had threatened the real ruler, and had been put to death after their period of office (see p. 139). However, there is no other evidence for the practice of the substitute king at such an early date. Another suggestion is that the principal burials were priests and priestesses who had played the part of the god and goddess in an enactment of the Sacred Marriage (see pp. 52–4). But where we have concrete evidence for the sacred marriage, at least one participant was royal, so that this would not preclude their being royal burials. A serious objection to linking these burials to the sacred marriage ritual is lack of evidence that this ritual ended in death for any of the participants. Furthermore, the Sacred Marriage rite was an annual event, so that if in the ED IIIa period it did end in death, one would expect, for the period covered by the Ur cemetery, more than the sixteen tombs actually found.

Chapter Four

AGADE,
THE FIRST EMPIRE

THE CITY-STATE REMAINED the basic unit of political organisation in Babylonia throughout the third millennium. Even rulers, such as Mesilim of Kish, who succeeded in extending their authority far beyond their own territory, still accepted the sovereignty of other city-states subject to recognition of their overlordship. In the second half of the third millennium this began to change, as conditions became favourable for wider political relationships. Trade had long flourished beyond the bounds of individual city-states, and the marks of advanced culture – writing, social organisation, cities – had accompanied trade as far away as the Mediterranean.

The first to make a major impact in the direction of larger political units was Lugalzagesi, ruler of the city-state of Umma, who, after conquering first Lagash and then Uruk, set himself up as king of Uruk and of south Babylonia, and then went on to defeat Kish in north Babylonia. He now claimed control not only of all Babylonia, but also of the routes from the Persian Gulf to the Mediterranean. But his imperial success was limited and short-lived, and he was overthrown by Sargon of Agade.

The first empire

It was Sargon of Agade who made the first successful attempt at empire.[1] Dates proposed for his succession range from 2469 BC to 2242 BC; we take it as 2371 BC. SKL gives us a bald outline of Sargon's career: it says he was a gardener who became cupbearer to a king of Kish named Ur-Zababa; he built the city Agade, became king himself, and reigned for fifty-six years.

Further dubious details of Sargon's origins come from a legend, known only from first-millennium copies, reminiscent of the story of Moses in the bulrushes. Told in the first person, its introductory lines read:

I am Sargon, the mighty king, king of Agade.
My mother was a high priestess; I do not know who my father was.
My paternal kinsmen inhabit the steppe.
My city was Azupiranu, set on the bank of the Euphrates.
My mother, the high priestess, conceived me, bore me in secret.
She put me in a reed-basket, she caulked my door with pitch.
She cast me into the river . . .

The legend goes on to tell how a water-drawer, appropriately named Aqqi ('I drew out'), found the baby and brought him up as his own son. Sargon became a gardener, and because the goddess Ishtar loved him he became king.

One version of the legend has a variant in place of 'I do not know who my father was'. This reads 'I had no father'. At first sight either form might be taken to imply that Sargon was illegitimate; but since the whole text is setting out to glorify a great hero, it would be strange for it to cast a deliberate slur on Sargon's legitimacy. It seems more probable that it was playing down his father in order to emphasise his high-priestly mother. A high priestess was always of noble and sometimes of royal blood, and enjoyed the status of wife of a god. She was, at least at some periods, permitted to marry a human husband, but she was not supposed to bear children. This explains why, according to the tradition, Sargon's mother had to abandon him to the river. But his mother's status made it clear that Sargon had good blood and perhaps, in view of the question mark over his paternity, even an element of divinity.

The rest of the legend deals with Sargon's later exploits, but only in general terms, saying little more than that he repeatedly crossed the mountains, and conquered Tilmun (somewhere in Iran or the Persian Gulf) and places on the Elamite frontier.

This, for what it is worth, is almost all we know about Sargon's origin. His Akkadian name, Šarru-kīn ('the king is the true one'), and the fact that his inscriptions were predominantly in Akkadian, suggests that his mother-tongue was Semitic. This has sometimes been taken as evidence that he belonged to a major wave of Semitic-speaking immigrants who had entered Mesopotamia shortly before. But this does not necessarily follow: as we have seen earlier (see pp. 29–31), speakers of a Semitic language had been prominent in north Babylonia centuries before Sargon.

There are several other sources of data for the careers of Sargon and his successors. First there is archaeological evidence, which chiefly takes the form of remains of temples or palaces of Sargonic rulers or monuments they set up. There are inscriptions of the Sargonic rulers themselves, some of them originals, the others copies made not later than the Old Babylonian period. They are mostly written in Akkadian, with a few in Sumerian and some bilingual. The information they give is reliable but patchy. Some economic documents remain from the period; and there are also later traditions. These last often give the fullest information, but their reliability is suspect. They comprise principally such types of text as epics, legends, chronicles, and allusions in omens; there is also a geographical survey of the empire.

All earlier power centres in south Mesopotamia had been cities founded before history, but Sargon's capital, Agade, was a new creation. The late Th. Jacobsen of Harvard, a distinguished Sumerologist, offered a credible hypothesis of its origin and name. According to SKL, Sargon had been a high official at the court of Kish, and Jacobsen concluded that when Lugalzagesi of Uruk conquered that city, Sargon withdrew to his family estates. There he founded a new town, which he called by the Semitic name Akkadê, meaning 'ancestral town'; this was rendered Agade in Sumerian.

The site of Agade remains unidentified. It must have been on a river, since it became a major port for Persian Gulf shipping. Most scholars look for it on an old course of the Euphrates, near either Babylon or Kish. An alternative proposal is a site on the Tigris, in the neighbourhood of modern Baghdad, but this is highly unlikely. There is a text which speaks of shipping plying between Agade and Nippur, and Nippur was without question on a branch of the Euphrates, not on the Tigris; therefore the same must have been true of Agade, unless at that time an otherwise unknown canal system linked the Euphrates and Tigris in north Babylonia.

The first step in Sargon's rule was to overthrow Lugalzagesi of Uruk, former conqueror of Kish. Sargon's treatment of the defeated Lugalzagesi shows he already had imperial ambitions, for he presented him in a neck-stock to the national god Enlil at Nippur, thereby demonstrating with maximum publicity that national supremacy had passed to himself. Further successes followed, which Sargon recorded in his inscription, telling of the defeat of Ur and other southern cities. His actions here went beyond earlier practice; he was not content merely to receive the submission of these cities, but in each case he destroyed their ramparts, and installed citizens of his capital Agade as governors. Beyond the bounds of south Mesopotamia, the important trading entrepot of Mari on the middle Euphrates became a client, as did also Elam in south-west Iran. This gave Sargon control of a considerable commercial empire.

In other inscriptions Sargon sums up further successes, both military and economic. Altogether, he claims, he won thirty-four battles, destroyed city ramparts as far as the Persian Gulf, and took fifty city rulers prisoner. Boats from Meluhha (north-west India), Magan (the region of the Gulf of Oman) and Tilmun (perhaps Bahrein) anchored at the quay of Agade. North-westwards his control now extended past Mari to take in the great commercial centre of Ebla south of Aleppo, and went as far as the 'cedar forest' (the Amanus) and the 'silver mountain' (the Taurus). Other texts speak of conquests by Sargon in the southern Zagros and south-west Iran, where he overthrew Elam and its associates, and took booty.

These details tell us something of the nature of Sargon's empire. Mari and Ebla were both great trading centres. At Ebla, for example, excavators found much lapis lazuli, including more than twenty-two kilos unworked, and since the only source of this semi-precious stone available to the ancient Near East was Afghanistan, this indicates extensive trading links. Also, there was obvious commercial significance in the fact that shipping from the Persian Gulf and beyond anchored at Agade. Elam in turn was important for overland trade across Iran to Afghanistan and north India. Precious stones reached Mesopotamia at this time even from east Africa; analysis of a copal

40 Above *A first-millennium* BC *cuneiform map of the world as seen from Babylon, to illustrate the exploits of the third-millennium conqueror Sargon of Agade.*

39 Above *The Agade kings took many thousands of prisoners in their wars, often restraining them in neckstocks, as here.*

41 Below *No remains have yet been found of the third-millennium ships which plied as far as India, but bitumen models, such as this one from Ur, show the type of vessel in use.*

(resin from tropical trees) found in a grave at Eshnunna in the Diyala valley and approximately datable to the Agade period shows that it can only have come from the Zanzibar–Madagascar–Mozambique region,[2] although we have no idea of the trading mechanism. Thus Sargon's empire was not so much a power-structure seeking to dominate populations by military force as a means of ensuring that international trade should flourish, largely for the benefit of the capital city. None the less, the dynasty did not hesitate, when their commercial interests demanded it, to use crushing military force to subjugate opponents and to ensure that key areas remained in their hands.

Sargon's own texts establish an empire stretching at least 1450 km (900 miles), from the north-east corner of the Mediterranean to east of the head of the Persian Gulf. Later tradition ascribed to him even wider dominion. An Old Babylonian omen alludes to him as 'Sargon who ruled the entire world', and an epic poem, *King of Battle*, has him penetrating as far as Cappadocia in central Anatolia, to safeguard oppressed merchants in the region of modern Kayseri. Was this truth or legend? Some question it, but it could contain a kernel of fact. At the beginning of the second millennium there was an Assyrian merchant colony in that area, of whose antecedents we are largely ignorant, and one cannot exclude the possibility that this was carrying on a tradition established centuries earlier. Sargon's grandson Naram-Sin certainly had links with this area.

Still more extravagant are the claims which a geographical survey makes for the extent of Sargon's empire (see fig. 40). It says that he conquered everything under the sky, and includes in the empire the whole territory from the Mediterranean to the Zagros and from central Anatolia to beyond the end of the Persian Gulf, as well as Anaku ('Tin-land', unidentified) and Kaptara (perhaps Crete) beyond the Mediterranean coast. However, this document was compiled only in the first millennium, and must be used with caution. There may be material in it which goes back to the third millennium, but its primary object was probably to flatter Sargon II of Assyria (722–705 BC) through the supposed exploits of his earlier namesake. Even though this text probably exaggerates the empire's boundaries, it does accurately reflect its essentially commercial basis, when it refers to people from all regions bringing tribute.

Whatever their precise boundaries, Sargon and his successors clearly established new and wider political horizons, and their inscriptions offer insights into factors behind their success. These involved policies radically different from those of their predecessors. Unlike most earlier major rulers, Sargon was not content with mere paramountcy; he wanted real rulership over the whole land. To this end he slighted the walls of other cities to make any future resistance ineffective; he installed citizens of his own capital, doubtless personal friends and perhaps kinsmen, as administrators in other city-states to preclude any independent policy; and he made sea-going vessels tie up at Agade, to gather control of all foreign trade into his own hands. His expedition up the Euphrates to the major trading centres of Mari and Ebla and to the Amanus and Taurus showed an equal determination to control trade with the north-west, while his incursions beyond the Zagros did the same for the east.

The Sargonic rulers were also not afraid of using military might. In one of his texts,

Sargon speaks of himself as 'Sargon, the king to whom Enlil gave no rival; daily 5400 men ate bread in my presence'. Clearly, these thousands of permanent attendants represented an embryonic standing army. This must have been the nucleus of a much larger conscript army, for one tradition about Naram-Sin refers to his having 360,000 troops at his disposal. One need not take this number as a precise count, but it does imply an army numbered in hundreds of thousands rather than tens of thousands. Everything points to a deliberate strategy designed to turn the city-state of Agade into the centre of a commercial empire with a military arm.

There was another significant factor in the dynasty's realpolitik: sheer ruthlessness. Its rulers were prepared to use overwhelming force, regardless of how many victims they killed, to deal with any city that stood in their way. Sargon's immediate successor, Rimush, brings this out clearly. In the records of his conquests, he gives figures for men killed, taken prisoner, or 'set to *karašim*' (see below), and these run into tens of thousands. For one city the three categories together totalled 54,016, and in other cities the numbers for killed alone ranged from nearly nine thousand to over sixteen thousand. Allowing for comparable massacres in conquered city-states for which figures are lacking, we may conservatively estimate that Rimush was responsible for the death of well over 100,000 of his fellow countrymen, apart from victims outside Mesopotamia. These figures allow us, incidentally, to make a rough estimate of the population of Mesopotamia at the time. Assuming that battle casualties were as high as twenty per cent, that all able-bodied men between the ages of fifteen and forty were combatants, and that male expectation of life averaged fifty, 100,000 war victims would imply a population of two million. If battle casualties were lower than twenty per cent, the figure for population would increase proportionately.

'Set to *karašim*' has been variously interpreted. There were two different words *karašim*, one of which meant 'camp' and the other 'slaughter', so that it was formerly disputed whether the reference was to putting prisoners into forced labour camps, or to slaughtering them. The former always seemed more probable, but the numbers concerned – running into thousands – seemed to some scholars unduly large. However, an archive of the Sargonic period has now been identified which clearly relates to a labour camp on that scale.[3] It was on the borders of Iran, on the route between Agade and Susa. The texts give information about personnel, both freemen and slaves, and also deal with issues of rations and tools. Among the tools, which were made of copper, were what were designated 'breaking tools'; this description, and the fact that they weighed about 3.5 kg (8 lb) when newly cast, identify them as sledge-hammers. Figures are given for work done by the labour gangs, expressed in terms of volumes excavated, and inasmuch as the quantities are too small to apply to work on building or irrigation, these must refer to extracting some material. One category of personnel mentioned is 'stone men', which, with the other data, puts the purpose of the labour camp beyond doubt: it was there for the quarrying of stone or ore. Reports of deaths among personnel show a relatively heavy mortality rate, and show how harsh living conditions were.

Sargon and his descendants also used family connections to their political ad-

42 *This stone disc shows En-hedu-anna, daughter of Sargon of Agade, high-priestess of Ur and a noted poet.*

vantage. The most striking example of this was Sargon's installation of his daughter, who bore the Sumerian name En-hedu-anna ('Lord, the ornament of heaven'), as high priestess of the Moon-god Nanna in the southern Sumerian-speaking city of Ur. This was a prestigious office which gave the holder great influence with the city and temple authorities. A stone disc from Ur, unfortunately smashed, depicts En-hedu-anna with three attendants (see fig. 42). She was evidently a person of outstanding ability, who left a reputation as a poet of distinction. A collection of hymns in honour of a number of temples was attributed to her, and although her contribution here must have been mainly the editing of older works rather than the creation of new ones, she certainly wrote and signed at least one major poetic composition, and there may have been others.[4] In the composition in question, a hymn in honour of the goddess Inanna, she poignantly expresses her grief when she was expelled from Ur by a certain Lugalanne, who led a rebellion against one of Sargon's successors. Sargon's grandson Naram-Sin also used members of his family to strengthen his position; like Sargon, he installed a daughter as high priestess in Ur, and at least two of his sons were governors of cities.

Sargonic imperial success owed much to a favourable economic policy. All traditions agree that the city of Agade enjoyed considerable prosperity, which must have ensured enthusiastic support from the population. There is no indication of opposition within the capital beyond traditions in Babylonian omens that the second king Rimush, and the last major king Shar-kali-sharri, died at the hands of their servants, but if these traditions have any basis the action against Rimush may have been no more than a palace rebellion, perhaps instigated by his older brother, who succeeded him.

The Sargonic rulers seem to have made a conscious attempt to extend their secure home base, by courting the support of other northern cities. This applied particularly to Kish, to which both Sargon and his successors showed special favour, perhaps because of Sargon's early links there, perhaps on account of its prestige as an ancient and powerful city. But this policy sometimes failed, and in the reign of Naram-Sin Kish headed a revolt. Naram-Sin complained of the city's ingratitude: 'Kish', he said, 'was not an enemy for me but my brother'.

The Sargonic period saw a significant shift in land ownership in favour of the crown. Until this time much land still remained in the hands of extended families, and, as in Israel much later (see the story of Naboth's vineyard in 1 Kings 21:1–16), a ruler had no legal power to compel a family to surrender ancestral land. But sale documents from the Sargonic period show that some families were now selling their land to the ruler, and at a price so low that it represented barely more than the value of one season's crop. We have no clear idea of the factors behind this. Perhaps some families had suffered such heavy losses in the Sargonic wars that they lacked the manpower to cultivate all their hereditary land. It seems equally possible that the unprecedented power of the Sargonic rulers put them in a position to exert pressure upon some free landowners.

Sargonic imperialism did not go unchallenged. Every one of the Sargonic rulers, not excepting Sargon himself, faced revolts, some on a large scale. In view of the long-standing tradition of independent city-states these revolts were to be expected; what is remarkable is not the revolts but the fact that these kings were able to contain them for over a century. Two factors contributed to this: the difficulty opponents found in taking joint action, and the immediate military response of Sargonic kings to potential opposition. Even rulers outside Mesopotamia learned such respect for the dynasty's armed might that they were ready to link themselves by treaty to an overlord in Agade. An extant treaty between Naram-Sin and the king of Elam gives an instance of this. Though written in Elamite, which is difficult to interpret, enough can be understood to show that Elam was the junior partner in the alliance.

Successors of Sargon

Sargon was succeeded by two sons in inverse order of age, firstly Rimush and then Manishtusu. They were competent rulers, who managed to consolidate much of their father's empire, suppressing several revolts and being particularly active in the southern Zagros and south-west Iran. But a much greater figure than either of these was Manishtusu's son, Naram-Sin (2291–2255 BC), the last major king of the dynasty.

Whether because of the awe in which he was held, or from his own deliberate policy, Naram-Sin became regarded during his own lifetime as a divine being, a status reflected in the writing of the prefix denoting 'god' before his name. He was certainly a great man. Later traditions make him equal in achievements to his grandfather Sargon, and contemporary texts and archaeological finds support this estimate. He certainly penetrated deep into central Anatolia, for one of his inscriptions names a town he took there, and a British expedition found the ruins of a palace he built at Tell Brak in north-eastern Syria. Further north, a stele with his image and inscription was found near Diyarbakir in Turkey, and if one goes to Kurdistan one can still see an

43 Above *Ritual trough (late third millennium) from north Syria, with snakes as symbols of supernatural powers.*

44 Below *This relief of one of the Agade kings, probably Naram-Sin, represents a victory over mountain folk. A very similar rock relief still stands high in a pass in the Qara Dagh range in Kurdistan (north-east Iraq).*

45 Below *Very soon after the invention of writing, it was being used for other systems than that of south Mesopotamia. This tablet from Susa (in south-west Iran) was inscribed in a little-understood language known as proto-Elamite.*

image of Naram-Sin leading his troops, on a rock-relief in a mountain pass not far from Sulaimaniyeh (see fig. 44). And statues and bricks bearing his name, found at Susa, leave no doubt that he exercised solid control over south-west Iran.

Yet, although tradition knew and admired Naram-Sin's successes, it also saw him as the victim of what the Greeks called hubris, that arrogant disregard of the will of the gods which brings down divine retribution. A Sumerian poem, *The Curse on Agade*, brings this out. It begins with all going well. The national god Enlil, having overthrown Kish and Uruk in turn, bestowed the kingship on Sargon of Agade. Sargon built a temple in Agade to the great goddess Inanna, and under her aegis Agade prospered mightily. All was joy and music. Foreign peoples flocked there with tribute of exotic animals; gold, silver, copper, tin and lapis lazuli were heaped up in the warehouses like corn. The old people were wise, the young ones happy. Under Agade all lands lived in security.

So it continued into the time of Naram-Sin; the western nomads delivered flawless cattle and goats, and peoples from the north and east, from as far away as Meluhha (north-west India), were still bringing their goods. But a shadow appeared. It was only the sanctuary of Inanna in Agade which benefited from all this prosperity; Ekur, the great national temple of Enlil in Nippur, was neglected, and its oracle fell silent. Inanna was alarmed and abandoned her sanctuary and withdrew her protection. Other gods likewise withdrew their guidance from Agade, and the city was troubled. Naram-Sin saw in a dream the bleak future of Agade, but would not accept it. He sought omens from Enlil to reverse the prediction of the dream, but in vain. Finally he attacked and sacked and looted Nippur's temple Ekur.

Enlil, enraged because his beloved Ekur had been violated, brought down from the mountains the Gutians, ferocious people with the semblance of humans but the savagery of dogs and the faces of apes. They covered the earth like locusts; nothing escaped them. Trade by land and water ceased; agriculture broke down; hyperinflation set in; people died of famine and lay unburied. And the great gods put a curse on Agade, that it should for ever remain desolate and be no more a place of habitation.

This was manifestly propaganda, behind which one may see the hand of the priesthood of Nippur, intent that all rulers should recognise the need to show favour to their temple. There are elements of history in the poem, insofar as it gives a fair picture of Agade's widespread commercial empire and its consequent prosperity, but in detail it is tendentiously distorted. In particular, it has telescoped events. If Naram-Sin did indeed ever attack Nippur, it can only have been at the beginning of his reign, when a revolt broke out headed by Kish, and a number of other ancient cities, including Nippur, joined the Kish federation. In view of the importance of Nippur as the chief shrine of the national god Enlil, complicity in a rebellion would very likely bring it under attack. But the text concerning this revolt explicitly says that the enemy did not get into Agade, and we know of no other occasion during Naram-Sin's reign when Agade could have been sacked. The only evidence for the Gutians being active in Mesopotamia under Naram-Sin is a later chronicle, which says that they invaded towards the end of his reign. Even if this record is reliable, this invasion could not have brought about the destruction of Agade, since that city was still the capital in the reign of Naram-Sin's son.

Other traditions about Naram-Sin may be still further divorced from history.[5] One such, *The Cuthaean legend of Naram-Sin*, tells of a massive invasion by seven kings, brothers, who ravaged the length of the empire from Anatolia to the Persian Gulf and Meluhha. The king named as the father of the brothers was a real ruler, since there is a rock-relief of his in a pass in the Zagros, but there is little to support other details. They are probably a distorted echo of a second widespread revolt, late in Naram-Sin's reign.

Ebla

Both Sargon and Naram-Sin claimed to have conquered a city-state called Ebla in Syria, whose territory included 'the cedar forests and the silver mountains', that is, the Amanus range and the adjacent Taurus. Ebla has now been identified; in 1974–5, Italian archaeologists excavating at the site of Tell Mardikh, 65 km (40 miles) south of Aleppo, found cuneiform inscriptions which proved that this was the site of that ancient city. Subsequent finds have brought the number of largely complete tablets up to over 2600, with more than 11,000 further fragments or chips. The calligraphy on some of the texts dates their origin to the ED III period (*c.* 2500 BC), while others may be as late as the twenty-third century). A sequence of twenty-two kings of Ebla suggests that the kingdom covered approximately the period 2700–2300 BC. The existence of the Ebla archive during at least the latter half of this period is informative for the history and spread of cuneiform writing.

The spread of writing

Between the Uruk period and the end of ED III, writing underwent major changes. Its appearance altered; it became more complex; it came into use for purposes other than the economic and administrative records for which it had been devised; and it was adapted for languages other than Sumerian.

First, its changed appearance. In the Uruk period many signs, and in Jamdat Nasr some signs, still showed their pictographic origin. During the Early Dynastic period, the practice developed of impressing signs with a triangular stylus instead of incising them. This resulted in pictographic forms becoming completely superseded by signs composed of impressed wedges. In addition, the direction of writing changed. In the earliest forms, the typical direction of writing was in columns from top to bottom, beginning at the right side of the tablet. Soon the practice developed of turning the tablet ninety degrees to the left, so that the signs were now written in horizontal lines starting from the left, and lay on their backs relative to their original shape. Opposite are some examples of the changes:

Pictogram (Uruk period)	Linear form (Early Dynastic period)	Cuneiform form (Early Dynastic and later)

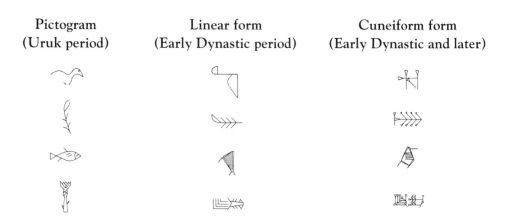

Writing began as a mnemonic system, in which the scribe used only sufficient signs to remind him of the transaction, so that the text was very brief. Here is the transcription of an early four-line text:[6]

> 7 BA
> 1 GI
> [unintelligible personal name]
> 6

That is all. But since BA meant 'give' and GI 'return', this record was intended to recall something like '7 bushels of barley were given as rations, one bushel was returned by [the person named], six bushels were disposed of.'

The writing system underwent further changes by the addition of morphological elements, that is, elements which indicated time reference or person in verbs, and the relationships between nouns and other elements in the sentence. Another change concerned word order. Because the earliest writing was essentially mnemonic, there was originally no need for signs to be consistently written in an order which represented the syntax of the language as spoken. During the Early Dynastic period this was gradually adjusted.

In the earliest writing system, pictographs were used as signs to denote an object (logograms) or a concept (ideograms). A major development came when some signs were divorced from their sense as logograms or ideograms, and used to represent syllables. For example, the sign KA, which originally meant 'mouth', 'to speak' and related ideas, could be used as a syllogram to represent the sound *ka*, carrying no implications related to 'mouth' or 'to speak'. This greatly increased the scope.

Cuneiform writing was a difficult and cumbersome system, which needed years of application to master. The spread of cities brought an increasing need for scribes, and early in the third millennium scribes who were already competent began to compile material for teaching purposes. This teaching material initially took the form of lists of all kinds. Typical of texts for scribal education in the first half of the third millennium were lists of signs with an indication of their pronunciations, lists of nouns, and lists of gods. Later these lists were elaborated; the nouns, for example, were given translations. By the beginning of the second millennium these lists had been edited into multi-tablet series. By that time grammatical texts had also been compiled to teach scribes the structure of Sumerian, which by then had become a dead language.

As the writing system became more flexible, it was no longer limited on one hand to economic and administrative records within the bureaucracy and on the other to scribal education. It could now be used inter alia for transmitting information over a distance, and for preserving material for posterity. A Sumerian epic, *Enmerkar and the Lord of Aratta*, registers what its author supposed was the first instance of the use of writing for diplomatic purposes. This came about when a ruler in Iran was negotiating, through a messenger, with the ruler of Uruk. Because his message was very complex, he committed it to writing.

During the first half of the third millennium, writing came into use for recording categories which by modern criteria count as literature more narrowly – epics, myths, hymns and Wisdom literature (see p. 152). There is currently no extant material before the Fara (ED IIIa) period, but works of this kind are likely to have been in oral circulation earlier. One of the finds at the site of Abu Salabikh (ED IIIa) was an archaic version of a hymn known from later times. In Uruk there was a scribal school which was particularly industrious in collecting tales of ancient heroes, and it attached a cycle of these as written works to three heroes of its First Dynasty: Enmerkar, Lugalbanda and Gilgamesh (see pp. 109–12). Nine Sumerian epics of third-millennium origin are now known in whole or part. Shortly before the end of the third millennium, scribes began to compile catalogues of Sumerian literature.

The growing versatility of writing allowed it to be used not only for a much wider range of texts, but also to represent languages other than Sumerian. Already by 3000 BC the undeciphered language proto-Elamite was being represented with a parallel although different writing system (see fig. 45), but the first language to which the developing Sumerian system was applied was Akkadian. This, a Semitic language, had major differences from Sumerian not only in vocabulary but also in structure and phonology, but problems were overcome in two main ways. One was to continue to use Sumerian ideograms, but with an Akkadian value. For example, the Sumerian for 'king' was *lugal* (invariable) and the Akkadian *šarru* (with different case endings). In Akkadian texts the Sumerian sign LUGAL was written for 'king', but was pronounced as *šarru* with the appropriate case-ending. The other adaptation was to break up Akkadian words into syllables, and to spell them in syllograms.

In some circumstances syllabic writing was also used for writing Sumerian. The chief instance was to write a Sumerian dialect called *emesal*, distinct from the main form of the language. Scholarly opinion is divided over this, but there is a good case for regarding *emesal* as meaning 'women's language', that is, a form of the language which used special words and pronunciations considered more proper for women; other languages provide ample parallels for this practice.[7] Emesal occurs mainly in epics and some hymns and prayers; it was used for the speech of women and goddesses and also the speech of their servants, who would normally have been eunuchs.

Wherever Sumerian civilisation went, cuneiform writing accompanied it, and with writing went scribes. By the first half of the third millennium, it is attested not only in cities throughout south Mesopotamia, but also in Syria. Ebla presents a striking example of this. Whether or not it was founded by settlers from south Mesopotamia, there was certainly south Mesopotamian influence from before the middle of the third millennium, as the archaic titles of its kings show.

Many of the Ebla tablets are inscribed in Sumerian, and some in Akkadian, and they correspond to contemporary forms in Mesopotamia. But in some of the tablets a third language is represented. This is of the Semitic group, and most scholars take it as being a distinct West Semitic language, which they refer to as Eblaite or Eblaic. This language illustrates how Mesopotamian cuneiform could be adapted to the needs of languages elsewhere. The signs employed are basically those used for writing Sumerian, but some are given rare or hitherto unknown values. Consequently, although it is often possible to identify enough words in Eblaite texts to get an idea of the subject matter, it is quite rare to be able to offer a full detailed translation with confidence. For example, one text has eight occurrences of verbal forms meaning 'I bind' or 'I bind you', which show that it is probably a magical incantation, but beyond this details are obscure. Another composition contains lines which say 'O Sun-god, you make the bricks, you build the house of Illilu [Enlil], father of the gods', which look like the beginning of a hymn to the Sun-god, but other parts lack an intelligible context.

It is clear that Ebla had scribal schools based on Mesopotamian models, for some texts are evidently concerned with scribal education. Here is an abridged extract from one which gives Sumerian ideograms with an indication of their pronunciation:

Sumerian ideograms	Pronunciation
lugal an-ka	nu-gal a-gi
nu-GEŠTIN	nu-du-bù
ki-gin$_7$	gi-gi-in
nu-KAB	nu-du-gú-wi-in

Lugal an-ka, in the left column of the initial line, is Sumerian for 'king of heaven and earth', and may have been the beginning of a hymn or myth. Nu-gal a-gi in the right-hand column represents how these words sounded to trainee scribes at Ebla whose native tongue was not Sumerian. Similarly, the third line means that the Sumerian signs written as ki-gin$_7$ were pronounced as gigin. The use of capital letters for GEŠTIN and KAB in the second and fourth lines is a modern convention to show that scholars do not otherwise know how these signs are pronounced in the context; however, the right-hand column tells us that here they were pronounced respectively dubu and duguwin.

After control of Ebla's trade passed into the hands of the rulers of Agade, the local script declined in importance, and when the empire of Agade itself collapsed, the civilisation of Ebla vanished with it.

Chapter Five

THE THIRD DYNASTY OF UR

TRADITION LINKS THE END of the Agade dynasty to invasion by the Gutians (Guti, later Quti), a people remembered as uncouth savages, barbarians and destroyers, but the different strands of tradition are inconsistent in detail. One has the Gutians devastating Agade during the reign of Naram-Sin in punishment for his treatment of Nippur, but another, the so-called *Weidner Chronicle*, gives a different reason:

> Naram-Sin destroyed the settlements of Babylon;
> Twice (Marduk) brought against him the army of the Gutians ...
> (Marduk) handed over his kingship to the army of the Gutians.

Yet Naram-Sin certainly cannot have destroyed Babylon, since if it existed at all in his time, it would have been no more than a village.

SKL does not introduce the beginning of Gutian domination until after the reign of Naram-Sin's son and successor, Shar-kali-sharri. Despite this king's name, which meant 'king of all kings', his reign began under pressure and ended in collapse. He faced not only revolts at his accession, like all his predecessors, but also invasions, with raiders attacking from the Zagros, from Elam, and from the middle Euphrates. His death was followed by anarchy, which SKL sums up in the laconic phrase: 'Who was king? Who was not king?', naming four dubious rulers covering three years. Much of the former empire had by now been lost, but it seems that stability must have returned to the central area, for two further kings of Agade followed, Dudu and Shu-Durul, with reigns which totalled thirty-six years.

The end of the Sargonic dynasty

For SKL, it was the end of Shu-Durul's reign which marked the demise of the Agade empire, perhaps because Nippur, the site of the shrine of the national god Enlil, had slipped from its grasp. But before it reaches 'the horde of the Gutians', it enters a further thirty years of another dynasty of Uruk. SKL attributes to the Gutians 91 (variant, 125) years of domination, after which supremacy in south Mesopotamia passed briefly to Uruk again, under King Utu-hegal, and then to the founder of the Third Dynasty of Ur.

These traditions abut the Guti raise problems. Who were they? Where did they come from, and when? Why their unparalleled reputation for savagery? Were they really the chief cause of the downfall of the Sargonic empire?

Although some traditions link the Guti with Naram-Sin, no contemporary record mentions them before the time of Shar-kali-sharri, whose date formulae record several clashes. There are few clues on where these took place or where the Gutians' homeland was, but we can make surmises. The Gutians harassed the Agade empire so effectively that they were credited with destroying it, whereas powerful federations of city-states had never been able to make a successful challenge. This implies some military advantage over city-states, which can hardly have been other than greater mobility. They must have been able to make surprise attacks, and this may explain why the Gutians were viewed with so much fear and regarded as so ferocious. There was a second factor. Agade normally reacted to opposition by attacking the enemy's major cities and neutralising his bases, but there is no hint of such measures against the Gutians. Since Agade armies showed themselves able to overwhelm cities as far afield as north Syria or south-west Iran, there can have been only one reason why they did not attack Gutian cities: there were none. This points to the Gutians – who may not have been a single ethnic group but a mixture of peoples – being hillsmen without major towns, which, in the context of third-millennium Mesopotamia, suggests a homeland in south-eastern Kurdistan. It is consistent with this that, as archaeology shows, it was cities to the north and north-east of Mesopotamia which suffered the worst destruction during the Sargonic period, presumably from Gutian attack. References to Gutians in the second and first millennia also put them in this region.

Despite tradition, attack by Gutians was probably not the direct cause of the collapse of the Agade empire, although fierce hillsmen disrupting the international trade routes which gave Agade its prosperity must have had major consequences. The Agade empire had large organised armies which it was not afraid to use, and it held potentially hostile cities in check by slighting their fortifications and by installing non-native governors backed by garrisons. However, the advantages such measures gave would gradually diminish as other cities or states learnt to counter them. There was probably another factor in Agade's decline – climatic changes outside Meso-potamia. There are indications of an extended period of drought in Syria, which set migration under way, bringing new pressures upon south Mesopotamia and adversely affecting trade routes. The considerable drain of manpower in Agade's imperial wars could also have had an effect. The main relevance of Gutian attacks upon Sargonic cities was that, although in themselves they were not sufficient to destroy the empire, they showed subject city-states that Agade was not invincible, and in an empire weakened by other factors this was sufficient to precipitate its final overthrow.

Few undoubted Gutian inscriptions are known, chiefly a dedication in Old

46 Above left *Until very recently this mace-head was the only object known bearing a Gutian inscription.*

47 Above right *A copper peg figurine buried at the building of the temple of Ningirsu in the city of Girsu in the city-state of Lagash, in the reign of Gudea (late twenty-second century).*

48 Above left *Diorite statue of Gudea, the powerful ruler of Lagash after the collapse of the Agade empire, in a pose exuding self-confidence.*

49 Above right *Diorite figurine, c. 15 cm (6 in) high, of Ur-Ningirsu (late twenty-second century), son and successor of Gudea. It bears on its back a dedication to the god Ningizzida.*

Akkadian on a macehead (see fig. 46), and there are virtually no details of Gutian rule in Mesopotamia. In the south of the country their control was quickly brought to an end as old city-states began to reassert themselves. The most prominent of these was Lagash, which, a generation after Shar-kali-sharri, was a flourishing independent city-state under Ur-Bawa, who commanded enough wealth to build or rebuild ten temples and to found a dynasty. His successor, his son-in-law Gudea (see fig. 48), who left extensive inscriptions, was powerful enough to mount a military expedition against Elam in south-west Iran. Contemporary inscriptions prove the existence of several other independent city-states, among them Umma, Shuruppak and Uruk. According to SKL, it was a ruler of the last-named city, Utu-hegal (2123–2113 BC), who succeeded to kingship after the horde of the Gutians had been overthrown. Utu-hegal described his campaign in detail, claiming personal credit for expelling the Gutians, whom he called 'that viper . . . , the enemy of the gods, who filled the land with evil'. But his campaign sounds more like action against a bandit chief than against a major king, for he found the main body of the Gutians not in central Babylonia but on the banks of the Tigris. Clearly, their power was on the wane.

Gutian chronology is confused. In its usual way, SKL represents all power centres in Mesopotamia as consecutive, and gives the following figures for the period between Naram-Sin's death and the rise of the next empire, the Third Dynasty of Ur (abbreviated III Ur):

King Shar-kali-sharri	25 years
Period of confusion	3 years
King Dudu	21 years
King Shu-Durul	15 years
Dynasty at Uruk (five kings)	30 years[1]
Gutian horde (21 kings)	91 years[2]
King Utu-hegal of Uruk	7½ years

This would make 167½ years between the end of the reign of Shar-kali-sharri and the beginning of III Ur. That is too long. Shar-kali-sharri's date formulae tell us that the Guti were already in Mesopotamia in his time, so their 91 years should be calculated from the beginning of his reign, not from thirty years after the reign of Shu-Durul. Also, the two periods of rule by Uruk were probably contemporary with the Gutian period, not one at each end. On these assumptions, the interval between the collapse of the Agade dynasty at the death of Shar-kali-sharri and the rise of III Ur was no more than 66 years (91 minus 25). Some reduce it to as little as 30 years, taking the supposed 91 years of the Gutian hordes to include an earlier time when they had a stronghold on the upper Euphrates.

The Third Dynasty of Ur

It was a king of Uruk, Utu-hegal, who finally overthrew the waning Gutian power, but some other southern cities had also recovered their importance. The chief of these was Ur, which vied with Uruk in antiquity and wealth. Ur lay within the territory over which Utu-hegal claimed kingship, and as his governor here he appointed a certain Ur-Nammu, whom some have seen as a kinsman. Ur-Nammu soon showed expansionist aims by picking a territorial dispute with Lagash. But he had wider ambitions than border conflicts, and within seven years he had overthrown his suzerain and made himself ruler of Babylonia (see fig. 50). There remain hymns which were composed for his coronation. Ur-Nammu's accession marked the founding of the Third Dynasty of Ur, and the beginning of a century of remarkable achievement. The enormous number of economic and administrative records of the III Ur bureaucracy make this the best documented century throughout the whole period that cuneiform was in use.

Ur-Nammu reigned for eighteen years. Except for action to expel the last remnants of the Guti from Mesopotamia, and conflict in south-west Iran, everything he did was directed to achieving economic and political stability. He made a diplomatic marriage with a daughter of a governor of Mari to augment his authority, and took measures for the security of trade routes. He gave considerable attention to cutting canals, with weirs to control water levels, partly in the interests of irrigation and partly to serve water-borne trade. He made it possible for ships from Magan at the far end of the Persian Gulf to reach Ur once again, as they had reached Agade under the former empire. Such measures brought a prosperous economy and made it possible for

50 *Fragments of a stele of Ur-Nammu, from Ur. The middle register shows the king twice, to the right (broken) approaching the seated god and to the left approaching the goddess. In the bottom register, Ur-Nammu shows his piety in temple-building by carrying tools on his shoulder.*

51 *The ziggurat of Ur during excavation, founded in the third millennium and restored in the sixth century* BC.

Ur-Nammu to undertake considerable works of temple building in his capital and other cities. At Ur his greatest work was the building of the great ziggurat, of which the main mass still stands (see fig. 51). At Nippur he rebuilt Ekur, the temple of the national god Enlil, and by virtue of his control of that city he was able to adopt the title 'King of Sumer and Akkad', which now meant southern and northern Babylonia. Ur-Nammu formerly received credit for the earliest known collection of laws, but a newly found fragment, which restores missing parts of the prologue, indicates that these were in fact the work of his successor, his oldest son, Shulgi.[3] Ur-Nammu died in battle, as we learn from a hymn telling of the despair that followed his death, the tumult in the netherworld, the sacrifices and offerings made, and the wailing for the walls of Ur he had not finished.[4]

The second king of III Ur, Shulgi, ruled for forty-eight years, and date formulae, which named years after notable events associated with them, give a framework for the reign. Those for the first nineteen years are mostly concerned with temple building and cultic activity, but in the twentieth year comes a reference to arming the people of Ur as spearmen, and subsequently about half the date formulae touch upon military actions. This suggests some shift of emphasis in the second half of the reign. Shulgi's early concern with temple building may have been directed to winning the support of the temple estates, which exercised considerable influence and power throughout Babylonia; if so, he was successful, for there is no evidence during his reign of significant opposition to him within Mesopotamia.

Hymns composed in Shulgi's honour give us some knowledge of the man himself. There are two main classes: hymns addressed to gods, with passages praising the king

85

52 Above left *Shulgi continued an ancient tradition of lion hunting. This basalt fragment representing a lion hunt is from the Jamdat Nasr period.*

53 Above *Copper figurine of Ur-Nammu, showing him as basket-bearer during the building of a temple. Such figurines were buried in the foundations of temples in order to keep the good works of the ruler permanently in the memory of the deity.*

54 Left *A dedication tablet of Shulgi (2095–2048 BC), from one of the temples he rebuilt at Ur.*

or praying for him, and those addressed to the king himself. The latter type normally centres on a narrative, which may be historical or, more often, religious. An historical narrative may recount how Shulgi acted in some campaign, or how he opened up routes for travellers and set up rest-houses with wardens. Religious narratives refer to cultic activities, such as Shulgi in the Sacred Marriage (see pp. 52–4) or his visits to temples. One religious narrative has him improbably running from Nippur to Ur and back,[5] a total distance of 320 km (200 miles), part of it in a tempestuous storm. But whatever the details, the hymns to Shulgi always emphasise his exemplary piety and his kinship with the gods.

These hymns became part of the curriculum of the scribal schools which flourished from III Ur to the Old Babylonian period. About twenty-three[6] of them are known from Old Babylonian copies, some found as far away as Susa in south-west Iran. Shulgi wrote one of them himself – it is in the first person throughout – and the others were the work of court poets.

If everything the hymns claim for Shulgi's qualities and skills are to be believed, he was a very great man. Even allowing some discount for hyperbole, it is beyond question that he was a man of high intelligence, considerable attainments and sound principles. His hymn in the first person brings this out very well. As a youth he studied in a scribal school (edubba, literally 'tablet house') and became top boy, gaining a perfect command both of the scribal art and of mathematics. He enjoyed success as a war leader, and was an expert in the use of all weapons. He was a skilful and courageous hunter of lions, wild bulls, wild boar, and wild asses, but – here a very modern touch – he had a feeling for conservation, and would not allow wild ass foals to be killed. He was, he claimed, so fleet of foot that he could outrun a gazelle, and he never tired. In divination he was so perfectly qualified that he could keep an eye on the professionals' extispicy procedure (inspection of entrails), so that if one slipped up he could check the omens for himself. He was a dedicated and skilful musician: he could play any stringed or wind instrument, he had a grasp of finger techniques, and he understood different types of composition. He composed songs, both words and music, and endowed scribal schools both at Ur and Nippur, with the hope (in the event borne out) that they would collect his songs and preserve them for ever. He ensured the fertility of his land by attention to watercourses. He knew foreign languages as no courtier did. He had a concern for justice, and spoke so well that he dominated the proceedings of the assembly. He even had kinship with the gods, for his mother was the goddess Ninsun, and the sun-god Utu was his brother and companion. In short, he was of all kings the greatest.

Even allowing Shulgi a touch of megalomania, the claims he makes for himself, and those made by others, do in essence correspond to programmes of administrative and economic reforms which he initiated and saw through. An instance is his concern for justice. Earlier kings had recognised their duty to protect the weak from the mighty, and some had attempted reforms, but Shulgi was the first yet known to promulgate a collection of laws (see p. 102), formerly attributed to his father. He explicitly states that these laws were intended to protect the economically weak against the powerful, or, as he put it, 'I did not deliver the orphan to the rich man, the widow to the mighty man, the man with one shekel to the man with one mina, the man with one lamb to the man with one ox.' Women were given a measure of protection in the event of divorce: a wife married as a virgin received one mina of silver compensation, and a former widow half a mina, but a woman who had merely cohabited without formal marriage received nothing. If a father accepted someone as potential husband for his daughter, but then married the girl to another suitor, he had to pay recompense to the wronged man. If a person injured another, he paid a penalty, but as a fine in silver, not on the principle of 'an eye for an eye'. Murder, robbery and some cases of rape were punished by execution. Other laws controlled the proper use of land. Thus, a farmer became liable to a penalty if he flooded another person's field by careless irrigation, or if he hired an arable field and then allowed it to become waste.

There were other areas in which Shulgi initiated reforms. He divided Babylonia into provinces; he introduced a new calendar for use throughout the whole empire; he standardised weights and measures; he brought in new accounting procedures in the Sumerian language; and he unified the administrative system throughout all Babylonia. He distributed royal land among military personnel and administrators as payment for their services. He set up factories employing thousands of weavers, carpenters, smiths, leather workers and the like, who worked under the control of the central government. He planted gardens. He took steps to bring under royal control the considerable resources of temple estates. This he did by placing all temple estates under the provincial governor, with the duty of ensuring that their surplus revenues reached the central government. Redistribution centres were set up, the best-known one being at the site today called Drehem near Nippur. Taxes previously assessed were paid into these centres in goods appropriate to the products of the province, such as livestock, cereals, reeds or timber, and provinces could make withdrawals against their own contributions. Military settlements in peripheral areas north-east and east of Babylonia had their own tax-collection and redistribution centre.

All these measures required administrators, and Shulgi took steps to provide them. There must have been scribal schools since early in the third millennium, in the sense of groups of learners working under experts, but Shulgi put this on a formal footing by endowing academies under his patronage. In these academies potential officials and members of the religious hierarchy learned writing, mathematics and other administrative skills. Because of the scribal schools, Sumerian literature flourished, with old literary works being revised, oral traditions recorded, and new literary works, including hymns to Shulgi, created. But this was not a Sumerian renaissance as a popular movement; it represented the use in a scholastic context of a language which as a spoken tongue was dying or already dead. All potential administrators had to pass through the scribal academies to gain literacy, and Shulgi was consciously using these academies to indoctrinate his administrators in a particular ideological ethos, which bound them together in loyalty to the king. To the same end Shulgi had himself proclaimed a god.

Ancient Mesopotamian cities were theocratic, in the sense that the city-ruler supposedly acted on behalf of the city-god. Shulgi conformed to this concept, but developed from it the claim that he himself was divine. This idea was not entirely strange to ancient Mesopotamia; in the third millennium one of the king's functions was to play the role of the god in the Sacred Marriage ritual, and this emphasised the closeness between a king and a god. Moreover, ancient kings such as Lugalbanda, Enmerkar and Gilgamesh were remembered as being divine or partly divine during their lifetimes, and unquestionably so after death. During the Agade dynasty, both Naram-Sin and Shar-kali-sharri had made an overt claim of divinity during their lifetime by placing the divine determinative before their name, and Shulgi's father, Ur-Nammu, became regarded as a god after his death. But it was only from about the middle of Shulgi's reign and during the rest of his dynasty and the one that followed, that the king regularly claimed to be a god during his lifetime.

It was in about his twentieth year that Shulgi first made his overt claim to divinity, by placing before his name the prefix DINGIR which denoted a divine being. Hymns addressed him in corresponding terms. His long series of good works towards temples earlier in his reign had prepared public opinion for this, and the narrative hymns emphasised Shulgi's kinship with the gods as a theological justification for his apotheosis.

During his reign of forty-eight years, Shulgi brought the empire of Ur to the peak of its prosperity. This empire was markedly more stable than that of Agade, although geographically less extensive. In the north-west, direct rule did not go beyond Mari on the middle Euphrates, but friendly relations with independent governors enabled Shulgi to exercise influence as far as the Mediterranean coast. Along the Tigris, Shulgi held the region as far north as the city of Ashur, and from there north-eastwards to Erbil, where he had to take military action towards the end of his reign. From Erbil the bounds of the empire stretched to Rania in Kurdistan and then southwards along the Zagros to Elam.

Shulgi claimed to be essentially a man of peace, not given to the destruction of cities, and there is indeed no indication of violent conflict in any of the cities of Babylonia during his reign. Cities elsewhere were a different matter, and Shulgi took vigorous action to seize and hold the whole region east of the Tigris as far as the Zagros. In one hymn he describes how the gods called upon him to destroy the *kur*, meaning the lands along the Zagros. He was to wipe out or enslave their populations, and to plunder their cities. He carried out these instructions with zeal. There were two main reasons why Shulgi was so much concerned with the lands of the Zagros. One was trade routes; several of these came from the east through passes in the Zagros, bringing such luxury goods as lapis lazuli from Afghanistan and carnelian from India. The other reason was security. Hillsmen from the Zagros had always been ready to raid into the plains below at any sign of weakness, and Shulgi was determined that there should be no repetition of the Gutian invasion; he sometimes referred to the hillsmen as Gutians. What made the hillsmen a particular threat at this time was probably that they themselves were under pressure from a new people pushing southwards from Armenia.

This new ethnic group was the Hurrians, who by the second millennium were to become an important ethnic element in north Mesopotamia and Syria. A letter reveals that Shulgi's attempts to control the region east of the Tigris included diplomatic missions. But the main instrument was a string of garrison settlements; there were at least ninety of these, each manned with between three hundred and twelve hundred soldiers,[7] giving a total army in the region of between sixty thousand and a hundred thousand.

Shulgi also took steps, both military and diplomatic, to ensure his control of Elam. He married two of his daughters to rulers in the area, appointed a governor in the capital Susa, and enlisted Elamite troops. He showed his keen interest in Elam by claiming in one hymn to know Elamite as well as he knew Sumerian.

The heart of the III Ur empire was Babylonia, including the Diyala region, divided into over twenty provinces roughly corresponding to old city-states. Each was under a system of administration manifestly designed to ensure that ultimate control rested with the central government. In each province there was both a governor and one or more military commanders. Both governors and military commanders were under the authority of the king through his vizier. In most cases the governor came from the old local aristocracy of the area, and this office, like many others both civil and religious, tended to become hereditary during the III Ur period. To preclude a dangerous local concentration of power, however, the military governor was not of that class, and in many cases bore a non-Sumerian name, usually Akkadian, sometimes foreign. Towns other than provincial capitals were under a mayor. Babylon, earlier a minor town, had now become important enough to have its own governor.

During Shulgi's reign there seems to have been a total absence of rebellion within Babylonia. This success, so different from the endemic revolts under the Agade empire, owed much to the administrative and economic measures just outlined and also to attention to security. Shulgi made a great point that travellers should be able to move safely throughout the land, and describes how he established a chain of rest-houses for them along the main routes.

Slavery and non-free labour

There is little mention of slaves in records of the III Ur period, but this need not mean that slavery was of diminishing importance. Only large-scale emancipation could have significantly reduced slavery, and of this there is no trace. On the contrary, Shulgi specifically states that in his wars east of the Tigris, he took the young people captive. Possibly their legal status was not that of slaves, but they were certainly used for forced labour, which can have differed from slavery only in name. In addition, the increased power of the central state meant that many who were not legally slaves became subject to forced labour, either in the army or in industrial production.

The III Ur empire continued for over forty years after Shulgi's death, through the reigns of his two sons, Amar-Sin and Shu-Sin, and his grandson Ibbi-Sin. The cause of its final collapse was largely the pressure of immigrating West Semitic Amorites.

The Amorites

To the west and north-west of Babylonia, beyond the Euphrates, lie the deserts of north Arabia and Syria. These are steppelands, which, though ill-supplied with water, provide seasonal vegetation adequate to support communities whose economy is based on the rearing of sheep and goats. Such communities have always needed to make seasonal migrations to find pasturage, but, before the camel came into wide-spread use at the beginning of the first millennium BC, their range was more limited than that of modern Bedouin, and it is customary to speak of them as semi-nomads.

Babylonia has virtually no natural defences to the west and north-west except the Euphrates, so it has always been subject to a trickle of immigration from the desert fringes. Under the impact of climatic deterioration or other factors, this has some-times swelled into migrations of whole tribes. A movement of this kind began in the Agade period, reached a climax at the end of the third millennium, and continued into the beginning of the second. It brought major social and political consequences, and dislocated communications and food supplies in Babylonia so severely that it contributed largely to the collapse of the III Ur empire.

The natives of Mesopotamia used several names for these semi-nomadic im-migrants from the desert. One, a Semitic term, was Didanum or Didnum (possibly to be read Tidnum).[8] This came to imply 'nomad', although some think that originally it was the name of a particular tribal group. The earliest term in Sumerian was written with the signs MAR.TU, probably pronounced Marru, corresponding to the Semitic term Amurru. In Old Testament Hebrew the latter term occurs as 'Amori, rendered Amorite in English. Biblical 'Amori were not necessarily ethnically identical with third millennium Amurru.

Something must have triggered the MAR.TU into moving outside their normal range, and there are indications that the main factor was climatic change. Excava-tions at sites of ancient cities in Syria north of the Euphrates suggest that drier conditions set in at about this time, and this could have dramatically affected the availability of pasturage in the Jebel Bishri region (see p. 92). Similar conditions could also have affected regions further east and north, since peoples of other ethnic groups, notably Hurrians (the Horites of the Old Testament), were beginning to push into Mesopotamia from east of the Tigris, although on nothing like the scale of the Amorite movement. The drier period appears to have continued for several centuries, during which the pressure of immigration grew.

By the reign of Shulgi's second son Shu-Sin (2038–2030 BC), the menace had become so intense that the imperial power built a great wall against the invaders, running for 270 km (170 miles) across country from the Euphrates to the Tigris north of Babylonia, with the banks of both rivers breached to fill a moat. This defence system, known as 'Fender-off-of-the-Bedouin', failed to stop the immigrants, and under the last king of III Ur, Ibbi-Sin (also transcribed Ibbi-Suen, 2029–2006 BC), they were operating as organised armed bands within Mesopotamia itself. The authorities attempted a military response, and the year formula for 2013 BC claimed the overthrow of the MAR.TU. But this was merely an ephemeral success. Soon after came a letter to the king telling of the Bedouin breaking through and taking one fortified place after another; royal authority was beginning to collapse. Datings on economic documents confirm this picture; the convention was that such a document bore a date giving the regnal year of the current monarch, and in the second year of Ibbi-Sin his name disappeared from datings in the Diyala region, and in subsequent years from more and more cities.

The first significant reference to these semi-nomads comes in the date formula for Shar-kali-sharri's first year, 2254 BC. This reads: 'the MAR.TU were in the Basar mountains'. The Basar mountains were the steppe region now called Jebel Bishri, a region rising to about 850 m (2800 ft) between the middle Euphrates and Palmyra in Syria. North of this region passed the trade route which followed the Euphrates upstream into north Syria. This trade route was vital to the Sargonic rulers, and the record implies that the semi-nomads had moved so close to the Euphrates that their presence had become a threat.

From the beginning of the second millennium we meet other terms for these sheep-rearing semi-nomads. Documents from Mari mention peoples called Haneans, Benjaminites, and Suteans, who were migrating, raiding, and gradually settling in the riverine areas along the Euphrates and in the Habur valley, as well as further west. They differed from each other mainly in their grazing grounds and in how far they were prepared to co-operate with the kingdom of Mari and place military contingents at its service.

The names of the many individuals designated as MAR.TU or Amurru in cuneiform documents are not of uniform West Semitic type. Also, there were some people described as MAR.TU in places east of the Tigris and even in Elam. On these grounds some scholars formerly distinguished two different migrations of MAR.TU (Amurru), and called the supposedly earlier group, those east of the Tigris, 'East Canaanites'. However, evidence now available points to a steady stream of migration over several generations rather than separate earlier and later waves. The differences in name type came about because Amorite families which had already become assimilated tended to give their children Sumerian or Akkadian rather than West Semitic names.

When migrant peoples and settled populations come into contact, tensions often develop. This may be exacerbated if the settled people are agriculturalists and the newcomers animal herders, bringing competition for land use. Yet such encounters are not wholly negative; each group may bring economic benefits to the other, leading to eventual mutual acceptance. This happened with the Amorites. Several literary texts allude to their way of life, showing that the city dwellers thought of them as in some ways odd: they did not cultivate corn; they lived in tents, not houses; they had no towns; they wore skins; they ate their food raw; they had perverted sexual customs; and when they died they were not buried according to the proper rites. But such comments implied amusement rather than rejection. On the positive side, they bred good cattle, sheep, goats and donkeys, and they made good soldiers.

A myth, *The marriage of Martu*, reflects this mixture of attitudes. The myth begins with Martu, eponymous god of the Amorites, asking his mother to find him a wife. Just what she advised we do not know, since the text is damaged at this point, but afterwards we find Martu at a city festival, distinguishing himself in wrestling matches. He made such a favourable impression that the city ruler offered him a gift of silver and precious stones, but Martu rejected these, and asked instead for the ruler's daughter in marriage. The ruler was willing, but one of the girl's friends sought to dissuade her from the alliance. She pointed out the uncouthness of Martu, and thereby of the nomads he represented:

> He is a tent-dweller,
> He eats raw food,
> He has no house during his lifetime,
> He is not properly buried when he is dead.[9]

But the girl was undeterred and the marriage went ahead, reflecting the peaceful assimilation of the semi-nomads as they settled.

Babylonian literature gives some clues to the way of life of the Amorites before they settled. It is clear that in their original homeland they did not practise agriculture, but lived by animal-herding, supplemented by gathering wild foods, as we learn from a text which refers to them digging up truffles. They were organised in tribes, with sheikhs called 'father' of the tribe. The language they spoke in their homeland was unintelligible in Babylonia, since there is mention of an 'interpreter of the Amorites'. Before they began to settle they had trading relations by means of donkey caravans with Syrian cities, and probably also with Babylonia, for their envoys came there, and Babylonia sent envoys to the Amorites in their mountain homeland.

The myth mentioned above, *The marriage of Martu*, points to Amorite-Babylonian intermarriage in the top social strata, and other texts indicate corresponding marriages at a lower level. Of Amorite religion little is known beyond a few indications from god-elements in personal names. Names of the type 'El is father', 'El lives', show the prominence of the god El, with whom Yahweh of the Hebrews was identified (Genesis 14:22), and some names reflect his attributes. For example, 'El indeed saves' proclaims El's readiness to deliver his worshippers from perils around them, and names meaning 'Beloved of El' and 'El is my rest' reflect belief in his love and benevolence. 'Haddu is lofty' and 'Strength of Haddu' are references to the West Semitic Thunder-god Hadad. 'Lim raises' contains the name of another deity well known at Mari. Amurru as a god was obviously the eponym of the tribal group. These names do not represent the total Amorite pantheon, but they form a substantial part of it, and indicate that polytheism was less developed among the Amorites than in Mesopotamian city-states.

We have seen that by the reign of Shu-Sin, Amorite immigration had become such a serious threat that it required the building of a great defence wall. Under Ibbi-Sin the situation became still worse. A figure who came to dominate the situation was a certain Ishbi-Erra. Originally he had been governor of Mari on the middle Euphrates, which, as the first major city between the Jebel Bishri and south Mesopotamia, early came under Amorite pressure. After initial successes against the invaders, Ishbi-Erra moved to a more southerly base at Isin, from where he held other cities of north Babylonia as Ibbi-Sin's representative.

Ishbi-Erra was an energetic and capable administrator, and when Amorite occupation of cultivated lands began to bring food shortage in Ur and with it inflation, he took counter-measures. He bought up grain supplies and stored them in Isin, and offered them to Ibbi-Sin if he could provide the six hundred barges needed to transship them to Ur. But Ibbi-Sin was quite incapable of this, and offered double payment if only Ishbi-Erra could produce the necessary shipping; he even took valuables from the temple of Ur to pay for the grain. However, the transfer did not come about. Instead, at the end of Ibbi-Sin's twelfth year (2018 BC), Ishbi-Erra renounced allegiance and set himself up as an independent king in Isin. From there he ruled a group of northern cities which included Nippur, Kish and Eshnunna.

Major Amorite immigration and incipient famine were not Ibbi-Sin's only problems. Elam, formerly firmly within the III Ur empire, broke away as soon as the imperial decline became apparent. Its capital, Susa, ceased to recognise Ibbi-Sin as king after his third year, and later conflict broke out. Ibbi-Sin allowed himself the fond hope, as we learn from one of his letters, that the national god Enlil would play his troubles off against each another, by calling in the Amurru to overthrow Elam and to catch Ishbi-Erra. But there was no such miraculous intervention, and finally the Elamites with their tribal allies closed in on Ur, sacked it and took Ibbi-Sin into captivity (2006 BC). Archaeological evidence attests the destruction of temple buildings and other structures at Ur.

The impact of the sack of Ur gave it a permanent place in Mesopotamian tradition. Omens linked portents to it, and poets composed laments on the disaster. But these laments were overlaid with themes which had little to do with history, and spoke of devastation in major cities other than Ur which never happened at this time. These references may have been literary embroidery based on theological considerations, or incidents recalled from some other period. The only city we know to have faced the full wrath of the Elamites at this time was Ur.

The collapse of the III Ur empire did not leave a total vacuum. The old city-state administrations still functioned, and Ishbi-Erra had taken advantage of this to create his major kingdom ruling from Isin. Other city-states quickly re-established themselves in limited areas, some under Amorite leaders. The most prominent of these others was Larsa, under a king who bore the good Amorite name Naplanum. Because of these two leading dynasties, the century following the collapse of III Ur is often called the Isin-Larsa period. Both eventually fell to another dynasty of Amorite origin, which established itself at Babylon, formerly an unimportant city. This became known as the First Dynasty of Babylon. Under this dynasty Babylon became supreme over the whole of south Mesopotamia, which thereby became known as 'the land of Babylon' or 'Babylonia'. The term 'Old Babylonian' is commonly applied to the whole period from the collapse of III Ur, through Isin-Larsa, down to the end of the First Dynasty of Babylon at about 1600 BC.

Chapter Six

THE OLD BABYLONIAN PERIOD

THE DYNASTY WHICH Ishbi-Erra founded at Isin had a line of fourteen kings said to have ruled for over two centuries. Because Isin controlled Nippur, the city of the national god Enlil, SKL considered it the legitimate successor to the III Ur empire. But it was never in full control of all Babylonia; it always shared power with other city-states, particularly Larsa in the south.

Ishbi-Erra retained what he could of the organisation of the III Ur empire. The old royal ideology, the state institutions and official titles and responsibilities continued as far as possible, but inevitably the break-up of the empire brought changes. This was particularly so in the economy. Under the III Ur empire, a considerable part of the economy had been a state monopoly, in two sectors, one being the temple estates, managed by their own administrators but with their profits going to the king, and the other the royal domain. Included in the latter were state factories, royal flocks and herds, and royal land. In the factories thousands of women weavers worked to make woollen textiles, of which some went for export. Part of the royal land was used as payment to military and other personnel for their services to the king, typically in plots averaging 36 ha (90 acres).[1] The loosening of the tight control exercised by the III Ur state reacted on all this, and brought an increasing emphasis upon the private sector. There had been a private economic sector under III Ur, comprising merchants, craftsmen, and private landholdings, but it had been of little significance, although it was beginning to grow towards the end of the period.

We can trace the trend away from state control in documents relating to the foreign trade of the city of Ur.[2] In the reign of Ibbi-Sin (2029–2006 BC), the temple of Nanna was central. Merchants drew garments, wool, oil, leather and barley from the temple for their sea voyages to Magan at the far end of the Persian Gulf to buy copper and semi-precious stones; clearly they were acting not independently but as agents for the temple, and were under state control. By the reign of Sumuel of Larsa (1894–1866 BC), changes can be seen. The sea journeys were shorter, only as far as

55 Bronze figure of a man carrying a basket on his head in building operations. Dedicated by Warad-Sin (1834–1823 BC), a king of the Larsa Dynasty, the man represented may have been Warad-Sin himself.

Tilmun (Bahrein) half-way down the Persian Gulf, and the merchants paid a tithe to the temple; by now the merchants were no longer acting as agents of the temple, although the temple retained some vestigial rights. By the reign of Rim-Sin of Larsa (1822–1763 BC), there had been further changes. The voyages were now financed by capitalists and run by business partnerships who travelled to Tilmun to buy copper for dealers. No tithes were paid to the temple, although the royal authority levied taxes.

As king, Ishbi-Erra took over some of the royal traditions of his predecessors at Ur. One was to claim divine kingship, by placing the sign DINGIR ('god') before his name. He also adopted titles which implied sovereignty over the whole land, such as 'king of the four world regions, king of the land', or even 'god of the land'. We obtain a general picture of his activities as king from date formulae, economic texts, literary texts such as hymns, and an inscription in his own name. Omens also offer some hints; one of them refers to conflict with Elam.

Date formulae during the Old Babylonian period emphasise the building or rebuilding of city walls or other fortifications. This would be expected during the reign of Ishbi-Erra, when there was a need to repair installations damaged during the Amorite incursions, but the trend continued for two centuries or more. This excessive concentration upon city defences can only be explained as a reflection of political uncertainties and anxieties at a time of competing city-states.

During the reign of Ishbi-Erra, Isin was the predominant state of Babylonia, controlling cities as far south as Ur, and engaging in trade with places as far afield as Elam and the Upper Euphrates. But it had several potentials rivals. One was Eshnunna in the Diyala region and south of that there was Der east of the Tigris, controlling one route to Elam. Other city-states in Babylonia which came to exercise a measure of independence included Uruk,[3] Kish and Sippar.

The rival which proved most enduring was Larsa in the south, where a certain Naplanum (2025–2005) founded a dynasty at about the same time as Ishbi-Erra. His name indicates his Amorite descent. The rulers of Isin and Larsa generally maintained peaceful relations, within which Larsa made gradual advances, until under Naplanum's fourth successor, Gungunum (1932–1906), Ur came into the hands of Larsa. The sequel showed that religious considerations could outweigh politics. At the time of the changeover the high priestess of the main temple in Ur was a daughter of the king of Isin, but the change in the ownership of Ur did not affect her status; the lady in question simply continued to perform her duties as high priestess under Gungunum.

Gungunum's contemporary at Isin was Lipit-Ishtar, who was probably the most important of Ishbi-Erra's successors, and evidently had a strong sense of social justice. One facet of this was his claim that he had 'made justice'. This claim, not unusual among Old Babylonian rulers, referred to the cancellation by royal decree of certain debts, such as any which had forced free people to sell themselves or their families into slavery; details are best known from a decree of Ammisaduqa (1646–1626 BC), one of the later kings of the First Dynasty of Babylon.[4]

Lipit-Ishtar was also one of the minority of rulers who promulgated a collection of laws. These laws, of which only about half are preserved, are written in Sumerian, by that time a dead language. The extant laws are largely economic, dealing with such matters as the hiring of boats, lease of orchards, slaves, marriage, inheritance, divorce, and liability for damage to a hired ox. There is another collection of laws which may have originated at about the same time, although the extant copies are a century or so later. It belonged to the city-state of Eshnunna, but the copies were found at a small site on the outskirts of Baghdad. Much of the Eshnunna laws correspond in substance to the laws of Hammurabi[5] (see pp. 101ff.)

Dozens of dynasties sprang up from the ruins of the III Ur empire, mainly with an Amorite background, but most of them had political importance only as part of a larger federation. The dynasty which was ultimately most successful in south Meso-potamia was that which established itself at Babylon as its First Dynasty. A later tradition held that the origin of Babylon went back to the gods in primeval times, but this was an invention in the days of its glory, when it was inconceivable that such a great city should be an upstart. In fact, there is no mention of Babylon until the reign of Shar-kali-sharri (2254–2230 BC), when it was of no more than minor importance. Natural factors probably contributed to its rise. At about the end of the third millennium, the Euphrates, whose main channel had previously run down the middle of the land through Nippur, shifted its main bed westwards. Babylon was now at the northern end of the main stream of the Euphrates, and this gave it increased importance, both commercially and strategically.

The original name of the settlement was Babil or Babila. This was pre-Semitic, being perhaps an instance of the so-called 'substratum language' (see p. 30). But the Babylonians gave it a bogus interpretation, taking it as an Akkadian phrase *bab ili*, which meant 'gateway of the gods'.[6]

The First Dynasty of Babylon was unquestionably Amorite in origin, for a gen-ealogy traces its kings back to Amorite chieftains of nomadic times. The first to settle as a local ruler in Babylon was Sumu-abum (1894–1881 BC), a contemporary of the seventh kings of both the Isin and Larsa dynasties. In Sumu-abum's time Babylon was still a city of minor significance, but date formulae show that he and his successors steadily concerned themselves with two activities likely to alter that: the defences of their city, and measures to assist agriculture, for example the building or clearing out of canals. Such undertakings provided the basis for later expansion.

At the time of Sumu-abum, there were already important political and economic centres further north. Mari on the middle Euphrates had been a major trading centre for half a millennium, and a line of energetic kings had long been established in Assyria. Already in the twentieth century one Assyrian ruler, Ilu-shuma, had been able to make an expedition as far into Babylonia as Der commanding a route to Elam, apparently to safeguard trading relations.

At the end of the reign of the fourth king of Babylon a general of Amorite descent named Shamshi-Adad (1813 to after 1781 BC), son of a petty prince in the Middle Euphrates area, overthrew the old Assyrian dynasty and established a kingdom with centres at Ashur, Ekallatum, and Shubat-Enlil (somewhere near the Habur river, perhaps Tell Leilan). Soon afterwards he annexed the kingdom of Mari. This gave him an empire in which, through dynastic marriages, allies and vassals, he dominated the whole region from the Mediterranean into north Babylonia. He was a man willing to delegate authority and used his two sons as sub-kings, the senior, Ishme-Dagan, over part of Assyria, the younger, Yasmah-Adad, over Mari.

It was during the reign of Shamshi-Adad of Assyria that Hammurabi (see fig. 56) succeeded to the throne of Babylon, still, although it now included the city-states of Sippar and Kutha, no more than a petty kingdom in north Babylonia. Throughout his reign Hammurabi conscientiously continued his predecessors' policy of devoting unceasing attention to defences, canals and agriculture. Although during his first decade he was only a minor figure, alliance with the powerful Shamshi-Adad, either as a junior partner or a vassal, permitted him to make some limited southward expansion, subjugating inter alia both Isin and Uruk.

Shamshi-Adad was still alive in Hammurabi's tenth year, as we know from a Babylonian document of that year in which an oath was sworn by Hammurabi jointly with Shamshi-Adad. He probably died soon after this, although some scholars argue that he lived on until Hammurabi's seventeenth year.[7] Whenever he died, Shamshi-Adad's death gave Hammurabi a freer hand, and removed any restraint upon action against potential rivals. Of these, the two most powerful were Ibal-pi-El II of Eshnunna and Rim-Sin of Larsa (see fig. 57), with a third at Mari after the death of Shamshi-Adad, when a scion of an earlier dynasty made a successful coup.

Hammurabi was, however, a skilled diplomatist, and supplemented his diplomacy with another valuable quality – patience. By means of this, despite occasional friction, during his first thirty years he generally maintained good relations with the kings of Eshnunna, Larsa, and Mari. Each of these kings had ambassadors at the courts of the others, where their duties were to watch over their masters' interests; in some cases they interpreted this to include espionage on political and military developments by means of a local intelligence network. Rulers in friendly relationship might in times of crisis give each other military assistance to the extent of thousands of troops; on one occasion Hammurabi received a contingent from as far away as the district of Aleppo in north Syria.

There are abundant sources for Hammurabi's reign. He left building inscriptions and a collection of laws[8]; there are documents in which his contemporaries mentioned him; and there are date formulae and a chronicle. In addition hundreds of

56 Above left *This votive monument shows the great king Hammurabi of Babylon (1792–1750 BC)*.

57 Above right *Copper foundation figurine of Rim-Sin I of Larsa (1822–1763 BC)*.

letters remain from his chancellory, and these show how assiduous he was in his correspondence and what detailed attention he gave to the administration of his kingdom.

Three decades of skilled diplomacy and statecraft left Hammurabi the strongest power in Mesopotamia, and he now set out upon a major expansion. Date formulae trace the course of his conquests. That for his thirtieth year records the defeat of a coalition east of the Tigris, and in the same year he subjugated his main rival in the south of the country, Rim-Sin of Larsa. This gave him control of all south Babylonia. Then in his thirty-second year he turned to the east and north, where he gained victories over the kingdom of Eshnunna in the Diyala valley, Subartum (meaning part of Assyria), and the Gutians. He then went on to conquer Mari, where Zimri-Lim, a member of an Amorite dynasty which had ruled there earlier, had expelled Shamshi-Adad's son. After consolidating his position at Mari, Hammurabi moved northwards, and eventually took Nineveh, so that by his thirty-eighth year he controlled the whole of Mesopotamia. He went on to conquer areas in the north-eastern mountains, important to him because they controlled the routes from beyond Iran which brought lapis lazuli and other luxury goods. In the end he controlled much the same territory as the old III Ur empire.

Long-distance trade

Babylonia's lack of metals, building stone, semi-precious stones and good quality timber could be overcome only by plunder or trade. The Old Babylonian period favoured trade.

The goods Babylonia had available for trade were principally foodstuffs, of which it usually had a surplus, so long as it kept its irrigation system in order. This was an important resource, since there were parts of the ancient Near East, dependent upon rainfall, which not infrequently suffered crop failures and famine. Throughout Babylonian history there are repeated references to export of grain from Mesopotamia to alleviate shortages abroad, often in west Iran. Other important exports were wool, textiles, probably leather goods, and manufactured ornaments. Babylonian cylinder seals and ornaments have been discovered from as far away as Egypt and Crete, but how they got there we do not know; they may have been passed on from city to city rather than brought in by merchants direct from Babylonia. Babylonia also acted as a middleman by reselling goods previously imported, such as tin from Afghanistan.

There seem to have been two possible mechanisms for trade in the Old Babylonian period. One was for merchants to travel or reside abroad, selling articles they had brought in and buying others, and making their profits on the transactions. The other was for a merchant in one city to have a contact in another, and to use an agent to carry goods as required. The laws of Hammurabi legislate for relations between merchants and their agents. Thus:

> §100 If a merchant gave silver to an agent for buying and selling, and sent him on a journey ... and he has seen a profit where he went, he shall calculate the interest on as much silver as he took and they shall count up the period which has elapsed, and he shall pay his merchant (accordingly).
> §101 If he has seen no profit where he went, the agent shall double the silver he received and give it to the merchant.

Clearly, it was envisaged that the merchant would receive a minimum return of one hundred per cent on his capital. A subsequent law makes provision for a different kind of business relationship between merchant and agent.

Merchants or their agents might operate far from home. A letter mentions two natives of Babylon passing through Mari on their way home after living in Hazor in Palestine, and although they are referred to as messengers and not merchants or agents, it is difficult to see why they should have been residing so far from home except in the interests of trade. Although overland trade was considerable in total, individual trading expeditions were normally on a small scale, using as their means of transport only a few donkeys, not hundreds. Payments were normally in silver. Even in cases including an element of direct barter, the value of goods bartered was expressed in terms of silver.

In addition to metals, timber and semi precious stones, other imports into Babylonia included wine, perfumes, aromatic oils from cedar-wood and the like, and slaves. The main sources of slaves were regions to the north and north-west and the Zagros, and two of Hammurabi's laws concern slaves or slave-girls bought abroad. A document of 1637 BC contains an order for healthy Gutian slaves to be delivered within one month; oil to the value of just over one-third of a mina of silver had already been sent to pay for them.[9] The source of the cedar-wood and aromatic oils was the Lebanon and the Amanus, and the wines came from Carchemish and Cilicia. Babylonia shipped barley southwards to Tilmun in the Persian Gulf,[10] and trading vessels plied on the Euphrates between north Syria and Sippar and Babylon. We learn from a letter that there was a checkpoint in north Babylonia where shipping was examined; only vessels with a passport issued by the king were allowed to proceed.

The best-attested trade during the early part of the Old Babylonian period was linked to Assyria rather than Babylonia. The Assyrians had established merchant colonies in Anatolia, and the archives from one of them, the ancient city Kanesh near modern Kayseri in Cappadocia, give some idea of how they operated. The Assyrians needed copper, and paid for it with either tin or textiles, sent from the Assyrian capital Ashur to central Anatolia, along a route of rather more than 1100 km (700 miles), by caravans of donkeys, each carrying about 100 kg (2 cwt). The journey took about two months, there could be trouble from bandits, wolves or weather, and donkeys might die on the way. The textiles used in payment for copper certainly link this trade with Babylonia, since a letter proves that at least some of the textiles came from Babylonia, and Babylonia may also have been the intermediate source of the tin, which must originally have come from deposits in Afghanistan. Later, in the time of Hammurabi and Shamshi-Adad, a letter to Hammurabi from Shamshi-Adad's son mentions an Assyrian caravan which had gone overland from Mari to Tilmun by way of Babylon. Mari was another transit town for trade in tin, and is known to have traded as far away as the Mediterranean ports and Crete.

The Laws of Hammurabi

In December 1901 French archaeologists digging at Susa in south-west Persia found a large piece of an inscribed monument of black stone. A month later they discovered a join which produced an almost complete stele well over 2 m (6 ft) high (see fig. 58). The stele was inscribed in columns of cuneiform surmounted by a relief showing a king before a seated god. When deciphered a few months later, the text proved to be a series of laws promulgated by Hammurabi.

Since some of these laws were markedly similar to laws associated with Moses, they aroused keen biblical interest. They were several centuries earlier than Moses, which led some scholars to conclude that Moses had borrowed directly from Hammurabi. Others proposed to see Hammurabi's name in the Bible, in the form 'Amraphel king of Shinar', mentioned in Genesis 14:1 as one of four kings who clashed with Abraham. Subsequent discoveries disproved both these assumptions: the Amraphel identifi-

58 *Stele bearing the laws of Hammurabi of Babylon (first half of the eighteenth century* BC).

cation is historically impossible, and similarities between Mosaic laws and others exist because they were legislating for similar problems.

The relief at the top of the stele shows Shamash, God of Justice, giving Hammurabi his charge. The bearded god sits on a throne, wearing a helmet with triple horns which denote his divinity. Before him stands Hammurabi, bearded, with his right hand raised in an attitude of reverence before his face. The god holds in his right hand a rod and ring, symbols of justice, and extends these towards the king.

Hammurabi's stele remains the most striking legislative monument, and his laws are still the longest and most complete collection from south Mesopotamia, but they have been robbed of their priority. In the 1940s some tablets and fragments in the University Museum in Philadelphia, excavated long before at Nippur, were recognised as containing Sumerian laws of Lipit-Ishtar of Isin, a king who antedated Hammurabi by more than a century and a quarter. Soon after came the publication of two further tablets of laws, this time in Akkadian. They were excavated on the outskirts of Baghdad between 1945 and 1949 at a small site, Tell Harmal, which proved to represent ancient Shaduppum. This was an outlying town of the kingdom of Eshnunna in the Diyala valley, and the laws were the laws of Eshnunna. They probably originated at about the same time as Lipit-Ishtar's laws, although the copies from Tell Harmal are later. After this came the finding of parts of the earliest laws of all. These laws, in Sumerian, were originally attributed to Ur-Nammu, founder of III Ur, but later joins have proved them to be the work of his son Shulgi. There are a few other unplaced fragments of ancient laws, both Sumerian and Akkadian.

Ancient compilers of laws conventionally set them between a prologue and an epilogue. Hammurabi began his prologue with a theological section which he used to express his view of his achievements:

> When the exalted Anu, king of the pantheon, and Enlil, lord of heaven and earth, ... decreed ... that Marduk the first-born son of Ea should have the divine lordship, ... and when they called Babylon by its exalted name and made it pre-eminent in all quarters, ... at that time Anu and Enlil called me by name, Hammurabi, the reverent prince who fears the gods, to render good to the people, to make justice shine in the land, to destroy the evil and wicked, (to ensure) that the strong do not oppress the weak.[11]

Hammurabi then noted his care for shrines, among them Nippur, Eridu, Babylon, Ur, Sippar, Larsa, Uruk, Isin, Kish, Kutha, Borsippa, Dilbat, Mari, Agade and Nineveh. In the epilogue Hammurabi took up other aspects of his piety, claiming to have been a faithful shepherd of his people in accordance with the will of the great gods, so that they could live in peace and safety. He had, he said, set up his monument in order that the strong might not oppress the weak. He ended by calling down blessing upon any future ruler who heeded his monument, and curses upon one who disregarded it.

Part of the laws on the stele was obliterated in antiquity by the Elamite king who had taken it off as booty. Later copies of the laws on clay tablets supply part of the gap. Altogether they originally comprised, on the conventional sub-division, 282 clauses, but of these over twenty are either missing or represented by only a few words on one of the copies.

Several eminent jurists have analysed the laws with respect to their juristic characteristics and place in the history of law. Here we are concerned only with their relevance to ancient society.

The best-known biblical laws are presented as commands direct from God in the form 'Thou shalt not kill'. Many others, however, take a different form, for example: 'If a man shall steal an ox, or a sheep, and kill it, or sell it; he shall restore five oxen for an ox, and four sheep for a sheep' (Exodus 22:1). The Bible makes it evident that laws of the second class originated not as specific decrees from God but as decisions given by duly appointed judges, or in hard cases by Moses himself (Deuteronomy 1:9–17).

The laws of Hammurabi exclusively take the second form, being represented not as divine decrees handed down by the gods, but as decisions the king had made in certain cases; in the epilogue Hammurabi actually called them 'the decisions of the land'. Some were judgements that Hammurabi had actually given, while others were expansions from one actual judgement to cover related cases which might arise in the future. We see a good example of this in a group of six laws about a man striking a pregnant woman, which differ only in the social status of the woman and whether she died or only miscarried. It is hard to suppose that Hammurabi would have been called upon to decide separately six different cases of this kind; most probably five of the cases were hypothetical elaborations from a single instance which actually happened.

Hammurabi's laws are broadly arranged according to subject matter, such as: the administration of justice; land law; commercial law; laws centred on women; assault; surgeons and builders; agricultural work and rates of hire and wages; and slave ownership. But these broad headings can cover legislation upon several disparate topics. Thus, laws covering women include marriage, inheritance, slander, cohabitation, adultery, remarriage, divorce and bigamy. The heading 'surgeons' also covers laws relating to veterinary surgeons and barbers, including payments for successful treatment and penalties for failure.

Hammurabi's laws, although more systematic in their arrangement than their predecessors, are not complete enough to be called a code, and make no distinction between civil and criminal law. In the epilogue Hammurabi states what he saw as their purpose: 'Let a man who has been wronged and has a cause, go before my stele called "King of Justice" and let him have my words inscribed on the monument read out.' This gives an interesting sidelight on literacy, recognising that most people were illiterate and would need the services of a scribe. A second unstated purpose of the laws must have been to achieve uniformity of legal practice across Hammurabi's now extensive kingdom, where earlier there had been substantial variations. For example, we know from Shulgi's laws that the *lex talionis* ('an eye for an eye' principle), so marked in Hammurabi's laws, had no place in Ur.

By modern standards Hammurabi's laws were harsh, with death the penalty for a wide variety of offences. These included false accusation of manslaughter, sorcery or any capital offence (§§ 1, 2, 3); theft of property of a god or the palace (§ 6); receiving stolen property (§ 7); kidnapping (§ 14); helping a slave to escape (§§ 15–16); housebreaking, robbery or arson (§§ 21, 22, 25); and irregularities in performance of royal service (§§ 26, 33). Other penalties included blinding; breaking a limb or tooth; lopping off the hand, ear, tongue or breast; putting the offender's daughter to death; having the head shaved; torture; impalement; burning; the river-ordeal; being thrown into the water; reduction of a married woman to the status of slave-girl; disinheritance; whipping and banishment. In other cases an offender might have to forfeit property or pay a penalty in silver. Some examples may give something of the flavour of the laws.

> §5 *Administration of justice*
> If a judge rendered judgement and gave a decision and had a sealed document made out, and afterwards he changed his judgement, and they proved by witnesses that he changed the judgement he had rendered, he shall pay twelve-fold the amount of the claim in that case. And in the assembly they shall remove him from his seat of judgement and he shall not again sit with the judges in a case.

From this we learn that cases were heard in the public assembly of a city before a bench of judges. When the judges gave their decision, they recorded it on a tablet and endorsed it with cylinder seals.

> §15 *Control of slaves*
> If a man has caused a slave or slave-girl of the palace or of a *muškenum* to go out of the great gate (of the city), he shall be put to death.

This demonstrates the tight control kept on the movement of slaves. Other laws legislate for a slave or slave-girl being caught in the open country.

> §§22, 23 *Robbery*
> If a man committed robbery and was then caught, he shall be put to death.
> If the robber has not been caught, the robbed man shall establish (by oath) before the god whatever he has lost, and the city and the mayor in whose territory or district the robbery was committed shall replace for him whatever he has lost.

The local authorities were responsible for the policing and security of their areas.

> §§28, 29 *Royal service*
> If there is either a *redû* or a *bā'iru* [two classes of military personnel] who is taken captive while on service in a royal fortress, and his son is capable of doing his service, the field and orchard shall be given to him and he shall do his father's service.
> If his son is a minor and incapable of doing his father's service, a third of the field and orchard shall be given to his mother, and his mother shall bring him up.

Military officers and others doing service (Akkadian *ilku*, literally 'a going') for the king received grants of royal land and orchards by which to support themselves and their families. The grantee could not sell such land. Hammurabi made considerable use of land grants, and there remains a whole archive of his letters written to an official named Shamash-hazir in charge of such allocations in Larsa. These laws show the strength of the principle of heredity, by assuming that in normal circumstances a son would take over the *ilku* duties of his father and succeed to the associated land rights. The laws also demonstrate the rudiments of a social security system, since even if the heir were too young to render service, provision was still made for the family.

> §32 *The state's responsibility to royal officers*
> If there is either a *redû* or a *bā'iru* who is taken captive on a royal mission, and a merchant has ransomed him and so enabled him to reach his city, if there is in his house the wherewithal for ransoming, he himself shall pay the ransom. If his house lacks the wherewithal for ransoming him, he shall be ransomed by his city's temple. If there is not the wherewithal for ransoming him in his city's temple, the palace shall ransom him. His field, his orchard or his house shall not be given for ransom.

In the last resort responsibility lay with the state. In view of the considerable wealth of temples at some other periods, it is interesting to find the possibility that a temple might be too poor to pay a man's ransom.

> §132, 127 *Accusation of adultery*
> If the finger has been pointed against a man's wife in connection with another man, but she has not been caught lying with the other man, she shall jump into the holy river for her husband.
> If a man has caused the finger to be pointed at a priestess or a man's wife and has not proved his accusation, they shall beat that man in front of the judges and shave off half his hair.

The river ordeal was used to obtain the god's decision about the truth of an accusation. But wives had some defence against unwarranted accusations, for a man who falsely slandered a married woman was flogged and publicly disgraced.

> §§196–9, 203–5 *Injury and assault*
> If a man has put out the eye of a man of the free class, they shall put out his eye.
> If he has broken a bone of a (free) man, they shall break his bone.
> If he has put out the eye of a man of the *muškenum* class, he shall pay one mina of silver.
> If he has put out the eye of a free man's slave or has broken a bone of a free man's slave, he shall pay half his price.
> If a man of the free class has struck the cheek of a man of the free class of his own rank, he shall pay one mina of silver.
> If a man of the *muškenum* class has struck the cheek of a man of the *muškenum* class, he shall pay ten shekels of silver.
> If a man's slave has struck the cheek of a man of the free class, they shall cut off his ear.

Differentiation of penalty according to class clearly illustrates the stratification of society.

MARRIAGE AND FAMILY LIFE

Hammurabi's laws accepted marriage as basically monogamous, with enough exceptions to show that the social force behind this was not moral considerations but inheritance. A man might have children by a slave-girl as well as by his wife, and this carried no stigma, but such children only became free if he formally adopted them. A man and woman could live together without social condemnation, but the woman only became a wife in the legal sense if she had a written contract:

> §128 If a man has taken someone as a wife but has not drawn up a contract for her, that woman is not a wife.

A marriage might be brought about by negotiations between the fathers of the two parties (§166), or between the bridegroom himself and the bride's father (§§159–61). It could be arranged while a girl was still a child, in which case she would remain in her father's house for the time being; she was already legally a wife, although still a virgin (§130).

When agreement was reached on a marriage, the bridegroom or his father gave a present and made a payment of what is sometimes translated 'bride-price', although the bride was not actually sold to her husband. (Conservative Iraqi society practises a corresponding custom to this day, the amount of the 'bride-price' – sometimes fictitiously inflated – being regarded as an index of the desirability of the girl.) On completion of the marriage, the husband might give his wife a marriage-gift, intended to support her if he died, while the bride's parents paid over a dowry, which was substantially more than the bride-price (§164). The dowry represented a daughter's share of her father's estate; it was also paid if a man's daughter became a priestess. The husband managed his wife's dowry but it never became his property; the wife retained a life interest in it and at her death it passed to her sons (§162), or if she had no sons it went back to her paternal household.

A wife's primary duty was to produce sons for her husband. If she was a priestess of a class not supposed to bear children, she could do this by proxy by giving her husband a slave-girl for the purpose (§144). Once the slave-girl had borne sons, she could not be sold (§146). If a wife failed to provide her husband with sons, he had the right to divorce her, but he must return her dowry and also pay her a sum equal to her original bride-price, or, if no bride-price had been paid, a weight of silver fixed by his social status (§§138–40). A man could divorce a priestess who had provided him with sons, but had to make over to her half his land and chattels until the sons were grown up (§137). If a wife behaved so badly that she brought disgrace upon her husband, he could be rid of her without penalty, but only after bringing the case before the courts and substantiating his complaint. He might then either divorce his wife without compensation or marry another woman and reduce the original wife to the status of slave-girl in his house (§141). A wife also had rights; if her husband had misbehaved so grossly as to bring disgrace upon her, she could bring the case to the authorities and, provided she herself were beyond reproach, take her dowry and leave him (§142).

A man could not divorce his wife on account of illness, although in some circumstances – for example, if she became afflicted with a certain skin disease – he had the right to marry a second wife. However, he was not permitted to divorce his first wife and must maintain her in his house as long as she lived; she, on the other hand, had the right, if she so chose, to reclaim her dowry and depart (§§148–9).

Adultery by a woman could be a serious matter (see p. 105). If she were caught in adultery, both she and the man were drowned, unless the husband chose to spare his wife, in which case the man must also be spared (§129).

A man could will his property to his wife rather than his sons, and she might choose a son to manage it for her (§150). A widow could not, however, sell property left her, and after her death her estate went to her sons (§173).

Hammurabi's achievements

Although Hammurabi left behind the longest and most important collection of laws from the ancient Near East, he was not the first lawgiver, and although his voluminous correspondence shows his ability as an administrator, his older contemporary Shamshi-Adad of Assyria was at least as able in attention to the administrative details of his empire. Yet even with these achievements discounted, Hammurabi still has a claim to greatness, for it was he who gave Babylon, a formerly insignificant city, a status which it never lost. He raised it to be for a millennium and a half the national capital, and the city after which the whole of south Mesopotamia received the name *mat Babili*, the

59 A geometrical text of the Old Babylonian period.

Land of Babylon. And although it was superseded politically towards the end of the first millennium BC, Babylon remains significant as a cultural symbol even to the present day.

Another achievement associated with the period of Hammurabi, although not due to him personally, was development in mathematics, mainly at Nippur. Here scholars reached a level of attainment in the solution of algebraic and geometrical problems (see fig. 59), with tables to calculate reciprocals, square roots, cube roots and so on, which has been compared to that of the early Renaissance.

Literature in the Old Babylonian period

By the beginning of the Old Babylonian period Sumerian was dead as a spoken language, but some of the old Sumerian myths and epics were considered important enough to be translated into Akkadian. Relevant here are what became the Akkadian myth *Anzu* (see p. 151) and some creation myths, but the most notable were traditions about Gilgamesh, an ancient hero of Uruk, which became a major Akkadian epic. This was so highly esteemed in the ancient world that pieces of it have been found as far afield as Megiddo in Palestine, and near Harran in south Turkey, and it was even translated into Hittite and Hurrian, as fragments found in north Anatolia show.

The Akkadian text of the *Gilgamesh Epic* is preserved in part in two forms, one fragmentary from the Old Babylonian period, the other from the first millennium, mainly on tablets from the royal library at Nineveh, and about three-quarters complete. The two forms show significant differences, leading some scholars to suggest that Old Babylonian *Gilgamesh* texts were still, like the Sumerian originals, a number of loosely linked stories about the hero and not yet a single integrated epic. This might tie in with a tradition which attributes the epic to a scribe of the Kassite period named Sin-leqe-unnini. But the fragment of the epic found at Megiddo and the translations into Hittite and Hurrian come from the second millennium, and suggest that a form of the *Gilgamesh Epic* as a unitary whole went back before Sin-leqe-unnini. The tradition about Sin-leqe-unnini's authorship could mean no more than that he substantially reworked an Akkadian epic which already existed. The final standard version is divided into twelve sections (or 'tablets', as the scribes called them), and the twelfth tablet appears to be a secondary addition; this could have been added by Sin-leqe-unnini. We therefore take this epic as going back to the Old Babylonian period, with later re-editing.

The *Gilgamesh Epic* is a major literary creation, in which the Sumerian sources have been not merely translated, but reworked with considerable skill. Its enduring value is that it explores some basic problems of the human lot, notably the inevitability of ageing and death.

The epic in its final form begins with a prologue in which the narrator is speaking: he will, he announces, tell the story of 'him who saw everything'. He points to the glories of the city of Uruk, its incomparable temple Eanna, and its great walls of baked brick. Inside that city, he says, is a copper tablet-box. Inside that box lies a tablet of lapis lazuli. And on that tablet is inscribed the story of Gilgamesh.

The story proper now begins. Gilgamesh was son of the king Lugalbanda. His mother was the cow-goddess Ninsun, by virtue of whom he was two-thirds divine. He was a great king who crossed the ocean and reached the edge of the world in his quest for eternal life. But Gilgamesh was a tyrant: he conscripted all the young men and claimed sexual rights over all the young women. The gods heard the complaint of the people of Uruk and called on the Creatrix-goddess to create a rival. This she did, making Enkidu – the equal of Gilgamesh – in the form of a wild and shaggy-haired man. He fed and watered in the open country with the wild animals, and protected them by filling up the hunters' pits and springing their traps. A hunter, catching a glimpse of this formidable being, was frozen with fear. He told his father, who gave him wise advice. He should go to Uruk to Gilgamesh, and obtain the services of a prostitute. She would expose herself to the wild man, who would become powerless in his desire.

All happened as planned, and Enkidu and the prostitute made love for six days and seven nights. But when Enkidu, sated, went back to the wilds, the beasts fled from him. There was nothing for him but to return to the prostitute, who persuaded him to come into Uruk to savour the pleasures of civilised life.

Now follows an account of two dreams of Gilgamesh. When he told them to his

60 *Mask representing Humbaba, the monster guarding the forest, who was slain by Gilgamesh.*

divine mother, she interpreted them as meaning that a friend would come to him, who would be his equal in strength, and whom he would love like a woman. (This was idiom; it does not imply a homosexual relationship.)

When Enkidu came into Uruk, Gilgamesh was on his way to exercise his *jus primae noctis*. Enkidu confronted him, and a titanic battle ensued; but they proved equal in strength, and became firm friends. Now follows a series of adventure themes, originally separate in Sumerian, but in the Akkadian epic interwoven with great skill.

Gilgamesh proposed an expedition to the 'coniferous forest'; although later interpreted as the forests of the Lebanon, the underlying Sumerian epic shows that this originally referred to the beginning of the exploitation of the great trees which once covered the Zagros range east of Babylonia. Counsellors sought to dissuade Gilgamesh; it was a dangerous enterprise, they said, for the forest was the abode of a supernatural giant Humbaba, whom the god Enlil had set there to protect it. But, undeterred, the two set out, armed with great bronze axes and swords.

On the long journey Gilgamesh had a series of ominous dreams, obscure to us because of damage to the text. Finally they reached the forest, and encountered the terrible Humbaba (see fig. 60). Gilgamesh called upon the Sun-god Shamash, and with his magical aid overcame the giant. Humbaba pleaded for his life but, at Enkidu's urging, Gilgamesh slew him. He died with a curse on his lips. Gilgamesh and Enkidu felled the trees they wanted, and returned home.

Back in Uruk, the goddess Ishtar saw Gilgamesh, splendid in clean robes, and called on him to be her lover. But (in a passage which is certainly later in origin than the Old Babylonian period) the hero rejected her advances with contempt, describing her as 'a back door that keeps out neither blast nor storm, ... pitch that fouls its bearer's hand, ... a shoe that nips its owner's foot.' He went on to catalogue the fate of former lovers of hers. One, the god Dumuzi, was fated to be lamented yearly[12]; another she had turned into a bird which continually cries *kappi kappi* ('My wing! My wing!'); and a third, a shepherd, she had turned into a wolf, now hunted by his own hounds. There were others.

Ishtar went up wrathfully to heaven and raised a clamour with her father, the supreme god Anu. If he did not send down the Bull of Heaven to avenge her, she would release the dead from the underworld. Reluctantly Anu acceded to her demand and she led off the Bull to Uruk. There it wrought havoc among the warriors, until Enkidu and Gilgamesh together seized the fearsome beast and slew it.

Then Enkidu had a dream, in which he saw the great gods in council. Anu said: 'Because they have killed the Bull of Heaven and Humbaba, one of them must die'. Enlil replied: 'Let Enkidu die, let not Gilgamesh die'. And although the Sun-god Shamash pleaded Enkidu's innocence, Enlil stood firm by his decree.

Enkidu began to pine away. His first reaction was bitterness, in which he called down curses on the hunter and prostitute who had brought him from the wilds. But Shamash reminded him of the good things of civilisation, and of his place of honour as Gilgamesh's friend. And at this he transformed his curse upon the prostitute into a blessing.

As he lay there stricken, Enkidu described to Gilgamesh another dream. He had been seized and dragged down to the underworld, which is described, in anticipation of Shakespeare, as 'the country from whose bourn no traveller returns', a place

> whose dwellers are deprived of light,
> where dust is their sustenance and clay their bread,
> where they are clad in feathers like birds,
> and see no light and dwell in darkness.

Day by day Enkidu grew weaker, and finally he died. Gilgamesh uttered a eulogy over his friend and called upon craftsmen to make a memorial statue. But as he mourned, the realisation struck him: 'Shall I not too die like Enkidu?' Seized with a dread of death, he resolved to seek out a deathless ancestor, Uta-napishtim, to learn from him the secret of eternal life.

He set out and reached the Mountain of Sunrise, guarded by scorpion-men. Recognising him as two-thirds divine, they allowed him to pass. On he went through a region of deep darkness and a land of precious stones, until he reached an inn. There he inquired of the hostess the way to Uta-napishtim. She was not encouraging. It was, she said, impossible to reach Uta-napishtim, for he lived over the waters, which it was death to touch. None but Shamash could cross them. His only hope was a ferryman, who made the passage of the lethal waters with the help of something called 'those of stone'. What these were is not clear, but when Gilgamesh met the ferryman, he smashed them. Without them the ferry could not cross. To replace their power the ferryman directed Gilgamesh to cut three hundred giant punt poles from the forest. He did this, and the ferryman took his craft out to sea. At the lethal waters, the ferryman instructed Gilgamesh to punt; he must use each pole once only, for it would be death for a drop of the waters to touch his hand. Finally Gilgamesh arrived, and explained to the astonished Uta-napishtim why he had come.

Uta-napishtim could offer no help. He assured Gilgamesh that to die was inevitable, for the gods had established death for mankind as well as life. But, asked Gilgamesh, how is it that you yourself, a man like me, have found eternal life? And at that Uta-napishtim told Gilgamesh the story of the Flood (see p. 39). Because he and his family had been the sole survivors, Enlil had blessed Uta-napishtim and his wife, and made them like gods, and set them to dwell for ever at the Mouth of the Rivers.

Even at the end of his Flood narrative Gilgamesh had not given up hope of eternal life, so Uta-napishtim made a challenge: let Gilgamesh remain awake for six days and seven nights, to show that he could bear eternal life. Immediately deep sleep overcame the hero, and for seven days he slept on. Each day Uta-napishtim had his wife bake bread and place it at the sleeper's head. When Gilgamesh at last awoke, he claimed he had just dozed off, but Uta-napishtim gave him the lie, by pointing to the line of loaves lying there, from dried up through stale and mouldy to fresh and newly baked. So Gilgamesh had to concede that he could not escape death.

Uta-napishtim gave Gilgamesh clean raiment, and set him on his homeward way. As he was leaving, Uta-napishtim's wife begged that he should receive some recompense for his journey, so Uta-napishtim revealed to Gilgamesh the secret of a magic plant for restoring youth, called 'Old-man-young-again', at the bottom of the sea. Fixing weights to his feet, Gilgamesh dived into the depths and retrieved the plant, and set out with it back to Uruk. But on the way, as he stopped to bathe in a pool, a snake crawled up and stole the plant. So it is the snake, and not man, that renews its youth by sloughing its skin. Gilgamesh returned to Uruk empty-handed, knowing he was destined to grow old and die, but he had one consolation: he could point out to the ferryman, who had accompanied him home, the splendour of the baked brick walls of the great city of Uruk, which would remain to his eternal glory.

Chapter Seven

KASSITE KINGS

HAMMURABI LEFT A kingdom with territory more extensive than modern Iraq. Its borders ran north-westwards from the Persian Gulf, up west of the Euphrates almost to Aleppo, northwards to the foothills of the eastern Taurus, eastwards to the Zagros, and south-eastwards as far as Elam in south-west Iran. However, this did not long survive him. Although the central part of the kingdom, north Babylonia, was sufficiently stable to endure through five reigns for a further century and a half, other parts, which had been seized and held only by Hammurabi's exceptional diplomatic and strategic skills, had no organic cohesion, and his successors were unable to counter growing external pressures.

The first signs of trouble came in the reign of Hammurabi's son Samsu-iluna (1749–1712 BC), whose date formulae reflect a series of problems. That for year nine mentions 'the army of the Kassites', implying a military clash. Previously these people were scarcely known, but they were destined to play a major part in Babylonian history for most of the second half of the millennium. The date formula for Samsu-iluna's tenth year reveals widespread disturbances – in north-eastern and eastern border areas, in Uruk in south Babylonia, and in Isin within 110 km (70 miles) of Babylon itself. And the formula for year twelve mentions a general rebellion of enemy lands. Samsu-iluna's own inscriptions identify the ringleader in these revolts as Rim-Sin of Larsa; he bore the same name as the king of Larsa who had ruled much of Babylonia before the rise of Hammurabi, and was probably his nephew. Samsu-iluna claims that he quickly defeated Rim-Sin and his allies, but although he may have won a battle, dangerous pockets of resistance remained. He had to take action against a usurper in Ur in his fourteenth year, and a general rebellion broke out in his twentieth year. By the end of his reign, Samsu-iluna had lost all the south of the country, the region known as the Sealands, where a certain Iluma-Ilum had established a dynasty and succeeded in extending his control as far north as Nippur.

A progressive decline in Babylonian territory followed. In the reign of Samsu-iluna's successor, Abieshu (1711–1684 BC), Babylon lost the middle Euphrates area, and there was a gradual further loss of territory subsequently. Despite this, judging by long reigns of the three remaining kings of the First Dynasty of Babylon, Ammiditana, Ammisaduqa, and Samsu-ditana, the central part of the kingdom remained stable. The second of these three, Ammisaduqa (1646–1626 BC), is best remembered for some observations of Venus from his reign, which are central to the calculation of chronology (see pp. 27–8) and for an edict cancelling certain debts (see p. 97).

The end of the First Dynasty of Babylon came with the reign of Samsu-ditana (1625–1595 BC). Babylonia was now so impotent that when in 1595 BC a Hittite king, Mursilis I, marched down the Euphrates to make a sudden raid on the capital, there was no effective resistance. Mursilis sacked Babylon and took away the statues of the city's tutelary deity Marduk and his consort. Since nothing more is heard of the royal family, they were presumably killed. The motive for the raid is unknown, but since Mursilis withdrew with no attempt at permanent occupation, it may have been nothing more than a looting expedition against a famous and wealthy city now *in extremis*.

The immediate aftermath of the Hittite raid is obscure. Babylonia's neighbours must have been interested in its fate, but minor states to the north-west along the Euphrates can have been of no military significance at this time, otherwise Mursilis could not have got through and back unopposed. The most powerful kingdom within reach of Babylon was now the Sealands to the south, and this may have seized the capital in the confusion after the Hittite attack. Favouring this view is an inscription on a *kudurru*, a so-called 'boundary stone' confirming a land-grant (see p. 122), which names Gulkishar, a king of the Sealand dynasty at about this time, as a king of Babylon. There is also a text about glass-making dated by the year in which Gulkishar became king in Babylon, and an entry in a king-list points to the same conclusion. But if Babylon was ruled by the Sealand dynasty it can only have been a brief interlude. The people who moved in permanently were the Kassites, who were to rule Babylonia for over four centuries (shortly after 1595 to 1157 BC).

The Kassites appear to have been another of the peoples from the Zagros, but their ethnic affiliations are uncertain. Too few Kassite words are known to provide any firm linkage on the basis of language, and although some see an Indo-European connection on the basis of certain Kassite god-names, this could be otherwise explained. They had clashed with Samsu-iluna in 1741 BC and later with his son, and, judging by Kassite names in economic documents, during the seventeenth century some of them were settling peaceably in Babylonia, including the area around the capital. There is no solid information on how the Kassites took over in Babylonia, but it must have been through an existing dynasty elsewhere which wrested control from the Sealand dynasty. One of the kings of Khana, a petty kingdom on the middle Euphrates, had a Kassite name, which may mean that some Kassites had already gained control there. If a group of Kassites had established themselves on the middle Euphrates under Hittite protection, this would explain why Mursilis was able to pass that region unopposed, and also how a Kassite dynasty could take over in Babylon in due course.

A king-list enumerates 36 Kassite kings, with a total of 576 years of rule, but these figures, if correct, must include kings who reigned elsewhere before the Kassites took over Babylonia. Since a Kassite dynasty did not gain control of Babylonia until after 1595 BC and the dynasty came to an end in 1157 BC, Kassite rule in Babylonia must have amounted to less than 440 years.

The Kassites were not the only ethnic group to come into prominence at this time. Another people, the Hurrians, were becoming an increasingly significant factor. Some scholars think they came originally from highland Armenia, but they could have been native to north Mesopotamia. In any case, they were moving further south within Mesopotamia from late in the third millennium. They had importance in several respects, but their most enduring cultural contribution was probably the part they played in bringing the horse into wider use. The horse was originally domesticated in Ukraine in the middle of the fourth millennium, and was known in Anatolia and Iran by 3000 BC and in north Mesopotamia and Susa by 2400 BC. Its Akkadian name, *sisû*, occurs first in the Isin-Larsa period.[1] It was already known in Mesopotamia as a riding animal in the Old Babylonian period, but in some quarters with some misgiving, for the writer of one of the Mari letters commented that it was undignified to ride a horse and that it would be more fitting for the king to ride a donkey. This attitude persisted throughout the Old Babylonian period. The Hurrians were certainly not the first to ride the horse, but seem to have been the first in Mesopotamia to recognise the full potential of the horse and to introduce the two-wheeled horse-drawn chariot for military purposes.

Another important cultural function of the Hurrians was to transmit features of Mesopotamian literature and religion to the Hittites, their neighbours to the north-west, and through them eventually to archaic Greece.

By the middle of the sixteenth century Hurrians were coalescing into kingdoms in Syria, Cilicia and north Mesopotamia. The most powerful of these, Mitanni, was centred on the Khabur east of the Euphrates. It was once held that this kingdom was ruled by an Indo-Iranian aristocracy, but this hypothesis is based entirely on about thirty words (numerals, god-names, personal names, and terms connected with horse-training) which may or may not be of Indo-Iranian origin. Mitanni expanded until by the middle of the fifteenth century it controlled parts of Syria and Cilicia to the west and had reduced Assyria temporarily to the status of a vassal. During the same period the Hittites in Anatolia had been advancing southwards into north Syria. Egypt had also entered an imperial phase and was expanding its boundaries north-wards through Palestine into Syria. Thus all three powers had an interest in Syria, and rivalry for control there brought them into close diplomatic relationship.

This gave rise to documents which shed some light on affairs in Babylonia. In the late nineteenth century a peasant woman digging in ruins at El Amarna in middle Egypt found something exceptional for Egypt – a collection of clay tablets inscribed in cuneiform, instead of the usual writing in hieroglyphics on papyrus. These tablets proved to be mainly diplomatic correspondence between Egyptian kings and rulers of the Hittites, Mitanni, Babylonia, Assyria and princes in Syria and Palestine from the early part of the fourteenth century. The Egyptian correspondents were Amenophis III and IV, the latter more commonly called Akhenaton. These documents, amounting to nearly four hundred, are today known as the Amarna letters, and their use of Babylonian (more accurately, Akkadian) cuneiform puts it beyond doubt that this had become the lingua franca of the civilised world, and reflects the international standing of Babylonian culture. Cuneiform could be used internationally even in contexts in which Babylonia and Assyria were in no way implicated, as for example in a treaty made at about 1280 BC between Ramesses II of Egypt and the Hittite king; there was an Egyptian version in hieroglyphics but the one in the Hittite capital was in Akkadian cuneiform.

Of Kassite rule in Babylonia before 1420 BC we know very little beyond the names and sequence of the kings, and in some cases not even that. A king-list names the first Kassite king as Gandash, and if we accept its figure of 576 years for the period of Kassite rule as accurate, and work back from 1157 BC when the dynasty came to an end, we reach a date of about 1733 BC for the beginning of the reign of Gandash. This is near enough to the date of Samsu-iluna's first clash with Kassite forces, 1741 BC, to suggest that the two were connected, and that Gandash established a dynasty somewhere – but not in Babylon – at this time. A first-millennium text which claims to be a copy of an inscription of Gandash (spelt Gaddash) refers to the conquest of Bà-bà-lam, which could perhaps be an allusion to the clash with Samsu-iluna in 1741 BC, although if so it is exaggerated, since Gandash certainly did not take Babylon then, even supposing he attacked it.

According to the king-list, the second Kassite king, the son of Gandash, was named Agum, designated *mahru*, meaning 'the first'. Thus there must have been at least one other king Agum and possibly a third. The second Agum, called Agum-kakrime, is known only from two seventh-century texts which claim to be copies of an inscription of his, and which recount how Agum II had brought back to Babylon divine statues which the Hittite raiders had taken off in 1595 BC. But there are doubts about the authenticity of this inscription. The text also mentions certain tax exemptions supposedly granted in connection with the restoration of the statues, so it may have been a forgery perpetrated to make out a case for continuing these exemptions. If, however, the text has a basis in fact, it shows that one of the earliest Kassite kings was already showing sensitivity for Babylonian religious traditions. Kassite kings also quickly began to enter into international relationships; the first mentioned in this connection is another sixteenth-century king, Burna-Buriash I, who according to a chronicle made a boundary treaty with Assyria.

The first Kassite king known from his own inscriptions was Kara-indash, datable towards the end of the fifteenth century; a chronicle records that he likewise made a boundary treaty with a king of Assyria, in his case Ashur-bel-nisheshu (1419–1411 BC). By now Assyria was beginning to free itself from Mitannian domination, but Babylonia was once again of major consequence on the international scene, and had come to regard Assyria as its vassal. Babylonia's international standing is reflected in Kara-indash entering into friendly relations with the king of Egypt, as one of the

Amarna letters reports. Such relations involved exchange of ambassadors, marriage alliances, and also so-called 'presents' from one king to another. These were in reality not mere courtesies but a form of trade, typically taking the form of ivory, ebony furniture, horses and chariots, silver, gold, and lapis lazuli. This commercial aspect becomes very clear when we find one of the kings specifying what he would like to receive, or complaining that the value he had received did not match what he had sent. The trade was by overland caravans which sometimes fell victim to banditry from nomadic tribes on the way.

Kara-indash's own inscriptions are on bricks from Uruk, where he built a new temple to Inanna; clearly by this time the Kassites had driven the Sealand dynasty out of the southern cities and were in full control of south Babylonia. An inscription on a clay tablet gives information about building work at Uruk, and calls Kara-indash 'mighty king, king of Babylon, king of Sumer and Akkad, king of the Kassites, king of Karduniash.' This last term was often used as a name for Babylonia from the Kassite period onwards.

The son of Kara-indash, Kadashman-harbe, reigned at about 1400 BC. Babylonia was again beginning to experience problems from pressure of nomads, since according to a chronicle he had to take military measures against the Suteans, a nomadic people along the Euphrates related to the Aramaeans. We also learn that he strengthened fortresses in a mountain region called Hihi which must have been somewhere in the Syrian desert. (The rest of this chronicle entry misleadingly mentions a rebellion which actually happened eighty years later.)

The next king was Kurigalzu. This can be a source of confusion, since there were two kings of that name, and more than 440 inscriptions mention a king Kurigalzu, in most cases leaving it unclear which one is meant. It is generally accepted that it was Kurigalzu I who created a new city, Dur-Kurigalzu, intended as a fortress against potential enemies east of the Tigris. This was built about 25 km (15 miles) west of where Baghdad now stands, and the massive remains of its ziggurat still survive as one of the most imposing of Iraq's ancient monuments (see pl. IX). Like his father's predecessor, Kurigalzu I maintained good relations with Egypt. One Amarna letter refers to an Egyptian king sending him gold, implying trading relations, and another implies that he had refused a Canaanite request to join an anti-Egyptian alliance.

The next two kings, Kadashman-Enlil and Burna-Buriash II, are also known from letters in the Amarna correspondence (see fig. 61). The Egyptian king wanted Kadashman-Enlil to send him a daughter in marriage, but Kadashman-Enlil was hesitant, since he had been unable to discover whether his sister, who had gone to Egypt earlier, was alive or dead. He proposed that he himself should receive an Egyptian princess in exchange, but the Egyptian king refused this, on the grounds that to send an Egyptian princess abroad was not customary. In consequence Kadashman-Enlil firmly declined to send his own daughter, even if the Egyptian king should send three thousand talents of gold. In home affairs, Kadashman-Enlil's firm control of his kingdom is shown by his undertaking building works on temples at Nippur and at Larsa in the south of the country.

61 *One of the cuneiform letters found at El Amarna in Egypt. It was written by Burna-Buriash II of Babylonia to Amenophis IV of Egypt.*

Burna-Buriash II (1375–1347 BC) was interested in trade with Egypt and proposed a reciprocal arrangement: 'What you want from my land, write and it shall be brought, and what I want from your land, I will write, that it may be brought'. But this did not work out to his entire satisfaction, since in one letter he complains that a 'present' he had received of two minas of gold was not enough. Burna-Buriash was very much on his dignity and wrote to complain that when he had been ill Egypt had sent no enquiries about him; he did not consider distance an adequate excuse for this omission.

Before the middle of the fourteenth century Assyria had freed itself from Mitannian control, so that its king Ashur-uballit I (1365–1330 BC) was able to send an envoy to the king of Egypt with a present of a fine chariot and horses and a jewel of lapis lazuli; he had instructions to open up diplomatic and trade relations and to report back. This displeased Burna-Buriash, who complained that Assyria was his own vassal, and should only have acted in international affairs through him. But Egypt disregarded this protest, and reciprocated Ashur-uballit's courtesy by sending its messengers to his court with a present of gold. Babylonia quickly came to terms with Assyria's parity, and Burna-Buriash married a daughter of Ashur-uballit I. A son of this marriage, whose name is doubtful, since he was variously called Kara-hardash or Kara-indash (II), succeeded on the death of Burna-Buriash, but the Kassite army deposed and killed him and enthroned a usurper. This murder of his grandson led Ashur-uballit to intervene in Babylonia to put down the revolt, and to place another son of Burna-Buriash, Kurigalzu II (1345–1324 BC), on the throne.

While Mitanni had been encroaching on northern parts of Assyria, the king of Babylonia had taken advantage of Assyrian weakness to move into its territory in the south, as far north as modern Kirkuk. The re-emergence of Assyria as a major power under Ashur-uballit led his successors to take steps to recover the territory which had been annexed. This brought repeated clashes, mainly resolved in favour of Assyria. Two chronicles report a battle on the Tigris between Kurigalzu II and his Assyrian contemporary, in consequence of which the boundary was readjusted south of the Lower Zab. A further boundary realignment in Assyria's favour came when Nazi-maruttash (1307–1282 BC) clashed with the Assyrian king Adad-narari I (1307–1275 BC). But these readjustments reflected Assyrian strength rather than any particular Babylonian weakness. Kurigalzu was strong enough to defeat Elam, as we learn from a chronicle, confirmed by two inscriptions found at Susa bearing Kurigalzu's name. This king must also have been active further north in the Zagros, judging by the finding in Luristan of a stone bead inscribed with his name. Nazi-maruttash also seems to have made a successful attack on Elam, for a text of his period about prisoners of war has a section on Elamites. He was also active in building as far south as Uruk.

By the end of the reign of Nazi-maruttash Assyria was indisputably the most powerful state in Mesopotamia, and for the next half-century little is heard about Babylonia. This period is covered by four Kassite kings, Kadasman-Turgu (1281–1264 BC), Kadashman-Enlil II (1263–1255 BC), Kudur-Enlil (1254–1246 BC), and Shag-arakti-Shuriash (1245–1233 BC). The first two were in correspondence with the Hittite king,[2] then a major international power, and the last undertook temple building in Sippar. Kudur-Enlil was the first Kassite king whose name was wholly Babylonian.

In Assyria Adad-narari I and his son Shalmaneser I (1274–1245 BC) had gained all of former Mitanni, and Shalmaneser's son Tukulti-Ninurta I (1244–1208 BC) continued an expansionist policy, first securing his kingdom to the east and north, and then turning to improve the line of his Babylonian border. The king who had succeeded in Babylonia, Kashtiliash IV (1232–1225 BC), failed to perceive the power-shift and reacted as his predecessors had done in the days of Babylonian dominance by invading Assyrian territory. The response of Tukulti-Ninurta was vigorous and decisive; he made a raid into Babylonia, captured Babylon itself and Sippar, and deported Kashtiliash. Chronicle P records:

> Tukulti-Ninurta returned to Babylon. ... He destroyed the walls of
> Babylon. He massacred the Babylonians. He brought out the property of
> the temple Esagila and Babylon as booty. He removed the great lord
> Marduk from his dwelling-place and set him on the road to Ashur. He
> installed his governors in Karduniash [Babylonia]. For seven years
> Tukulti-Ninurta controlled Karduniash.

A poet composed an epic to glorify the Assyrian achievement, attributing Tukulti-Ninurta's success to divine support. Marduk's statue apparently remained in Assyria until the early twelfth century. Its presence there had a consequence which Tukulti-Ninurta did not foresee and certainly did not intend, in that it brought an upsurge of Babylonian religious influence in the Assyrian capital.

Chronicle P tells us that as his means for controlling Babylonia Tukulti-Ninurta installed governors, but one of the king-lists names three kings who reigned in Babylonia during the seven years of Tukulti-Ninurta. Probably these were Babylonians whom Tukulti-Ninurta appointed successively as puppets to meet Babylonian aspirations for a native king, but they could have been rivals of Tukulti-Ninurta who enjoyed some brief and limited success. Certainly Tukulti-Ninurta's grasp of Babylonia was not as complete as Chronicle P or the epic might suggest. Elam to the east responded to the new situation by twice invading the country, capturing several cities, among them Nippur, and deposing two successive native kings, which favours the view that they were Tukulti-Ninurta's puppets. These deep Elamite incursions point to Assyrian forces being over-extended.

The Kassite royal family still found Babylonian support, so that one of its members, Adad-shuma-usur (1218–1189 BC), was able to seize the kingship in the south of Babylonia. Chronicle P takes this as ending Assyrian rule. But Assyria must have still maintained a presence in Babylon, for another chronicle implies that Adad-shuma-usur was not able to gain control of the capital until after a battle with Assyrian forces later in his reign. There is also an historical epic which alludes to a rebellion during the reign of Adad-shuma-usur, and this could have been fomented by Assyrians still in Babylonia.

Developments in Assyria favoured Adad-shuma-usur. The Assyrian capital had long been Ashur on the west bank of the Tigris, but after his Babylonian campaign Tukulti-Ninurta built a new capital on the east bank. No explanation is offered for this, but the move implies tensions between Tukulti-Ninurta and the citizens of Ashur. Certainly there were internal problems, for a rebellion broke out in which Tukulti-Ninurta was killed. Chronicle P attributed this to his treatment of Babylon: 'Tukulti-Ninurta, who had brought his hand for evil against Babylon, his son Ashur-nasir-pal and the magnates of Assyria rebelled against him, they took him from his throne, imprisoned him ... and killed him.'[3]

This left instability in Assyria, to Babylonia's advantage. Extensive building works show that during his thirty-year reign Adad-shuma-usur gained firm control of his country. Although he was in direct line of descent in the Kassite dynasty, his name was not Kassite but Babylonian, and the same was true of the names of three of his four successors. The Kassite dynasty, almost since its beginning, had been sensitive to Babylonian culture and traditions, and clearly the Kassite dynasty had become babylonianised in every respect.

Adad-shuma-usur was succeeded by his son Meli-shipak (1188–1174 BC) and his grandson Marduk-apla-iddina I (1173–1161 BC). These reigns appear to have been stable and, judging by building inscriptions and land-grants, even prosperous, but the

Kassite dynasty was nearing its end. The major new threat was the Elamites, who were now expanding north-westwards and beginning to take over the Diyala region, through which ran important trade routes. The next Kassite king, Zababa-shuma-iddina, lasted only a matter of months in 1160 BC. He suffered first an attack by Assyria under Ashur-dan I and then invasion by the Elamites, who deposed him and took off considerable plunder from north Babylonian cities. This booty included a victory stele of Naram-Sin and a stele inscribed with Hammurabi's laws, both looted from Sippar and in modern times discovered in the ruins of the Elamite capital, Susa. One further Kassite king, Enlil-nadin-ahi (1159–1157 BC), the last of the dynasty, continued the struggle for three years until he too was captured and deported to Elam. To demonstrate that Babylon's god was on their side, the Elamites also took back with them the statue of Marduk from Esagila.

Developments in the Kassite period

The absence of rebellion, or traditions hostile to the Kassite rulers, makes it clear that their rule was never found oppressive; royal charters reinforce this conclusion, showing these kings to have been scrupulous in accepting the established rights of citizens. They maintained internal stability, and before the end of the fifteenth century had once again reunified the country and retaken the south, where an independent dynasty of the Sealands had reigned since the time of Samsu-iluna.

It was only the earliest of the Kassite rulers who were ethnically distinct from the native Babylonian population. They seem to have used the Babylonian language (or for inscriptions, Sumerian) from the beginning, and later rulers of the dynasty were fully babylonianised, intermarried with Assyrian royalty, and, in the case of five of the last seven kings, bore Babylonian, not Kassite, names.

The Kassite rulers took all possible measures to encourage international trade. The Amarna letters show them in direct communication by trading caravans with Egypt, and in the fourteenth and thirteenth centuries trade also flourished between Babylonia and Assyria. Seals and other objects of lapis lazuli and carnelian indicate that luxury items were still imported from Afghanistan and India by way of Iran.

The Amarna letters show international diplomacy in operation. This was no new thing, since it went back to the Early Dynastic period, as we learn from the Sumerian epic *Enmerkar and the Lord of Aratta* (see p. 78), which concerns diplomatic exchanges in the interests of trade between Uruk in south Mesopotamia and somewhere in Iran. From later in the third millennium there is a treaty in Elamite between Naram-Sin of Agade and a king of Elam. The Mari letters, from the century or so after 1900 BC, often reflect a situation in which rulers joined in coalition for common defence. One letter refers to this explicitly: 'No king is powerful alone. Ten or fifteen kings follow Hammurabi of Babylon, an equal number follow Rim-Sin of Larsa and the king of Eshnunna, and twenty kings follow the king of Yamhad.' In such coalitions minor states were expected to conform their foreign policies to that of the suzerain, and to provide contingents in case of war, but in return for these obligations they themselves received protection in the event of attack. International agreements were always backed by religious sanctions. They could cover not only arrangements for mutual assistance in case of attack, but also matters concerning trade, embargoes upon trading with a hostile country, and even extradition arrangements. International treaties were sometimes reinforced by marriage between royal families, and we have seen a good example of such a dynastic alliance between Assyria and Babylonia (see pp. 118–19), when Ashur-uballit made a military intervention to protect the interests of the Babylonian royal family when a revolt broke out there.

From the beginning of the fourteenth century, considerable building work took place throughout Babylonia, which implies a sound internal economy. The Kassites continued and developed the Old Babylonian practice of making land-grants to servants of the crown, but showed no signs of attempting to operate a centralised economy. They introduced an innovation in the form of the type of document called a *kudurru* ('boundary stone') (see fig. 62). This was usually a stone monument, occasionally a large cone of baked clay, used to record a land-grant made or confirmed by the king, most commonly to a high official. In some cases, where the land had been in a family for a long time, the text records details of former lawsuits and royal decisions upon them. The text states the boundaries of the land-grant, which may have been considerable, names the witnesses to the grant, and concludes with curses against any future person who might dispute the grant or destroy or hide the boundary stone. A characteristic of *kudurrus* is groups of curious symbols at their top, such as an eight-pointed star, a crescent moon, a dragon, a snake, turtle, a spade, or a two-pronged fork (meaning lightning); these were the symbols of the gods under whose protection the land-grant was placed.

In art the Kassite period saw a new development in the decoration of the outer walls of temples with a series of niches in which divine figures, alternately male and female, were set in high relief (see fig. 63).

The second half of the second millennium also saw religious developments, markedly changes in the pantheon. Enlil, supreme in the third millennium, was supplanted as national god by Marduk, tutelary deity of Babylon, who usurped his functions and titles. From about 1200 BC onwards there was a marked trend for a number of the great gods to become regarded as aspects of one particular god. Thus in a hymn to Ninurta, of late Kassite origin, the god is told 'Your eyes, O Lord, are Enlil and Ninlil; Anu and Antu are your two lips; your head is Adad; your brow is Shala; your neck is Marduk, judge of heaven and earth; your throat is Sarpanitum, creatrix of mankind.'[4] This, although not yet monotheism, was the beginning of a movement which by the first millennium was to lead Babylonian religion increasingly in that direction.

Another cultural feature of the Kassite period was its considerable literary activity. There had been scribal schools (in Sumerian é.dub.ba, literally 'tablet house') in the III Ur period, and there had been a marked flowering of literary activity in the Old Babylonian period, when, although Sumerian as a spoken language was either already dead or rapidly dying, it remained a subject of keen study in scribal circles. Prominent

62 *The Kassites introduced this type of monument (called* kudurru, *usually translated as 'boundary stone') to commemorate grants of land or tax exemptions on land. This example is post-Kassite.*

63 *One of the innovations of the Kassite period was a frieze made from baked moulded bricks to form a temple façade, 2–3 m (7–10 ft) high. This reassembled example comes from the temple of Inanna at Uruk, late fifteenth century* BC.

among the Sumerian literature of the Old Babylonian period, known mainly from Nippur and Ur, were myths and epics, hymns to the praise of gods, temples and rulers, and laments over the destruction of cities and temples. Since Sumerian was no longer understood by the population generally, such categories obviously cannot have been intended for their entertainment or edification, putting it beyond question that its main objective was the education of scribes, who at all times learnt their craft by copying out works of literature written by experts.

Scribal experts during the Kassite period continued and even extended these trends. Some scribes earned a considerable reputation, and in later times there were scribal families who were able to trace their descent back to an ancestor of the Kassite period. The fact that we can speak of scribal families indicates an increasing tendency for the scribal craft to be largely hereditary.

New works were created in this period, among them some epics and some compositions exploring problems of conduct and belief which are usually called Wisdom literature. But the major literary achievement was the collection and revision of older works, and their editing into what was subsequently accepted as the standard (or 'canonical') form. This included the arrangement of material – for example, lexicography or omens – into a numbered group of tablets (in some cases up to a hundred of them) which we call a 'series'. Old Sumerian texts were provided with translations, and commentaries written on them. Sumerian remained important in scribal circles and in religion, and even as late as around 1200 BC Babylonian royal inscriptions on temple buildings were more often in Sumerian than Akkadian.

Babylonian scribal education had its influence as far afield as Ugarit in Syria, where from c. 1400 BC there were found various scholarly texts of Mesopotamian origin, such as lexical texts, grammatical texts, god lists and syllabaries. There were also vocabularies of Mesopotamian origin but adapted to the needs of scribes in Ugarit by being either trilingual, using Sumerian, Akkadian and Hurrian, or quadrilingual, with those three languages plus Ugaritic. Babylonian scribal techniques also left their mark in Anatolia during the Kassite period, and we have already noted that Egypt used Babylonian cuneiform for its international correspondence, even with countries outside Mesopotamia.

The Second Dynasty of Isin

After the collapse of the Kassite dynasty the predominant influence in north Babylonia for several years was the Elamites. But further south a new native dynasty emerged; a king-list writes its name with the cuneiform signs PA.ŠE, which denoted the city Isin, and this dynasty is therefore known as the Second Dynasty of Isin. It is not clear whether Isin was the dynasty's original power centre, or whether it was simply the city from which the ruling family emanated. As the Elamites withdrew, the dynasty established itself at Babylon.

For the ordinary Babylonian the significance of the new developments was not the change of dynasty, but the emergence of order and stability after the confusion which had followed the Elamite invasions. We know little of the first two kings of the dynasty beyond their names and approximate regnal dates, Marduk-kabit-ahheshu (1156–1139 BC) and Itti-Marduk-balatu (1138–1131 BC). The third king, Ninurta-nadin-shumi, was during his short reign (1130–1125 BC) strong enough to challenge Assyria by a raid deep into its territory east of the Tigris, where he penetrated as far as Erbil. But the high point of Babylonia towards the end of the second millennium came with the reign of Nebuchadnezzar I (1124–1103 BC).

The looting of the statue of the national god Marduk by the Elamites had made a powerful impression. By ancient thinking, this could only have happened because Marduk had been angry with the Babylonian cult centres. The Elamites still controlled some regions claimed by Babylonia east of the Tigris, and Nebuchadnezzar decided to rid the country of the Elamite threat. He announced that Marduk had now abated his anger and that he had commissioned him to take the road to Elam. He set out in high summer, whereby he encountered grave problems of heat and shortage of water:

> It was as though the roads burnt like flames.
> There was no water in the lowlands, the water supply was cut off.
> Even the best of the great horses came to a standstill,
> And the legs of the strong warrior began to fail.

> But the king, pre-eminent, goes on, the gods supporting him;
> Nebuchadnezzar leads on, he has no rival. . . .
> The mighty king hastened, to reach the bank of the Ulaya river.[5]

This comes from an inscription on a *kudurru* which recorded a grant of land rights. The beneficiary on this one was a colonel of chariotry, who had distinguished himself in the battle; in recognition of his services the king had granted him tax exemptions and other rights over certain villages which he hereditarily owned.

At the Ulaya river, the Elamites were waiting and gave Nebuchadnezzar no chance to rest his army before engaging the enemy. But the Babylonians were victorious and, as the text says,

> King Nebuchadnezzar stood in victory,
> He seized the land of Elam, he took its property as spoil.

As part of the booty from this campaign (or possibly of a subsequent campaign which some scholars would read into the texts) Nebuchadnezzar recovered the statue of Marduk, looted from Babylon at the end of the Kassite dynasty, and formally reinstated the god in his temple Esagila in Babylon. Some argue that this was the occasion at which Marduk was finally accepted as supreme deity in the Babylonian pantheon. However, there is a problem: did formal theological statements precede and shape popular beliefs, or did they follow them? The latter seems more probable. In that case, although this may have been the first time the headship of Marduk in the pantheon was formally promulgated as official doctrine, he may well have been widely identified as the supreme god in popular belief centuries before. An Old Babylonian hymn supports this interpretation, since it says of Marduk: 'In the pure Apsu he is Asaluhi; above in heaven his name is An'[6], and An (Anu) of this identification was traditionally the supreme god.

Nebuchadnezzar's titles point to other military activity beyond the borders of Babylonia. He is called 'despoiler of the Kassites' and 'the one who overthrew the mighty Lullubu'. Action against 'Kassites' can have no direct connection here with the dynasty which preceded his, but must refer to raids on groups east of the Tigris from where the Kassites originally stemmed, and the Lullubu lived in Kurdistan, probably not far from present-day Sulaimaniyeh. Another title of Nebuchadnezzar, 'conqueror of the Amurru', suggests military action west of the middle Euphrates.

Nebuchadnezzar was also active in temple restoration and in the regulation of temple revenues and temple duties, and he was generous in grants of land, or tax exemptions, to his supporters, both military and priestly. His inscriptions, and the *kudurru* already quoted, were written in elegant language, which points to a literary revival in which scribes sought to give fitting expression to what were felt to be glorious royal achievements.

Nebuchadnezzar was succeeded by a son, Enlil-nadin-apli (1102–1099 BC), who was a minor. Little is known of his brief reign. After him came a brother of

64 *Boundary stone, with a land-grant by Nebuchadnezzar I (1124–1103 BC) inscribed on the reverse.*

Nebuchadnezzar, Marduk-nadin-ahhe (1098–1081 BC), whose reign was overshadowed by his powerful Assyrian contemporary, Tiglath-Pileser I. The latter was vigorously resisting a new problem – Aramaeans who were attempting a massive migration into Mesopotamia from the Syrian semi-desert. This was soon to have a major impact upon the society of Babylonia itself. Tiglath-Pileser in his inscriptions designates himself conqueror of Babylonia, but his actual military activities against Babylonia amounted to no more than border skirmishes and a quick raid on the capital.

Chapter Eight

ARAMAEAN AND OTHER MIGRATIONS

SO LONG AS Babylonia's rivers were properly managed, it enjoyed the most productive cornlands east of Egypt. This had made it a natural objective for immigrants or invaders since agriculture began, and there were no significant natural defences to block their entry from the west, while from the east there were routes that gave easy access via the valley of the Karun river or through passes in the Zagros. There is the possibility that the earliest Sumerian speakers entered from Iran, and certainly the earliest population using a Semitic language in Mesopotamia came in from the western steppes. In the second half of the third millennium began the inward movement of the MAR.TU from the Syrian desert regions, and tradition attributed the collapse of the Agade dynasty to the Gutians from the Zagros. Then in the second millennium the Kassites who ruled Babylonia for over four hundred years came originally from somewhere east of the Tigris.

Another migration wave into Mesopotamia from the Syrian steppes got under way in the latter part of the Kassite period. This time it was the people most usually known as Aramaeans, although they or associated groups are sometimes mentioned under other names. Their initial penetration into Assyria and Babylonia had points in common with that of the Amorites a millennium earlier. The usual view is that both Amorites and Aramaeans had earlier been semi-nomads – the term used to distinguish them from peoples such as the Bedouin Arabs, who could practise nomadism deep into the desert after the camel came into widespread use as a riding animal late in the second millennium. On this view, both peoples lived primarily by sheep-rearing in the steppes centred on the highlands between Palmyra and the Euphrates. In recent decades some scholars have challenged this, and prefer to see them as in origin settled peoples who had been set in motion by adverse circumstances.

We do not know enough about the initial stages of either the Amorite or Aramaean migrations to compare them in detail. What is beyond doubt, however, is that both movements initially caused considerable disruption in Babylonia, but whereas the

Amorites developed local dynasties, some of which eventually took over first city-states and then the whole country, the entry of the Aramaeans had no corresponding long-term political consequences.

A land *Aramu* is mentioned as early as the third millennium, but there is nothing beyond a similarity of name, probably accidental, to link this place with Aramaeans. The first certain reference to this group comes in a letter of the Kassite period, which mentions 'the gold caravans of the Ahlamu' in south Babylonia,[1] indicating that at this time they were people on the move concerned with long-distance trade. 'Ahlamu' seems originally to have implied 'nomad', but by the twelfth century it was being used as virtually a synonym of 'Aramaean'. By the twelfth century the circumstances of the Ahlamu seem to have changed, for the Assyrian king Ashur-resh-ishi (1133–1115 BC) reported that he had clashed with an army of these people and scattered them, suggesting that the Ahlamu now were no longer simply nomadic traders, but that some of them constituted roving bands so menacing as to be a threat to outlying parts of Assyria.

Under the next Assyrian king, Tiglath-Pileser I (1114–1076 BC), the situation had become worse. He had to undertake repeated campaigns against groups who are now designated by the compound name Ahlamu-Aramaeans, whom he encountered over a very extensive region. One of Tiglath-Pileser's text indicates that they might be found anywhere from the Lebanon range to the city of Tadmor (now Palmyra) in the Syrian desert, and along the whole length of the Euphrates from the borders of Babylonia to Carchemish in the north. But their main centre seems to have been in the Jebel Bishri range of hills south of the middle Euphrates, since Tiglath-Pileser claimed to have destroyed cities here. It appears therefore that although some of these people practised a nomadic way of life, by this time they also had permanent settlements. Ashur-bel-kala (1073–1056 BC) made similar attacks in the same area, but referred to the people simply as Aramaeans.

The earliest mention of the Aramaeans, under the term Ahlamu, suggests that they acted as traders, and there is plenty of later evidence to support this. But another side of their economy was sheep-rearing. There is a biblical account of Jacob going to his Aramaean relatives in the Harran district, and the story (Genesis 29:1–8) centres on shepherds watering their flocks at a well; cuneiform documents also often mention sheep in connection with Aramaeans.

There must have been some particular factor or combination of factors which led the Aramaeans, who had long practised their pastoralism and trading from bases in the Jebel Bishri, to move out permanently into Mesopotamia and urban Syria. This movement began at about the same time as several other migrations in the ancient Near East; one may think of the Sea Peoples, of whom the Philistines were part, moving out of Anatolia into Palestine, and the Hebrews into Canaan, the 'land of milk and honey'. It seems likely that a major factor in setting the Aramaean and other migrations under way was climatic change. Textual, climatological and archaeological lines of evidence all lead to this conclusion. Ancient documents allude to crop failures and famine from about 1200 BC, which point to the onset of a drier period in the Near East. Climatological studies show that between about 1500 and 1200 BC there was a relatively cool period in Europe, and that this was followed by a warmer and drier period from 1200 to 900 BC. A corresponding sequence in the Near East is proved by evidence of changes in the volume of water carried by the Tigris and Euphrates, which reached a maximum between 1350 and 1250 BC, and then began to drop, indicating reduced rainfall. River flow rose sharply again from about 950 BC.[2] These changes seem to have affected Assyria as well as areas further to the west, for Ashur-dan II (934–912 BC) refers to his bringing back people of Assyria who had earlier left their homes because of famine.

Archaeology tells the same story of a period of drought. Excavation at Ras Shamra (ancient Ugarit) on the Syrian coast found in the twelfth-century stratum a yellowish-white powdery layer, distinct from normal soil, suggesting exceptionally dry conditions at the time. Since rainfall in the steppe lands of Syria, the original homeland of the Aramaeans, was at best only marginal, a prolonged decrease in precipitation would have brought aridity so severe that the population would need to migrate to find grazing grounds for their flocks.

The Aramaean migration was certainly under way before 1200 BC and may have started a century or more earlier. The migrants were by no means a homogeneous group. Although their basic way of life was pastoralism, the fact that some of them lived in towns in the Jebel Bishri region before they entered Mesopotamia, and that some quickly settled in Mesopotamian towns, shows that they included groups who were familiar with urbanism and the specialised activities and social organisation which accompanied that way of life.

Some of the Aramaeans moved westwards into Syria soon after 1100 BC and began to settle as far south as Transjordan, ultimately forming important kingdoms. Both the Bible and cuneiform inscriptions provide abundant evidence of their presence in these areas. Genesis 25:20, for example, speaks of Isaac's wife Rebekah being the daughter of an Aramaean of Paddan-aram (in the Harran area), and Deuteronomy 26:5 accepts that the Aramaeans were one element in Israelite ancestry, since on a specified cultic occasion it required Israelites to say: 'My ancestor was a nomadic Aramaean' (not 'a Syrian ready to perish' as Authorised Version). One of the earliest Aramaean kingdoms was Zobah, which according to the Bible clashed with the two earliest kings of Israel, Saul and David (1 Samuel 14:47; 2 Samuel 8:3). Solomon did a thriving trade in chariots and horses with foreign rulers who included 'kings of Aram' (1 Kings 10:29; some English versions misleadingly render this 'kings of Syria'). During Solomon's reign the main power centre of the Aramaeans shifted from Zobah to Damascus (1 Kings 11:23–5), and by the beginning of the ninth century the Aramaean kingdom of Damascus was powerful enough to be a serious threat to Israel (1 Kings 15:16–21). There were other Aramaean states, not mentioned in the Bible, which developed further north and east in Syria, in northernmost Mesopotamia and in southern Anatolia. These included Sam'al (based on Zencirli west of Carchemish), Bit-Khalupe near the mouth of the Habur river, Bit-Bakhiani along the upper reaches of the Habur, and Bit-Zamani along the upper Tigris near Diyarbakir. Another

Aramaean tribal group, on the east bank of the middle Euphrates south of Carchemish in north Mesopotamia, formed a powerful kingdom Bit-Adini, which Amos 1:5 refers to as Beth-eden (Authorised Version 'the house of Eden').

Other groups of Aramaeans attempted to migrate into Assyria. Although vigorous Assyrian resistance kept them out of the central part of the country, they managed to settle in the western fringes, along the middle Euphrates and south of Ashur. They also began to overrun Babylonia. By the end of the eleventh century the Aramaean semi-nomads had taken over regions along the middle Euphrates and a buffer strip between south Assyria and north Babylonia, so that the threat to merchant caravans of marauding tribesmen seriously affected Babylonia's trade routes through those regions to the north and west. For over a century the only major trade link available to Babylonia was the route from Iran by the Kermanshah-Hamadan road. This conclusion is based mainly on the fact that bronzes with Babylonian inscriptions and art motifs (the so-called 'Luristan bronzes'), found in this area from the third millennium onwards, are particularly abundant at this time.

The Aramaean immigrations also caused problems in some Babylonian cities. The one to suffer most initially was Sippar, understandably so, as it was the first city that immigrants coming down the Euphrates would encounter. Here pressures were so severe just before 1000 BC that food shortages made it necessary to discontinue the regular temple-offerings. Babylon and Borsippa were also badly affected. One indication of Aramaean presence around Borsippa is the existence there during the first millennium of a goddess called Sutitu, meaning 'the Sutean goddess' – Sutean was a name frequently used for a group of semi-nomads associated with the Aramaeans.

As to Babylon, conditions there were so unsettled that for two decades or so from about 1000 BC the central authority was near collapse and the nominal rulers of the country were two ephemeral dynasties not of native Babylonian origin. If a chronicle entry is correctly interpreted, at least some of these kings did not use the capital Babylon as their city of residence but lived at an unidentified city named Kar-Marduk. The first of these petty dynasties derived from a Kassite clan called Bit-Bazi, originally based on the Tigris; it comprised three rulers, a father Eulmash-shakin-shumi (1004–988 BC) followed by two sons who covered the next three years. This was followed by a still more shadowy 'dynasty of Elam' consisting of a single ruler, Mar-biti-apla-usur (983–978 BC), who though he had a Babylonian name was of Elamite descent. Nothing else is known of him, which reflects how impotent the central government was.

The next ruler was a native Babylonian, Nabu-mukin-apli (977–942 BC). In his reign there were serious problems in Babylon itself. We learn this from a chronicle, which reports for a number of his regnal years that: 'in the month Nisan, the Aramaeans were hostile, so that the king could not come up to Babylon, Nabu [god of the neighbouring city of Borsippa] was unable to come there, Bel [= Marduk] could not come out, and (the king) did not perform the sacrifices of the Akitu [= New Year festival].' The relevance of the mention of the Akitu is that an essential element of this festival was a journey in which the king escorted the gods to a temple outside the city walls (see p. 136). The fact that this was impossible shows either that the Aramaeans were such an immediate threat in the outskirts of the city that it was not safe to emerge, or, as the phrase 'the king could not come up to Babylon' seems to suggest, that the general insecurity had led Nabu-mukin-apli to reside elsewhere than in Babylon, as the kings of the Bazi dynasty had done.

Aramaeans must still have been causing problems around Babylon and Borsippa nearly two hundred years after Nabu-mukin-apli, for a chronicle records that as late as about 770 BC King Eriba-Marduk drove out Aramaeans and restored to the rightful owners fields and orchards they had taken from the people of those cities.

It was not only the cities that suffered. In the countryside the arrival of Aramaeans following a semi-nomadic way of life based on animal husbandry must have brought competition for land use with agriculturalists. Farmers could also feel that their lives were at risk when working in the open country, and this would discourage the maintenance of irrigation canals, on which agriculture depended. The threat to personal security from immigrant semi-nomads was a very real problem, for as late as the eighth century we find an Assyrian king referring to Aramaeans and an allied group, the Suteans, as 'dwellers in tents, fugitives, thieves, robbers'.

All this seriously hit the Babylonian economy, and this is reflected in the fact that economic documents from this period are relatively few. In at least some parts of the country there must have been a decrease in the urban population, since surface surveys show a reduction in the occupation area of old settlements. However, this does not necessarily prove a drop in total population, since there were probably new tribal settlements in areas not yet surveyed; but whether or not the population decreased absolutely, the proportion of Aramaeans in the population of Babylonia certainly increased.

As the Aramaeans settled, economic conditions gradually improved. The Aramaeans were rarely of overt political consequence, but they were not without cultural importance in the ancient Near East. This was shown mainly in two areas, which were inter-linked. Firstly, they played an important role in trade, and this involvement is attested almost from their earliest mention. We have met a reference to the gold caravans of the Ahlamu (see p. 129), and in the eleventh century Ashur-bel-kala (1073–1056 BC) attacked 'contingents' of Aramaeans at various cities, using a word (*harranu*) which often means trading caravans, and probably does here.[3] When Tukulti-Ninurta II (890–884 BC) took his army along the Euphrates he encountered cities associated with the Aramaeans, from whom he received tribute which included quantities of tin and iron, ivory furniture, vessels of bronze, linen and woollen garments, myrrh, and dromedaries, besides precious metals, cattle and food. The mention of tin implies international trade, since its main source in the ancient Near East was Afghanistan, and the myrrh must have come from as far away as south Arabia. Dromedaries also point to trading links with some part of Arabia. Ashur-nasir-pal II (883–859 BC) received similar tribute from Aramaeans near the beginning of his reign, and when he later came into conflict with the Aramaean kingdom of Bit-Adini west of the Khabur river he received equally rich booty, as did his son

Shalmaneser III (858–824 BC). The Aramaeans of Damascus were certainly merchants, since they required the king of Israel to give them a special area in Samaria for
trading purposes (1 Kings 20:34).

This trading role of the Aramaeans across all Syria and Mesopotamia had a
secondary consequence; it led to the gradual spread of their language to other ethnic
groups, until by about 400 BC it was for some purposes in use everywhere from Egypt to
Iran (see p. 142).

The Aramaeans in Babylonia never formed a single united group, and eventually
there were some forty Aramaean tribes there distinguished by name. One of the most
powerful tribes, the Puqudu, is mentioned (spelt Pekod) in Jeremiah 50:21 and Ezekiel
23:23; in the latter passage it is named alongside Babylonians, Chaldeans and others.
Two other important Aramaean tribes in Babylonia were the Gambulu and the Ru'ua.
The Ru'ua settled in central Babylonia around Nippur, the Puqudu north and east of
Ur, and the Gambulu south of the Diyala river towards the Elamite border. The
Gambulu tribe had at least one major city, Dur-Athara, sufficiently populous for
Sargon II of Assyria to deport over eighteen thousand inhabitants when he conquered
it.

The division of the Aramaeans into so many groups suggests a social structure
which made them disinclined to unite under a single leader. The manner in which
tribes were governed also points to the same conclusion, since at least in the case of
large tribes, there was a collective leadership involving groups of up to eight sheikhs
(Akkadian *nasiku*). Such factors made it difficult for the Aramaeans in Babylonia to
unite for common action, and more than once it happened in a struggle for control of
the country that different Aramaean groups supported different contenders. The
Assyrians, who were well aware of this fissiparous tendency, used it. Thus at the time of
the Mukin-zer rebellion in Babylon (see p. 154) we find a commander reporting that
he had offered freedom from corvée service to any Aramaeans who deserted from the
rebel leader.[4] A consequence of this was that the political influence of the Aramaeans
in Babylonia was always more limited than their wide distribution might lead one to
expect. The Aramaeans remained largely pastoral and had few large towns, although
individual Aramaeans often assimilated into Babylonian life. Personal names show
that Aramaeans were sometimes found at court; the particular evidence relates to the
Assyrian court, but there is no reason to think it was otherwise in Babylonia.
Aramaeans also served in the army, and one small tribe or clan, the Itu'a, are often
mentioned in Assyrian letters as policing conquered cities.

The Chaldeans

The Chaldeans (Kaldu) were first referred to in 878 BC as a people in south Babylonia.
Their antecedents remain in doubt. Some scholars suppose that they represented
another migration of Aramaeans, earlier than the rest, who settled in the southern
marshes to become regarded as a special ethnic group. But there is no proof of this;
cuneiform sources invariably make a distinction between the two peoples, and there

are features besides name which set the Chaldeans apart from the Aramaeans. One distinguishing mark was distribution. Whereas the Aramaeans were to be found not only throughout most rural areas of north and south Mesopotamia, but also in Syria and Transjordan, the Chaldeans as originally encountered were restricted to south Babylonia, and always remained predominant there. There is no conclusive evidence about their linguistic origins; at a later period the Chaldeans spoke Aramaic, but this proves nothing, since the same was true eventually of most peoples between Palestine and south Iraq. Before 722 BC all we know of their language is a few place-names and less than twenty personal names, and of the latter over three-quarters are Akkadian, not Aramaic. There is no hint of any non-Semitic linguistic background, but this does not preclude the possibility that their ancestry included elements from earlier groups who had ruled the south of the country, or from the Kassites. Some scholars suggest that they were originally of east Arabian origin; there is little positive evidence for this, but it is not impossible, and if they came in via the west coast of the Persian Gulf it might explain why they were in the main only in the south of Mesopotamia.

The Chaldeans were quite different in their social organisation from the Aramaeans. In contrast to the forty or so Aramaean tribes, they were organised in only five tribes, all designated *bit* plus a personal name, where *bit* meant 'household of', and the name represented an eponymous ancestor. The three principal tribes were Bit-Dakkuri, Bit-Amukkani, and Bit-Yakin, and there were also two smaller ones, Bit-Sha'alli and Bit-Shilani. By the eighth century Bit-Dakkuri and Bit-Amukkani occupied the region along the Euphrates southwards from Babylon, and the Bit-Yakin tribe lived from around Ur to the marshlands which stretched as far as the Persian Gulf and the Elamite border. It was this geographical association which led to the Bible designating Ur as 'of the Chaldees'.

The Chaldean way of life appears to have been based originally on cattle-herding, although they also came to engage in the cultivation of date palms. Although they retained their tribal structure and felt a strong tribal loyalty, they became assimilated into the Babylonian way of life more readily than the Aramaeans. They often took Babylonian names, and at least some of the more prominent of them settled in the old cities within their tribal areas, where they sometimes came to play an active role in Babylonian politics. Even the majority who did not settle in the older cities were often ready to adopt urban institutions, so that before the end of the ninth century they had begun to build their own fortified towns. By 700 BC, when Sennacherib undertook a major campaign against some of the Chaldean tribes, he listed eighty-eight fortified cities of theirs, many of them new creations, although a few were ancient Babylonian cities of which the Chaldeans had recently gained control. Commanding as they did long stretches of the Euphrates south of Babylon, and virtually the whole of the southern marshlands adjacent to the Persian Gulf and Elam, the Chaldeans played an important role in trade with regions further east. Whether or not they had a tradition as traders before their arrival in south Babylonia (assuming them to have been recent immigrants) we do not know.

MERODACH-BALADAN

The most important of the Chaldean leaders was the man who is mentioned in the Bible (2 Kings 20:12) as Merodach-baladan, the king of Babylon who sent a diplomatic mission to Hezekiah of Jerusalem. He was a descendant of Eriba-Marduk, who had made himself king of Babylonia at about 770 BC; by a literal interpretation of his own account he was this king's eldest son but he may have meant grandson. Eriba-Marduk, despite his tribal origins, left the reputation of dealing even-handedly with the settled population; according to a chronicle, he took action against Aramaeans who had terrorised the citizens of Babylon and Borsippa, and returned to the rightful owners the fields and orchards they had stolen. Merodach-baladan could thus properly claim to be of honourable royal descent.

He proved to be a consummate diplomatist, who held the throne of Babylon for a decade, and was a constant thorn in the side of Assyria in its attempts to control Babylonia. Assyrian royal records and state correspondence contain many references to him. His political career is discussed in chapter 10.

Other migrations affecting first-millennium Babylonia

Towards the end of the second millennium Indo-Iranian tribes began to move into north-west Iran from further north, and this was to have considerable consequences for Babylonia. The two main groups of migrants are known to us as the Medes and the Persians, both first encountered in Assyrian cuneiform records at about 836 BC. The Assyrians usually referred to the Medes as 'wide-spread', reflecting their early nomadism. They were famous for horse-rearing, which made them a tempting target for Assyrian raids. In the first half of the seventh century they were becoming a major political force, and King Esarhaddon made treaties with their leading princes, who undertook to support after his death the succession he had arranged for Assyria and Babylonia. Shortly after, they coalesced into a major kingdom with a capital Ecbatana near Hamadan, and this kingdom, in association with native and Chaldean forces in Babylonia, played a vital part in the overthrow of the Assyrian empire and the re-emergence of Babylonia as an international power.

During the second quarter of the first millennium the Persians were moving southwards in western Iran, eventually to settle in what had been Elam. Originally vassals of the Medes, in the mid-sixth century they became the dominant partner and went on to conquer Babylonia and bring its last native dynasty to an end.

The role of the king

We have seen that just after 1000 BC the presence of the Aramaeans around Babylon prevented the performance of the New Year festival. This illustrates one aspect of the central role of the king in Mesopotamian religion. A Mesopotamian king as we meet him in historical times combined the functions of what had begun as several distinct offices. Of these the three most significant had originally been to act as the primary human link with the gods, to organise the agricultural work of the city-state, and to serve as war leader. The king always retained the first function, so that in state religion there were some cultic situations where only he could officiate. The principal annual festival, called the *Akitu*, in later times specifically tied to the spring new year, was one such. One essential element of this festival was a procession of the gods to the Akitu temple, which was always outside the city. The presence of the king to escort the procession was central, and on occasions when the proximity of hostile Aramaeans made this impossible, the festival could not take place.

There had been one period, towards the end of the third millennium and at the beginning of the second, when the king had actually been considered divine. After this time the king in Mesopotamia never again enjoyed full divinity during his lifetime, but he always remained a sacral person, with a very close link with the gods. It was believed that the office of kingship was divinely ordained and had originally been let down from heaven, and that every legitimate king was chosen for that office by the gods, sometimes from the womb, a concept familiar to Jeremiah (1:5). Rulers from Hammurabi to the last native Babylonian king, Nabonidus, claimed to be called by a great god, and divine choice was more important than royal blood. Nabopolassar, who founded the Neo-Babylonian Dynasty in 626 BC, although he modestly called himself 'son of a nobody' could none the less claim to be king of kings, by virtue of the fact that he was 'called by Marduk', he was 'formed by the goddess Ninmenna', he was 'the beloved of Ea', and 'Nergal mightiest of the gods went at his side and overthrew his enemies'. Nabopolassar's son, Nebuchadnezzar II, in his turn was 'the favourite of Marduk' and 'the beloved of Nabu', and claimed that the goddess Ninkarrak loved and protected him. He was also 'the faithful shepherd who leads mankind, who guides aright the subjects of Enlil, Shamash and Marduk'. The essence of the royal role was that the king was charismatic in the original sense of that much abused word; that is, he was filled with *charis* (Greek for 'divine grace').

This ideology, which saw a special link between the king and the gods or God, was not limited to Babylonia but was found in varying degrees throughout the ancient Near East. It is very evident in Israel, where the king's relationship to God was so special that some scholars argue for divine kingship there; this is going too far, but the king was certainly called Yahweh's son (Psalm 2:7). The king of Tyre actually did claim to be divine, according to Ezekiel 28:2.

Divine favour carried with it certain responsibilities, and kings were always conscious of certain duties towards the people of their land. From the third millennium the first kings of Babylonia claimed that they maintained prosperity in the land, gave justice, destroyed the wicked, did not allow the strong to oppress the weak, maintained canals and dug new ones, and that they ensured that their people lived in security. The gods were accustomed to give overt signs of their approval of a king's rule; if the king pleased them, he would enjoy a long reign, he would be successful in war, his people would live in safety, and there would be bountiful harvests. There were corresponding marks of divine disapproval – famine, failure to have an heir, illness, defeat in war, rebellion and a reign cut short. It was taught everywhere that mankind had been created to do the work of the gods, and that the ruler was the vicegerent of the gods on earth. Piety therefore required a subject to conform to all demands of the ruler. Yet all this gave a king no safeguard against rebellion and usurpation; if a rival made a successful challenge for the throne, this in itself proved that the gods had found the previous ruler unworthy and had now chosen a new one in his place.

There was nothing in Mesopotamia to correspond to the situation in Israel, where prophets openly denounced the king for wrongdoing, whether cultic, moral or ethical. There was, however, a widespread acceptance that the king had a responsibility to the gods, and this was sometimes explicitly propounded as a caution against gross departure from custom. A text which originated in Babylonia, probably in the early first millennium, known from the library in Nineveh and a Nippur tablet, warns what will happen if the king or any of his officials offends against the will of the gods in some way. Written in omen form, part of it reads:[5]

> If (a king) does not heed the justice of his land, Ea king of destinies will change his destiny and keep after him with adverse intent.
> If he does not heed his nobles, his days will be short.
> If he does not heed a minister, his land will rebel against him ...
> If they bring citizens of Nippur to him for a verdict, and he accepts a present (from them) but treats them with injustice, Enlil lord of lands will muster a foreign army against him and bring about the downfall of his army ...
> If he mobilised Sippar, Nippur and Babylon all together, and imposed forced labour on these people, (or) they arranged corvée service for them at the call of the herald, Marduk, wise one of the gods, the prince, the counsellor, will turn his land over to his enemy ...
> If he gives fodder belonging to the citizens of Sippar, Nippur or Babylon to (his own) horses, those horses which have eaten the fodder will be led away for the yoke of the enemy ... Mighty Erra, who goes in front of his army, will smash the front of his army and will go at the side of his enemy.

There were other and more formal ways of ensuring that the king conformed to traditional custom. Prominent among them was the annual requirement for the king of Babylon to give the gods an account of his stewardship during the past year. This happened at the New Year festival, on its fifth day. The king had to present himself before the statue of Marduk, where the high priest took away his royal insignia and made him kneel. He then recited a confession, of which the following is part:

> I have not sinned, O Lord of the land,
> I have not been negligent to your divinity,
> I have not done harm to Babylon, ...
> I have not interfered with Esagila [the temple],

I have not been heedless of its rites,
I have not afflicted the people under your protection.[6]

This done, the high priest struck the king and pulled his ears; if he did it hard enough to make the king shed tears, so much the better, for this showed that Marduk was pleased with his land. The high priest then restored to the king the royal insignia. All this ritual expressed publicly that though the king was supreme in Babylon, he was responsible to the gods for the welfare of his land, and ruled only with their authority and as their agent. This was also true in Assyria, where down to the fourteenth century rulers almost always described themselves not as 'king' but as 'regent of the god Ashur'.

Although the king in Babylon was nominally sovereign of the whole country, after the third millennium he was not an autocrat, and by the first millennium there were in practice considerable checks upon his authority. In the first place, there were areas inhabited by Aramaean or Chaldean tribesmen which were often in practice virtually self-governing. Secondly, the country was organised into provinces under royal governors, and although these governors were nominally appointed by the king, they often came from powerful local families with an almost hereditary claim to high office, who were in a position to exercise a substantial degree of independence. Thirdly, some of the great cities and their associated temple-estates enjoyed considerable autonomy. Their citizens had acquired exemptions from taxes and conscription for military service or the corvée, and custom required that every king should confirm these privileges anew at his accession. Should the king attempt to encroach upon traditional rights and privileges of the citizens of such cities, there was the very real possibility of revolt. The cities sometimes strengthened their position relative to the king by association with Chaldeans in their area, who within their tribal structure had taken substantial steps towards adopting Babylonian institutions.

By the eighth century the royal position in Babylonia had become so weak that power struggles for the kingship almost totally superseded hereditary succession. The greatest beneficiaries of this situation were the Chaldeans; so successful were they in their political activities, backed by readiness and ability to use military force, that during the eighth century there was a king in Babylon from each of the three major tribes. But the Chaldeans failed to hold the kingship for long or to produce dynasties, because they themselves had no single leader.

An important aspect of the king's duties was temple building, and when a king built or restored a temple he always buried in the foundations an inscription recording his name and proclaiming his piety. This might incidentally give information to any later ruler who restored the building, but its overt purpose was to keep the king's piety in remembrance before the gods. To the same end the king would in some circumstances write a letter to the gods to report his activities and deposit it in the temple.

The closeness of the king to the gods made his person sacred, and he therefore had to be surrounded by taboos, which affected all aspects of his behaviour. In the event of unfavourable omens, he might be required to fast or go into seclusion or subject himself to particular religious rituals. One of the more unusual of these rituals was the institution known as the substitute king. Since the well-being of the land was intimately connected with the king, he had to be protected from all evil. Therefore if an omen predicted that some grave misfortune threatened the king, he temporarily handed over the throne to a substitute, upon whom the threatened evil would fall. The substitute was provided with all the symbols of kingship, including a queen, but enjoyed no executive power. At the end of the period of danger the substitute and his queen were put to death and the real king resumed his rule.

Chronology

There is a dearth of evidence about events in Babylonia and other parts of the ancient Near East between the period conventionally dated from about 1200 to shortly before 900 BC. This has brought an attempt (P. James et al., *Centuries of Darkness*, London 1991) to show that this period did not exist. Applying this to the Assyrian evidence, the authors argue (pp. 271–3) for an 'almost complete blank' for over 250 years from 1208 BC, although subsequently they accept the force of their 'almost' and reduce the alleged blank to the 122 years between the end of the reign of Ashur-bel-kala (conventionally 1056 BC) and the beginning of that of Ashur-dan II (934 BC). But there is no blank here. King-lists name eight kings within this period, and six of these are attested by contemporary inscriptions, and one more is named on one of these inscriptions as the king's predecessor. The supposed gap is thereby reduced to at most the seven years from 1019 to 1012 BC. The argument fails.

Chapter Nine

THE ARAMAIC
LANGUAGE AND
ANCIENT LIBRARIES

THE MAIN ENDURING influence of the Aramaeans lay in the spread of their language, Aramaic. This became so widespread and proved so enduring that a few minorities still use it to the present day. Several factors contributed to this. One was the extensive diffusion of the Aramaeans. The migration of these people had left groups of them along the main routes everywhere from Transjordan in the west to near the Persian Gulf in the east, and this gave their language international status and made it a useful vehicle of communication for traders and administrators.

Another factor was linked to the writing systems in use. Down to the second half of the second millennium, it was standard practice everywhere in the Near East except in Egypt and Crete, for cuneiform on clay tablets, mostly in the Akkadian (Babylonian) language, to be used for communications and often economic documents, and even in Egypt it was used in some cases. But Babylonian cuneiform writing was a cumbersome system; a great battery of ideograms and syllograms had to be learned, and this took many years to master. Before writing could spread beyond the minority of professional experts, something simpler was needed.

From the middle of the second millennium there were several attempts to devise a simpler form of writing. The principle of these new writing systems was to disregard ideograms and to reduce the hundreds of syllograms to a manageable number – in most cases thirty or less signs. That is, instead of having, like Babylonian cuneiform, separate syllograms for *ma, me, mi, mu, am, im, um,* they devised a single sign which would serve for any of these. We interpret the resultant simplified sign as simply *m,* although the inventors probably thought of it as *m* plus unspecified vowel.

The most successful of these new systems was the alphabetic script originally used for Canaanite and then for Phoenician, the form into which Canaanite developed from about 1100 BC. This was the basis of almost all subsequent alphabets. The Greeks borrowed the system from the Phoenicians at some time before 800 BC, and adapted it to become the Greek alphabet, from which eventually developed the various alphabets used throughout Europe. (Some scholars argue – mainly on the basis of the forms of the names of the Greek letters: *alpha, beta, gamma*, etc. – that the Greeks obtained the alphabet not from the Phoenicians but from the Aramaeans, but since the Greeks' primary Near Eastern trading area was the Phoenician coast and not inland where Aramaeans predominated, this seems unlikely.)

The Aramaeans also adopted the Canaanite–Phoenician alphabet, certainly not later than the first half of the ninth century, since several Aramaic inscriptions of this period have been found in Syria and the Jordan valley. With Aramaeans present across the whole region from Syria to Babylonia, and some of them engaged in international trade, the Aramaic language was particularly appropriate for commercial documents and international correspondence. It had the additional advantage that the Aramaic writing system could be mastered in months, instead of the years needed for cuneiform. Even in some circles where cuneiform had always predominated, Aramaic writing was being used as a supplementary system soon after the middle of the eighth century (see fig. 65). A bas relief of Tiglath-Pileser III provides direct evidence of this; it shows two scribes at work, one of them writing in cuneiform on a clay tablet, while the other is recording events on parchment or papyrus in what must have been Aramaic (see fig. 66). Also, some cuneiform documents directly refer to the writing of Aramaic. Thus, a cuneiform letter sent to the king by an official in Tyre at about 720 BC said it accompanied 'a sealed Aramaic document', which must

65 Below left *From the first half of the first millennium, Aramaic (as here in an ostracon from Ashur) was increasingly used alongside cuneiform on clay tablets, eventually replacing it.*

66 Below right *Two scribes of the Assyrian king Tiglath-Pileser III are making records, one in cuneiform on a clay tablet, the other in Aramaic on a scroll.*

have been a full report to which the cuneiform letter served as an introduction. Another royal letter of about the same period refers to a palace scribe receiving a roll of papyrus, which can only have been for writing Aramaic. The use of Aramaic was becoming so common at this time that even weights were marked with Aramaic characters, as examples found at Nimrud (ancient Calah) show. By the mid-seventh century cuneiform documents often mention Aramaean scribes as witnesses, and one dated 697 BC describes a person with an Aramaic name as 'palace scribe'.

Aramaic was commonly written on either parchment, papyrus or potsherds, although since the first two materials are unlikely to have survived physically in Mesopotamia, the only evidence for their use is references in cuneiform tablets. But potsherds remain, and proof of their use as a writing surface is provided by extant letters on sherds in Aramaic, such as one from the middle of the seventh century dealing with events in Babylonia.[1]

By the seventh century at latest Aramaic was also spreading as a spoken language where Akkadian had formerly held sway; from that time Aramaic words and grammatical formations are present in increasing numbers in cuneiform documents from Babylonia. But it was some centuries before Aramaic replaced Akkadian as the main spoken language in either Assyria or Babylonia, and Akkadian cuneiform continued to be written, although decreasingly, down to the Seleucid period. In scholarly circles cuneiform remained in restricted use for some specialised purposes, chiefly religious and astronomical texts, right into the first century of the Christian era.

The Bible is another witness to the spread of Aramaic. When the Assyrians besieged Jerusalem in 701 BC it was already accepted as a language of diplomacy, since the Judaean ministers wished to use it for negotiations, although it was not yet understood by the mass of Jews (2 Kings 18:26). By 539 BC, when the Achaemenids under Cyrus the Persian conquered Babylonia, Aramaic was spoken and written from the borders of Iran as far as Egypt, and Darius (521–485 BC) gave it a further impetus by employing a form of it (Imperial Aramaic) as one of the official languages of the Persian empire. When he set up an inscription in Old Persian, Elamite and Babylonian cuneiform on the rock face at Bisitun (see p. 10), he had Aramaic translations of the text sent as far afield as south Egypt, where fragments of it have been found at Elephantine. Aramaic inscriptions of this period have also been discovered as far east as Afghanistan. Aramaic remained the lingua franca of the whole region from Egypt to Iran until the conquests of Alexander in the late fourth century BC, when Greek began to replace it in some places.

In the Achaemenid empire Aramaic was not only an official language; it also came into widespread use as the tongue of common speech. Nehemiah 13:23–5, for example, records an incident which shows that by the late fifth century BC half of the Jewish children in Jerusalem knew only Aramaic and could not speak Hebrew. Parts of the biblical book of Daniel (2:4–7:28) and of Ezra (4:8–6:18 and 7:12–26) are in Aramaic, and there is one verse of Aramaic in Jeremiah (10:11) and two words in Genesis 31:47. By the time of Christ the common language of Palestine was West Aramaic, and there are translations of the Old Testament, called Targums, in this

67 *At some periods contracts were placed inside clay envelopes which bore a near duplicate of the terms. In case of dispute the envelope could be broken before judges to reveal the terms of the contract.*

dialect. Babylonia saw a corresponding increase in the use of the East Aramaic dialect for both common speech and documents over the same period. Jews in Babylonia spoke East Aramaic, and this is the predominant language of the Babylonian Talmud, which was composed mainly between the fourth and sixth centuries AD. A form of East Aramaic, known as Syriac, originally the dialect of Edessa near Harran, was used for Christian literature from the third to the thirteenth centuries, and played a part in the transmission of classical learning to the Arabs. West Aramaic lives on as a minority language near Damascus, and East Aramaic is still spoken by communities (mainly Christian) in north-west Iran, north Iraq and south-east Turkey.

Libraries

The first decade of major excavations in the mid-nineteenth century saw the finding of many thousands of cuneiform texts at Kuyunjik, the site of ancient Nineveh. They are now in the British Museum. In the circumstances of archaeology of the time, no exact record of find-places was kept, but later study of these texts made it apparent that they must contain material from at least three different groups. One group, comprising letters to Assyrian kings, mainly from the seventh century BC, must have come from a royal archive. A second group consisted of economic or legal documents dealing with such matters as court decisions, or sale of slaves, houses or land, and often bore cylinder seal impressions and a date (see fig. 67). Some tablets in this second group could have come from private archives. Tablets of both these classes were originals, with contents directly related to the time when they were written.

The great majority of the other tablets had features which set them apart from those in the first two groups. Firstly, most of the tablets with their ends intact had a colophon, which usually either stated explicitly or implied that the tablet had been copied from an earlier original. Secondly, in many cases a number of tablets bore duplicates of the same text. Thirdly, the contents of these tablets had nothing to do with current political, economic or legal circumstances; instead they were of a scholastic or literary nature. Many of them comprised series of omens, some dealt with various aspects of religion, the cult and the pantheon, and others were lists of cuneiform signs and vocabulary. There were other texts which recorded ancient traditions in various forms; some of these were legends, some were lists of kings, and some were chronicles. There were also myths and epics. Obviously texts of such categories represented the remains of some ancient library.

It was normal practice for a scribe to add a colophon when he copied a library tablet, and this can give invaluable information about a text and how it was transmitted. The scribe would state his name, the date, and information about the tablet. In the early period this information was very brief, but later it tended to be amplified. Typically it might name the series to which the tablet belonged, its position in that series, and the number of lines in the tablet. It would normally also include a formula of the type 'written, examined and checked according to its original'. If it was an excerpt rather than a complete copy, the colophon said so. The colophon might also specify the source of the inscription, naming both the place from which the original came (a particular city, temple, or house), and its physical form. This latter was most commonly another clay tablet, but in exceptional cases it could be a stele, a baked brick, a writing board of wood or ivory covered with wax, or a leather scroll.

There was a religious dimension in copying an ancient tablet, which is often clear from the colophon. A section of the colophon found on some of Ashurbanipal's tablets illustrates this:

> I wrote on the tablets the wisdom of Nabu ... and I checked and
> collated them. I placed them for futurity in the library of the temple of
> my lord Nabu ... in Nineveh, for my life, for the guarding of my soul,
> that I might not have illness, and for making firm the foundation of my
> royal throne. O Nabu, ... for ever bless my kingship. When I call on
> you, take my hand. ... Guard my steps continually. When this work is
> put in your house, and placed before you, ... remember me with favour.

Often a curse and a blessing were appended, the curse being aimed against anyone who damaged or destroyed the tablet and the blessing to fall upon a person who preserved it. All this puts it beyond question that behind the collecting of libraries lay a superstitious regard for the supposed magical powers of ancient writings; it was not a mere matter of antiquarian interest.

Study of the colophons on the Kuyunjik tablets proves that this library in its final form was the work of King Ashurbanipal in the seventh century BC. However, research has established that earlier kings had already taken steps in this direction and that some of these tablets had originally been in a library which Tiglath-Pileser I founded.

Registration numbers for Kuyunjik tablets amount to more than twenty-five thousand, but these are not all from Ashurbanipal's library. Some of these belong to the archives of letters and economic and legal documents already mentioned. Of the remainder, in many cases a number of fragments are part of a single tablet, which brings down the number of complete library tablets to around five thousand. Among these five thousand tablets, many contain duplicate texts, so that the total number of different texts in the library probably did not amount to more than fifteen hundred.[2]

We normally speak of the Kuyunjik library in the singular, but the colophons prove that the tablets were stored in more than one building. Some of the library tablets bear a colophon in which Ashurbanipal says: 'I placed [it] within my palace for my royal examination', whereas in other colophons he speaks of placing the tablet 'in the library [girginakku] of the temple of Nabu'. Clearly there were – in terms of place of deposit – at least two libraries in Nineveh in the time of Ashurbanipal. However, since the king was patron of both collections it is not unreasonable to treat them as sections of a single whole.

Archaeological expeditions have subsequently found collections of texts at many other sites, often in temples or palaces. Not all collections come from libraries; groups of letters or business documents are obviously likely to have belonged to family or state archives. But there are other collections of tablets whose contents are concerned neither with current correspondence nor with economic affairs. Their subject matter is traditional learning, often similar to what is found in the library tablets from Kuyunjik, and are not infrequently duplicates. This justifies us in regarding them as parts of further ancient libraries, even though not as extensive as Ashurbanipal's library, and probably not royal collections. In some cases such collections may have belonged to a temple, in others to a scribal school or even to an individual scholar who had built it up as a basis for scribal training.

Three collections of this kind are known already from the third millennium. There is one from Fara (ancient Shuruppak), another from Abu Salabikh (ancient name uncertain), and the third comes from Ebla in Syria (see p. 76). The first two are datable to the middle of the millennium, and the third is probably a century or so later. Before the end of the nineteenth century American excavators had found tablets from another important library at Nippur; these are datable to the Old Babylonian period more than a thousand years before Ashurbanipal. Ashur, the most ancient capital of Assyria, provided tablets from yet another library, discovered by German archaeologists in 1904–5. This was the library Tiglath-Pileser I founded in the late twelfth century; he began it with a nucleus of tablets plundered from Babylon or perhaps Borsippa, and later added newly made copies of further tablets.

Later discoveries of libraries include one at Nimrud (ancient Calah) in Assyria, another at Sultantepe near Harran in south-east Turkey, and others at Sippar, Borsippa, and Ur in Babylonia. None approached the size of the libraries of Kuyunjik. Excavations in the late 1930s at Ras Shamra (ancient Ugarit) in Syria found a further collection of tablets from a library from the second half of the second millennium. These tablets followed Mesopotamian models, but many of them were written not in Mesopotamian syllabic cuneiform but in a West Semitic language using a cuneiform alphabetic script invented in Syria.

68 *Cuneiform tablets were sometimes collected into libraries. This shows some of the shelving for a second-millennium library discovered at Sippar.*

Any collection of tablets demands some form of storage. Archaeological techniques in the middle of the nineteenth century were too crude to recover any evidence that may have remained to show how tablets were kept at Kuyunjik, but storage arrangements have been identified at some sites excavated subsequently. Evidence from a temple in Ashur shows that at about 1100 BC economic archives there were kept in clay jars. At Calah there were storage cabinets, made of large burnt bricks, about a foot and a half square. At Sippar the assyriologist Professor Farouk Al-Rawi pointed out a form of shelving used for the library (see fig. 68). In cases where a number of tablets constituted a consecutive work (a 'series'), these were sometimes corded together in groups with a docket for easy identification.

Although Ashurbanipal's library was in Nineveh, the capital of Assyria in his time, there is no doubt that most of its contents were ultimately of Babylonian origin. Some tablets make their Babylonian origin explicit by what is written in the colophon. There is also a letter which provides evidence about this. The letter, datable to the seventh century, is from an Assyrian king who, although not named, can only have been Ashurbanipal. The letter reads:

> Royal command to Kudurranu. ... As soon as you see my tablet, take charge of [three named men] and the scribal experts known to you in Borsippa, and collect all the tablets that are in their houses, and all the tablets deposited in the temple Ezida, (in particular):
> tablets (with texts) for amulets for the king;
> (tablets) for (purification rituals in) rivers for the days of the month Nisan,
> amulets for (purification rituals in) rivers for the month Tashrit, (and) for the (ritual called) 'house of water sprinkling';
> amulets for (purification rituals in) rivers; ...
> four stone amulets for the head of the royal bed and its foot; ...
> the incantation 'May Ea and Marduk give perfect wisdom'; all the

> series there are about battle, together with as many of their
> additional single-column tablets as there are;
> (the incantation) 'That in battle an arrow come not near a man';
> (the series) 'Returning to the palace from going in the desert';
> the rituals 'Raising of the hand';
> (any) inscription (about the properties) of stones and what is good for
> kingship; …
> any tablets desirable for the palace, as many as there are;
> and any rare tablets that are known to you and that are not in
> Assyria.
> Seek these out and send them to me. … No one is to withhold any
> tablet from you. And if there is any tablet or ritual which I have not
> mentioned to you and you get knowledge of it and it is good for my
> palace, search it out, confiscate it, and send it to me.[3]

This makes several things clear. Firstly, Ezida, the temple of Nabu in Borsippa, had its own library, with associated scribal experts, and private persons might also own tablet collections. Secondly, it is glaringly obvious that Ashurbanipal was not seeking texts to be read for aesthetic pleasure, or creative writing with excellence of form or style. It is true that the Kuyunjik library, and tablet collections elsewhere, do contain a minority of texts which by modern criteria have literary merit, but such qualities were of no concern to ancient royal patrons. In ancient belief the person who occupied the throne was particularly vulnerable to the slings and arrows of outrageous fortune, and what Ashurbanipal primarily wanted was supernatural protection for himself and his palace. It is for this reason that the commonest type of text in the Kuyunjik library comprises various omens. These are arranged in series, and record an extremely wide field of circumstances supposedly offering knowledge of future events.

In seeking particular omen texts and ritual series, Ashurbanipal's purpose was completely practical: omens might play a significant part in statecraft, or give warning of potential dangers to the state or the king, and associated rituals could forestall or counter evils predicted. There were many ways in which the gods might make their intentions known; it might be by the appearance and movements of animals, birds, and reptiles, by monstrous births whether human or animal, by conditions in cities, by dreams, or by astrological forecasts. In the words of Carl Bezold, who first catalogued these texts for the British Museum, 'there seems to have been scarcely any event, … however trivial, which was not provided for by this pseudo-science'.[4]

In Babylonia the supreme divination technique from the Old Babylonian period onwards was observation of features of the internal organs, particularly the liver, of a sacrificed sheep. The expert in this, the *bārû* (extispicy diviner) was a highly respected figure, and a whole pseudo-science grew up around his procedure, with clay models of animal organs, marked with the prognostication of various signs (see fig. 69).

The Kuyunjik library may have contained a small minority of texts specifically of Assyrian origin, but Ashurbanipal's letter, taken with the evidence of colophons, puts

69 *The most prestigious form of divination in Babylonia was by inspection of the entrails of a slaughtered animal. Clay models of organs, like this model of a liver, were made to provide a key to prognostications.*

it beyond question that the great majority of the tablets were representative of scribal literature recognised in Babylonia in the first millennium and earlier. They are the kinds of texts Babylonian scribes traditionally copied and preserved. Further confirmation of this comes from the fact that many of the Kuyunjik texts are duplicated in text collections found in Babylonia.

By comparing versions of the same text from different periods, scholars can obtain clues to the history of their transmission. In many cases scribes began to edit Mesopotamian literary texts into a standardised or so-called 'canonical' form in the Kassite period at about 1200 BC. This process continued into the reign of Nebuchadnezzar I (1124–1103 BC), and by the time of Ashurbanipal almost all ancient texts still in use had taken a standard canonical form, with rarely more than minimal differences between copies of the same text. Behind the form of the text as edited in the Kassite period there was often an Old Babylonian recension and sometimes behind that a third-millennium Sumerian original.

The ancient scribes themselves did not leave any system of text classification, although they sometimes provided rubrics indicating the circumstances in which they were to be used. Certain broad groups of texts can be described.

TEXTS FOR SCRIBAL EDUCATION

The organisation of Mesopotamian cities rested upon written records, and some system for training scribes was essential. Students gained scribal competence by copying existing tablets under the instruction of someone who was already an expert scribe, and this system provably went back to before the middle of the third millennium, and may have been already in use by 3000 BC. It presupposed the existence of collections of ancient tablets to serve as models, and the professors in scribal academies must have made their own collections for this purpose. Such collections were the basis of later libraries. To learn the scribal craft took many years, according to a text in which a scribe is told: 'You sat in the Tablet House from the days of your youth until your maturity'. 'Tablet House' (Sumerian *é.dub.ba*) was the name given to scribal academies, which by the final centuries of the third millennium at latest had a staff of experts in the scribal craft. King Shulgi of the Third Dynasty of Ur founded or developed such academies at both Ur and Nippur (see pp. 87–8), and claimed that he himself as a child had been educated in such an institution, where he excelled all other youngsters in the scribal art and arithmetic. Texts written in the academies give us a vivid account of the methods, curriculum and discipline of scribal schools.

Although scribal academies seem usually to have been independent, there must have been a close relationship between them and temples, since scribes played an indispensable part not only in the temple administration but also in cultic matters. For example, circumstances such as a coronation, or the installation of a new divine statue, or an outbreak of plague, or the death of a king in war, would require elaborate rituals, needing texts, either old ones adapted or new ones specially written, which only scribes could supply.

Scribes not only had to be able to write and compose in both the Akkadian and Sumerian languages, but when fully qualified also had to be able to deal in writing with any aspect of Babylonian life. Texts concerned with scribal education therefore included inter alia such categories as vocabularies (giving the Akkadian value of Sumerian or foreign words); sign-lists (giving the Akkadian value of cuneiform signs and combinations of signs); syllabaries; synonym lists; lists of archaic signs; grammatical paradigms; mathematical and astronomical texts; god lists; commentaries on ancient texts; geographical lists; texts dealing with such activities as glass-making; pharmaceutical texts; and lists of a diverse range of categories such as animals, buildings, offerings, temples, liquids, meals and officials.

RELIGIOUS AND MAGICAL TEXTS

The other main group of texts found in ancient libraries, excluding the minority which we would accept as literature in the narrower sense, were all in some way connected with the supernatural world. After omen texts (see p. 147), the next greatest in number were rituals of various types and associated incantations. These could touch on almost any aspect of life. They could be designed to avert real or threatened evils, such as illness or attack by witchcraft or demons; to give protection against possible hazards as when crossing a desert; to obtain good omens or supernatural favour when some new enterprise was to be undertaken, such as the king setting out on campaign or founding a temple; the temple authorities giving a ritual drum a new skin; or someone beginning to build a house or to dig a well.

In some cases incantations and rituals were collected into long series. Instances of this are those against evil demons, witchcraft and sin. The incantation series *Maqlû* was directed against witchcraft by practitioners of either sex, and the incantations *Šurpu* against sin, treated as a supernatural contagion. The greatest danger requiring magical protection was, however, attack by demons, who were as significant in Babylonian religion as the gods, and a greater danger, since although gods often

70 Above left *Amulet showing the fearsome she-monster Lamashtu, particularly active against pregnant women and small babies. This was worn to ward off her attack.*

71 Above right *Another much-feared demon was Pazuzu, shown on this amulet worn to ward off his attack. He probably originated as a demon of sandstorms, but his demonic attack later became more general.*

punished they were essentially just, whereas demons acted arbitrarily and were mostly ill disposed. The principal collection of incantations and rituals against demons was known as *Utukku Lemnutu* (Evil Demons).

There were many classes of demon, sometimes said to be formless and sexless, although the most dangerous, Lamashtu (see fig. 70), took the form of a woman. She was a particular danger to babies and women in childbirth, although she could also attack men; she sometimes bore different names in these different contexts. As well as being frequently mentioned in *Utukku Lemnutu*, Lamashtu had a whole ritual series directed against her, and amulets were also used for protection. Another particularly nasty demon was named Pazuzu who, although originally associated with sandstorms, came to be associated with demonic dangers in general. Magical amulets used against Pazuzu took the form either of a grotesque head, or of a creature with a lion's head, human body, wings and tail (see fig. 71).

There were some texts of religious content, primarily hymns and prayers, which could be considered as literary in the narrower sense. Hymns in the first millennium took rather a different form from earlier ones; in the third and early second millennia they were often in praise of temples or kings, whereas later ones, with rare exceptions, were directed exclusively to gods and goddesses.

TEXTS WHICH ARE NARROWLY LITERARY

First-millennium cuneiform libraries included myths and epics, most of which went back in origin to the second or even the third millennium, but received their final form in the Kassite period. *Enuma Elish*, known only from first-millennium copies although containing earlier material, linked two themes, a myth of cosmic creation, brought about by divine combat with a primeval monster Tiamat, and the exaltation of Marduk, god of Babylon, to supremacy in the pantheon. The linkage was achieved by editing ancient material to make Marduk the victor over Tiamat. Other old myths still in use in the first millennium included *Atrahasis, Anzu, The Descent of Ishtar to the Underworld*, and *Nergal and Ereshkigal*.

Atrahasis, which was basically another myth of creation, is first known in Akkadian from a three-tablet version of the Old Babylonian period; by the time of Ashurbanipal's library this had been revised into a two-tablet form. It presupposes a world without humans, where the junior gods themselves had to perform the heavy toil of canal digging. They did not like it, and went on strike and made a violent demonstration against Enlil. He consulted other leading deities, and it was decided to relieve the hardship of the gods by creating man to toil on their behalf. This was done by mixing with clay the blood of a slaughtered god – so that man had a spark of the divine. Later, mankind became so tumultuous that the gods had to take action to reduce the population, first by famine, so severe as to bring cannibalism, and then by a great flood. Included are fragments of rituals concerning marriage and childbirth.

Anzu, also known in an Old Babylonian version, concerned the defeat by the warrior-god Ninurta of a pre-anthropomorphic bird-monster of that name, who represented the storms which raged in the mountains (see fig. 11).

The Descent of Ishtar to the Underworld is a revised and shortened version of an old Sumerian myth. Ishtar set her mind upon going down to the Underworld, where her hostile sister Ereshkigal ruled. She was admitted, but had to pass through seven gates, at each of which she was stripped of some part of her insignia, finally arriving naked and helpless and unable to escape. Her absence from the earth robbed it of fertility, whereupon the god Ea used a male prostitute, who was not bound by the normal rules of access, to secure her release. The myth clearly originated in connection with seasonal fertility, and shows subsidiary themes related to the sexual cult of Ishtar.

Nergal and Ereshkigal is known not only from first-millennium copies but also from a short fifteenth-century version found at El Amarna in Egypt. Nergal behaved disrespectfully to Ereshkigal, Queen of the Underworld, and was sent down to her for punishment, but ended up as her husband. The concept of Ereshkigal as Queen of the Underworld goes back to prehistoric times, but Nergal's supremacy there did not begin until the late third or early second millennium. The myth offers a theological explanation of a changed concept linked to the gradual reduction in woman's status.

Another myth represented in ancient libraries was *Erra*, about the plague god (another form of Nergal), which arose out of disasters afflicting Babylon in the eighth century.

The main epics still widely known in the first millennium were the *Epic of Gilgamesh* (see pp. 109–12), *Adapa* and *Etana*. Adapa was a fisherman who broke the wing of the South Wind, which had upset his boat, and was called to account by the great god

72 *The myth* Etana and the Eagle *must have been of great antiquity, since early cylinder seals depict a hero borne by an eagle (here at right).*

Anu. Anu offered him bread and water of immortality, but the wise god Ea by a trick prevented him from partaking of them, so that mankind lost the chance of immortality. *Etana* tells of a childless hero, a king of Kish, befriended by an eagle, which took him to heaven on its back in the hope of obtaining a son. The story must have been very old, for third-millennium cylinder seals depict a hero on an eagle's back (fig. 72).

Other literary works in the Kuyunjik library include legends about early kings, such as the Birth Legend of Sargon (see pp. 66–7) and other texts linked to Sargon and Naram-Sin of Agade.

One might also include as literature in the narrower sense some Wisdom texts, that is, compositions in the category of the biblical books of Job and Ecclesiastes. The earliest known specimen of this is a Sumerian text from the mid-third millennium, which takes the form of a father's advice to his son. A major Wisdom text, composed in the Kassite period and attested at Kuyunjik and in other first-millennium libraries, was called *Ludlul bel nemeqi*, meaning 'I will praise the Lord of wisdom'. A nobleman describes the long series of calamities and humiliations he endured before the god Marduk restored him to health and well-being; like the Book of Job, but on a lower level, the work examines the problem of suffering. A second work of Wisdom literature, the *Babylonian Theodicy*, takes the form of a dialogue between a sufferer, who exposes facets of divine injustice, and a friend, who attempts to show on the basis of received beliefs that there has been no injustice. The work is a clever piece of scribal craftsmanship, taking the form of an acrostic in which all eleven lines of each stanza begin with the same syllable, and the syllables make up a sentence which names the author. It was probably written at about 1000 BC. Another work in dialogue form, *The Dialogue of Pessimism*, is a series of exchanges between a master and a slave; the master proposes various courses of action, the second always the opposite of the first, and the slave sycophantically agrees every time. This is satire, but satire intended to examine the purpose of life.

Chapter Ten

THE NEO-
BABYLONIAN EMPIRE

THE FIRST QUARTER of the first millennium saw Babylonia at a low ebb; it was politically unstable, its economy was stagnating, and it played little part in international affairs.

A factor in this may have been a westward shift in the main channel of the Euphrates in the late second millennium, bringing a reduction in irrigable land and population. But more significant was Aramaean migration. This also affected Assyria, but it recovered more quickly, so that Tukulti-Ninurta II (890–884 BC) and Ashur-nasir-pal II (883–859 BC) were able to recover lost territory as far south as the Diyala and make demonstration marches in Babylonia itself. Ashur-nasir-pal in 878 BC referred to the south of Babylonia as 'the land of *Kal-du* (the Chaldeans)', the first mention of these people.

Assyria was always concerned for stability in Babylonia because of trade routes, and Shalmaneser III (858–824 BC) made a formal treaty, which was triggered at the death of Nabu-apla-iddina (see fig. 73) of Babylonia in 851 BC, when the succession of his heir was disputed. Chaldeans must have been involved in the unrest, since Shalmaneser took action against tribesmen along the lower Euphrates. Shalmaneser's incursions were not anti-Babylonian; they were directed only against the Chaldean tribes who were destabilising the rule of the legitimate king, just as marches of Tukulti-Ninurta II and Ashur-nasir-pal II had been primarily directed against marauding Aramaean tribesmen.

In the reign of Shamshi-Adad V of Assyria (823–811 BC), Babylonia was so weak that the Assyrians were able to occupy Der, a key fortress east of the Tigris, and to take two successive Babylonian kings prisoner. But subsequent problems with northern neighbours prevented Assyria from intervening further in Babylonia for over half a century. The greatest beneficiaries of this were the Chaldeans, who during the first half of the eighth century were able to put on the throne of Babylon a king from each of the three major tribes.

73 Above left *Monument showing Nabu-apla-iddina, a ninth-century king of Babylon, being led by minor deities before the Sun-god in a shrine, holding symbols of justice.*

74 Above right *Stone tablet, early ninth century, recording a grant of land by Nabu-apla-iddina to a high official.*

A coup in Assyria in 745 BC put in command a vigorous new ruler, Tiglath-Pileser III (745–727 BC). In Babylonia a native king, Nabu-nasir, was ruling, and Tiglath-Pileser initially contented himself with a demonstration march in the Diyala border region, to give notice that he intended to protect Assyrian interests. There were already disturbances in Babylonia, but no major problems developed until Nabu-nasir died in 734 BC. Then followed a power struggle, and after two years Nabu-nasir's successor was killed in a rebellion. But the usurper, a former governor Shuma-ukin, survived only a month before the chief of the Chaldean Bit-Amukkani tribe, Nabu-mukin-zer (in shorter form, Mukin-zer) seized the throne. Tiglath-Pileser responded with vigour, but the Chaldeans were so strongly entrenched that it took him three years (732–729 BC) to capture Mukin-zer. Tiglath-Pileser deported 155,000 people from Chaldean tribes which had sided with the rebel leader.

A factor in Mukin-zer's defeat was Chaldean disunity. Chaldean leaders who supported Tiglath-Pileser apparently included Marduk-apla-iddina, known as Merodach-baladan, chief of the Bit-Yakin tribe. The rich tribute he sent Tiglath-Pileser after the Mukin-zer campaign shows that he already controlled considerable wealth, which must have derived from trade, for which the position of his tribe, straddling the border between south Babylonia and Elam, presented good opportunities.

In the absence of a reliable native Babylonian ruler, Tiglath-Pileser had himself installed as king of Babylonia for the remaining two years of his life (729–727 BC). His successor, Shalmaneser V (727–722 BC), followed the same course. Neither king attempted a major occupation of the country, but exercised control through garrisons. Tiglath-Pileser's direct rule set a precedent, so that almost continuously for a century Assyrian kings ruled Babylonia either in person or through an Assyrian sub-king or a Babylonian puppet.

Shalmaneser's reign ended in an insurrection, and Merodach-baladan used the instability in Assyria to make an alliance with Elam. In April 721 BC he seized the throne in Babylon, and with his Elamite ally planned an attack upon the major Assyrian outpost at Der towards the Elamite border. Sargon, Shalmaneser's successor, sent his army to meet the threat. A chronicle relates what happened:

> Humban-nikash king of Elam did battle against Sargon king of Assyria in the Der area. He forced Assyria to turn back and inflicted defeat on them. Merodach-baladan and his army, who had gone to the help of the king of Elam, did not take part in the battle and withdrew.[1]

This can hardly mean, as sometimes interpreted, that Merodach-baladan failed to arrive on time. He was a man of considerable ability, unlikely to risk his interests by such elementary carelessness. More probably Merodach-baladan was standing by to protect the capital in case the Assyrian army broke through.

Sargon could also claim victory, since he had held Der and prevented any further Elamite advance. But the mauling the Assyrian forces had received prevented any further action in Babylonia, and Merodach-baladan was able to hold the throne for the twelve years between 721 BC and 710 BC (see fig. 75).

Some scholars have seen Merodach-baladan as the man who rescued Babylonia from extinction, but there is nothing to suggest that Assyria ever planned to extinguish Babylonia. Whether Merodach-baladan's reign was a blessing or disaster depends upon who tells the tale. Merodach-baladan himself claimed exemplary piety, in 'fulfilling divine ordinances, carrying out rituals correctly, and renewing cult places and shrines of the great gods'. Archaeology partly confirms this claim, showing that he did restore certain temples, and texts indicate that in several cities he protected citizens' interests. He must also have concerned himself with the irrigation system, since a canal near Uruk was named after him.

Sargon told another side of life under Merodach-baladan; he spoke of caravans being looted, of citizens of Sippar, Nippur, Babylon and Borsippa being ill-treated and their lands seized, and of city gods being taken off from Uruk, Eridu and other cities. The truth probably lies between; people and cities fared well or ill under Merodach-baladan, according to whether they supported him or Assyria.

Not until 710 BC was Sargon in a position to mount another attack. It was well planned. He first neutralised Elam, and then, with support from native Babylonians, marched to expel the Chaldean leader from Babylon. The citizens and temple authorities of Babylon and Borsippa welcomed Sargon into the capital, where he presided at the New Year festival at the beginning of 709 BC, thereby formally becoming king of Babylonia. Outside Babylon, he deported some Aramaeans and Chaldeans and resettled others.

There was nothing exceptional in the welcome Sargon received in the capital, since after tribal disturbances Assyria represented a return to stability and conditions favourable for trade. The Assyrians also astutely promised that under Assyrian rule citizens would continue to enjoy their ancient privileges of exemption from taxes and conscription; a royal Assyrian letter specifically records such an undertaking by Tiglath-Pileser's commander to the citizens of Babylon at the time of the Mukin-zer rebellion.[2] In the south, the region most subject to Chaldean depredations, some cities remained pro-Assyrian well into the second half of the seventh century. In north Babylonia, however, support for Assyria began to wane much sooner. During his reign from 721 to 710 BC Mcrodach-baladan did all he could to encourage this trend, demonstrating his conformity to Babylonian traditions by such measures as maintaining the irrigation system, and restoring temples to show that the gods were on his side. He also proved that Chaldeans no less than Assyrians could guarantee stability, for he united all the Kaldu tribes for the first time and made an alliance with Elam.

After his defeat by Sargon, Merodach-baladan, supported by Aramaean allies, fled for refuge to his southern tribal area, seizing hostages from Babylonian cities en route. Reaching his capital Dur-Yakin, he strengthened its defences by cutting approach bridges and digging a great moat, but Sargon ferried his troops across and took and devastated Dur-Yakin. He released citizens of Sippar, Nippur, Babylon and Borsippa held prisoner there, and restored stolen divine statues to their sanctuaries.

75 Below left *A monument in black marble of the Chaldean chieftain Marduk-apla-iddina (Merodach-baladan of 2 Kings 20:12), who seized the kingship of Babylonia from 721 to 710 BC.*

76 Below right *Part of a bas-relief from Nineveh, showing a scene in which Assyrian troops have caught Chaldean rebels in the marshes of south Babylonia.*

Merodach-baladan, although wounded in the engagement, escaped to Elam.

In 705 BC Sargon died in battle defending his northern frontier, and was succeeded by his son Sennacherib, who was formally king of Babylonia from the next New Year festival.[3] But anti-Assyrian feeling was festering, and early in 703 BC a Babylonian official proclaimed himself king, to be displaced a month later by Merodach-baladan. The latter had been using his considerable diplomatic skills to forge a widespread anti-Assyrian alliance, for he not only received widespread support from native Babylonians, and paid for military assistance from Elam, but had also won the friendship of Hezekiah of Judah, who also rebelled.

Sennacherib's reaction was prompt and effective. He came south with his army and brilliantly out-generalled Merodach-baladan, who fled to the southern marshes. Sennacherib followed through the whole Chaldean area, where he claimed to have taken eighty-eight walled cities and 820 villages of Bit-Dakkuri, Bit-Sha'alli, Bit-Amukkani and Bit-Yakin. He returned with 208,000 captives, and many thousands of horses, mules, asses, camels, cattle and sheep, apart from the share which fell to his troops.

Some of the towns taken had names of Arabic form, and one of Sennacherib's captives was a brother of the queen of the Arabs. Clearly Arabs from the western desert had begun to involve themselves in Babylonia, and to settle among the more northerly Chaldean tribes.

Sennacherib reverted to the older practice of ruling Babylonia through a puppet king. His appointee was a Babylonian nobleman, Bel-ibni, who had been educated in Assyria. By 700 BC Bel-ibni had proved unsatisfactory, however, and Sennacherib removed him, placing on the throne his own son Ashur-nadin-shumi, the crown prince of Assyria. Merodach-baladan remained a threat, but renewed action failed to capture the Chaldean leader, who fled to Elamite territory; he must have died shortly afterwards, for we hear nothing more of him. Ashur-nadin-shumi governed Babylonia with apparent stability for six years.

Although Merodach-baladan had disappeared, his Bit-Yakin tribe remained a threat, and their position on the border meant that rebels could always take refuge in Elamite territory on the other side of a great tidal lagoon. Sennacherib decided on a final solution. He built a fleet in the north, sailed it down to carry his army over the lagoon, and thereby in 694 BC was able to attack the Bit-Yakin tribe and pursue them well inside Elamite territory.

The Elamites replied unexpectedly with a counter-attack into northern Babylonia, taking Sippar with considerable slaughter. This prompted an insurrection in the capital, where rebels captured Sennacherib's son and handed him over to the Elamites, installing a native Babylonian, Nergal-ushezib, in his place.

Not all Babylonian cities had turned anti-Assyrian, for the Babylonian Chronicle records that in the following summer Nergal-ushezib sacked Nippur. But he then over-reached himself and moved against the Assyrian army, only to be taken prisoner. The Assyrian army took its chance to ravage Elam, whose king had just been killed in a rebellion.

In Babylonia a Chaldean chieftain, Mushezib-Marduk (Shuzubu), seized the vacant throne, and, after robbing the main temple treasury in Babylon, bought military assistance from the new king of Elam, who mustered an enormous army from people from western Iran and Aramaean tribesmen. The Elamite force joined Mushezib-Marduk and his Chaldeans and marched north along the Tigris (691 BC), possibly intending an invasion of Assyria itself.

The Assyrian army met them at Halule, on a plain not far from the river Diyala. There was a major battle. Sennacherib described it in graphic terms, speaking of his horses plunging into streams of blood and corpses filling the plain. The Assyrian king stopped the Elamite advance, but at such a cost that he had temporarily to return to base, leaving the Elamite nominee ruling in Babylon. However, in 690 BC he was able to return, and after appointing a complaisant son of Merodach-baladan as governor of the main Chaldean tribal area in the Sealands, he put the capital under siege. At the same time an Assyrian force attacked an Arab stronghold at an oasis west of Babylonia, capturing the queen of the Arabs and five thousand camels, presumably to prevent Arab allies intervening to break the siege of Babylon. The city held out for fifteen months with growing famine, until when finally taken in early winter 689 BC its open places were filled with corpses.

Previously Sennacherib had shown patience; he wanted an accommodation with the cities of Babylonia, and regarded the main problem as the tribal peoples and their Elamite allies. But now, with all attempts at a settlement frustrated, and his oldest son murdered, he adopted a more severe policy. He first settled the score with the usurper Mushezib-Marduk, whom he executed, paying his weight in silver to the man who had captured him. He then began the systematic destruction of Babylon, sharing out the city's portable wealth among his army, and either smashing the images of the great gods or sending them off to Assyria. With Babylon now robbed of divine protection, Sennacherib burnt what would burn, and razed the rest of the capital to the ground. He spared neither houses, city walls, nor temples, and dumped their rubble into the main canal. The soil of the city he threw into the Euphrates, which, by his account, carried it as far off as the Persian Gulf. Finally he dug water channels across the city to make it a swamp; eleven years later Esarhaddon found large areas water-logged.

This was hubris. Babylon's cultural influence far exceeded its political or military power, and its destruction harmed Assyria itself, by bringing a significant decline in support for the imperial power. A letter, perhaps from the reign of Esarhaddon, refers to the unpopularity of Assyria, although Nippur, from where the letter came, remained pro-Assyrian, possibly because a substantial element in its population was non-Babylonian.[4] Dissent at the Assyrian court from Sennacherib's Babylonian policy may have been a factor in a palace revolution, in which, as the Bible records (2 Kings 19:37), Sennacherib was murdered by his own sons.[5]

Babylonia under Esarhaddon

For two months there was confusion. Then the nominated heir, Esarhaddon, in command of an army in the west, returned, defeated the regicides, and took the thrones of both Assyria and Babylonia. His reign in Babylonia began with certain advantages. Although the governor of the Sealands, Nabu-zer-kitti-lishir, a son of Merodach-baladan, initially attempted to assert independence, he gained no widespread support, and when he fled to Elam in the face of approaching Assyrian forces, the king of Elam had him arrested and executed. The dead leader's brother Na'id-Marduk promptly made submission to Esarhaddon, who appointed him governor in his brother's place. Esarhaddon secured the good will of the Arabs west of Babylonia by returning their divine images and by appointing as queen a young woman who had been a hostage in Nineveh. He won the submission of the Aramaean tribes on the eastern border by appointing their paramount sheikh, Bel-iqisha, as warden of the frontier against Elam. Elam had shown by its treatment of the rebellious Nabu-zer-kitti-lishir that it no longer wished to meddle in Babylonia, and subsequently made a treaty of friendship with Esarhaddon.[6]

Esarhaddon set to work to show his favourable intentions towards Babylonia, reinterpreting his father's devastation of Babylon as divine retribution for Babylonian impiety. Now, he proclaimed, the merciful Marduk had relented, and shortened the period of desolation from 70 years ($\mathbb{K}$ in cuneiform) to 11 ($\langle \mathbb{T}$). This brought its termination to near 680 BC, the year of Esarhaddon's accession. Esarhaddon took immediate steps to implement the decreed restoration, showing his good will by participating in person. He began by clearing derelict and waterlogged parts of the city, and then started reconstruction. Marduk's great temple Esagila was rebuilt and re-equipped with gold and silver vessels, and its rituals resumed. The ziggurat was restored, the capital was fortified anew, and in other cities temples were renovated and looted divine images brought back and set up in their cult-places.

When Esarhaddon found that the Chaldean tribe of Bit-Dakkuri had seized lands belonging to citizens of Babylon and Borsippa, he reversed this wrong and deposed the tribe's sub-king, replacing him by his son. Wherever possible Esarhaddon restored rights to citizens who had suffered hardship, as he recounts:

> For wronged citizens of Babylon, who had enjoyed privileged status, I established anew their freedom under the protection of Anu and Enlil. Those who had been sold and gone into servitude, ... I gathered together and brought back to Babylon. Their plundered property I returned. To those who were naked I gave clothing, and set their feet on the way back to Babylon. I encouraged them to live in the city, to build houses, to plant orchards, to dig canals. Their privileged status, which had ... fallen into disuse, I restored, renewing their tax exemption in writing. I opened the routes for them in all directions, so that they could establish (commercial) relations with all lands.[7]

This was a programme to win Babylonian support, and it succeeded. Allusions in letters and chronicles suggest occasional disturbances and conspiracies, but there was no major rebellion. Babylonia at peace enjoyed considerable economic advantages from its leading position in Esarhaddon's considerable empire. This was the largest unitary trading area the world had yet known, stretching from Cyprus and Asia Minor to Armenia, to the Hamadan region of Iran, into the fringes of Arabia, and to the borders of Egypt.

The situation was now sufficiently stable for Esarhaddon to initiate a new phase of imperial expansion, the conquest of Egypt, begun in 675 BC. This was only possible because Esarhaddon had developed good relations with Arab camel-tribes, indispensable as guides across the arid sands of the Sinai desert.

Esarhaddon wished to avoid after his death any recurrence of the crisis which had ushered in his own reign. His solution was a dynastic diarchy. This decision was formalised in 672 BC in the presence of provincial governors and vassals, who took oaths to support the settlement. Assyria was to be ruled by a younger son, Ashurbanipal; the king designate of Babylonia was an older son, Shamash-shum-ukin, already the senior administrator in Babylonia before his father's death.

Shamash-shum-ukin as king of Babylonia

Esarhaddon died in 669 BC, en route to Egypt, and the planned diarchy went into operation. Since Assyria had long been the more powerful state, Esarhaddon presumably intended the king of Assyria to be the senior partner; titles accorded to the two princes, and the positions of their images relative to Esarhaddon on a stele, seem to have made this explicit. Action by Zakutu, paternal grandmother of the two princes, also implied Ashurbanipal's seniority; shortly after the accession, she arranged for all senior administrators and Shamash-shum-ukin himself to swear an oath to reveal anything they ever came to know of treasonable intentions against Ashurbanipal.

Ashurbanipal always acted as though he were the senior, and for sixteen years Shamash-shum-ukin accepted this, even applying to his brother for decisions in some matters. Ashurbanipal assumed responsibility for Babylonia's defence and foreign policy, had his own intelligence network, and appointed officials in Babylonia, many of whom reported direct to him. Shamash-shum-ukin's independent authority was mainly limited to economic matters, such as questions of land-tenure, and in this area he seems to have had some success, for the economic texts during his reign indicate prosperity.

From 667 BC onwards Assyria was attempting to consolidate Esarhaddon's achievements in Egypt, by rule through native princes backed by Assyrian garrisons. In 664 BC came signs of fresh trouble in Babylonia. Although Elam had received generous food relief from Ashurbanipal during a devastating drought, it now invaded north Babylonia, in alliance with the formerly peaceable Gambulu tribe on its frontier. Since Elam withdrew on the approach of Assyrian forces, the invasion may have been primarily to divert attention from internal problems; that there were problems is indisputable, since a revolution broke out when the king died later that year.

In Egypt, the Assyrian position gradually became untenable from the early 650s BC, as native princes began to assert independence. This had repercussions elsewhere. In summer 653 BC Ashurbanipal received intelligence that Teumman, the new king of Elam, was mobilising to invade the Assyrian empire, and decided upon a pre-emptive strike, in which he caught and killed Teumman. He followed up with a punitive sweep through the territory of the Aramaean tribe of Gambulu, which had been implicated.

By early in 652 BC Ashurbanipal knew Shamash-shum-ukin intended to rebel, and wrote to warn the people of Babylon against involvement, condemning his brother's lying propaganda. What prompted Shamash-shum-ukin's rebellion is a matter of speculation, but to speak of sibling rivalry explains nothing. Possibly Shamash-shum-ukin had simply allowed himself to become the mouthpiece for the old combination of anti-Assyrian forces within Babylonia. Perhaps the rebellion had been intended to synchronise with an invasion by Teumman, a synchronisation which Ashurbanipal's prompt action frustrated.

When war came, at the end of 652 BC, it was fierce and protracted. Assyria had its formidable army, now wholly withdrawn from Egypt, and it enjoyed the support of several southern cities, of which the most important were Uruk, used as an army base, and the ever loyal Ur. A minority of Chaldeans and Aramaeans also took the Assyrian side. Supporting Shamash-shum-ukin were most cities of central and north Babylonia, most of the Chaldeans and of the two principal Aramaean tribes, and groups of Arabs. He also had the spasmodic support of Elam, now weakened by rival claimants to the throne.

Fighting for control of north Babylonia continued for eighteen months, with Assyria gradually gaining ascendancy. By July 650 BC Babylon was under siege, with Shamash-shum-ukin inside.

In the south, pro-Assyrian cities at first came under severe attack from Aramaean and Chaldean tribesmen, but by 649 Assyria was well in control. At Babylon the siege became so grim that people were driven to cannibalism. It finally fell in late 648 BC, when Shamash-shum-ukin died in a conflagration, perhaps by suicide. Ashurbanipal gave his brother's remains burial with appropriate rituals, but living rebel leaders met a more barbarous end. Ashurbanipal reports:

> the rest of those still living I destroyed at the colossi where my grandfather Sennacherib had been destroyed, making them a funerary offering for him. Their carved-up bodies I fed to dogs, pigs, wolves, eagles, birds of the heavens and fishes of the deep.

The customary deportations followed, remembered in Ezra 4:9–10 over two centuries later. Altogether, between the reigns of Tiglath-Pileser III and Ashurbanipal the Assyrians deported nearly half a million people from Babylonia, many of them Chaldeans.

77 *A bas-relief showing incidents from Ashurbanipal's campaign against the Elamites, after he had crushed the rebellion in Babylonia.*

78 *By the reign of Ashurbanipal (668–627 BC), Arabs were beginning to enter south Mesopotamia and involve themselves in the struggle for power. This bas-relief shows troops of Ashurbanipal taking action against them.*

As earlier, Elam gave sanctuary to fugitive tribesmen, including the Chaldean leader, Nabu-bel-shumati, a grandson of Merodach-baladan. Ashurbanipal resolved to deal with Elam once and for all. In two campaigns, in 647 and 646 BC, he marched over large areas and devastated them, carrying off their huge flocks, deporting the population, and sacking major cities (see fig. 77), among them the ancient capital Susa. Terrified, the king of Elam caught Nabu-bel-shumati but before he could dispatch him to Ashurbanipal, the captive and his groom stabbed each other in a suicide pact. As a mark of good faith, the king of Elam had Nabu-bel-shumati's body preserved in salt and transmitted with the head of the groom to Ashurbanipal.

Elam never recovered from Ashurbanipal's atrocities. Its destruction left a power vacuum which the Indo-European Persians, moving south at this time, eventually filled. This was to have far-reaching consequences for Babylonia.

One element in the Shamash-shum-ukin rebellion remained unpunished – the

Arabs of the western desert. Shortly after his Elamite operations Ashurbanipal made a summer campaign to capture key oases, bringing the surrender of leading chieftains (see fig. 78). Two of them he chained to dog kennels by gateways in Nineveh.

From this time until Ashurbanipal's death in 627 little is known about the political history of Babylonia. Although there is an abundance of economic texts, suggesting exceptionally high economic activity, this could be an accident of archaeological discovery.

Babylonian King List A records that after the death of Shamash-shum-ukin a king named Kandalanu ruled Babylonia on behalf of Assyria. The Ptolemaic Canon, a Greek text of the second century AD, supports this. But the native author Berossus (third century BC) says that Shamash-shum-ukin was succeeded by Sardanapollos, his spelling for Ashurbanipal. Was Kandalanu simply the name Ashurbanipal used as king in Babylonia, or was Kandalanu someone distinct serving as Ashurbanipal's puppet? Scholarly opinion remains divided on this.[8]

Kandalanu died in 627 BC and Ashurbanipal (if a different person) in the same year. Ashurbanipal was succeeded in Assyria by two sons successively, first Ashur-etil-ilani and then Sin-sharra-ishkun. The succession in Babylonia is uncertain. A chronicle records that disturbances at once broke out in both countries. The new element in the situation was the rise of a new Babylonian leader, Nabopolassar. Some surmise that he was of Chaldean origin, since he had some connection with the Sealands, but he may simply have been a high official there.

Nabopolassar left inscriptions, but they are almost totally concerned with building operations. Of his rise to power they tell us only that he was a 'son of a nobody' (so not of the house of Merodach-baladan), that he was born in Babylonia, and that he defeated Assyria, 'which from olden days had ... made the people of the land bear its heavy yoke'.

Chronicles are more illuminating. According to one, Nabopolassar attacked Babylon soon after the death of Ashurbanipal. Sin-sharra-ishkun, a son of Ashurbanipal and possibly the intended successor to the Babylonian throne, withdrew to Assyria, but left the Assyrian army in Babylonia, where it went on the offensive, driving Nabopolassar southwards. But at Uruk he stood his ground and forced the Assyrian army to retreat. After further fighting Nabopolassar took the throne in Babylon in November 626 BC. As a move to secure good will abroad, he returned to Susa Elamite gods which the Assyrians had taken as plunder.

By the following year Nabopolassar was so firmly in control of Babylonia that Assyrian attacks failed to dislodge him. By 617 BC he was in a position to move his army up the Euphrates as far north as the Balih, and up the Tigris to Kirkuk and the Lower Zab. In 615 BC he attacked the old capital Ashur, but the defenders forced him to retreat south to Takrit, where he himself came under siege. The Assyrians withdrew on receiving intelligence of an impending attack by the Medes from north-west Iran, who, formerly vassals of Assyria, were now, under their king Cyaxares, becoming a major power in the Near East.

In 614 BC the Medes moved into central Assyria, taking both Tarbisu, a fortress only 8 km (5 miles) from Nineveh which controlled its communication to the north and west, and Ashur. Nabopolassar arrived at Ashur shortly afterwards to make a formal alliance with Cyaxares, but instead of following up their success the two leaders led their armies home. The events of the next year explain this surprise withdrawal. Tribesmen along the middle Euphrates rebelled against Nabopolassar, clearly in alliance with Assyria, which sent an army to their support. The Medes had reason to fear an attack on their rear by Scythians from further north, a tribal people who had had predominantly friendly relations with Assyria since the reign of Esarhaddon, and who were now on the move.

In fact the Scythians (called Umman-manda in the chronicle), were on the side of Babylonia. In 612 BC Nabopolassar marched north and joined them and the Medes to put Nineveh under siege. The city as rebuilt by Sennacherib had the most powerful defences in the Near East, and might have been expected to resist for years. In the event it fell in a mere three months, according to Greek sources and the Bible (Nahum 1:8) because a tributary of the Tigris swept away a section of the defences. The city was sacked, and Sin-sharra-ishkun died in the destruction.

The Assyrian army, still a formidable force, withdrew to regroup at Harran in north-west Mesopotamia, where a member of the royal family, Ashur-uballit II, was proclaimed king, and called upon Egypt for support. The three erstwhile allies now each hastened to secure their share of the collapsing empire; the Scythians established themselves in Asia Minor, the Medes took Anatolia, and Nabopolassar occupied central Assyria and the middle Euphrates region.

In 610 BC the Scythians began an attack on Harran, forcing Ashur-uballit to withdraw. In the same year a new pharaoh, Necho II, ascended in Egypt and to safeguard Egyptian interests in Palestine and Syria decided on massive support for Assyria. But Nabopolassar had been active in diplomacy, and as Necho moved northwards through Palestine in 608 BC he met opposition both from Gaza (Jeremiah 47:1) and from Judah (2 Kings 23:29). Despite this, Necho's forces arrived in Syria, and made a joint base with Ashur-uballit at Carchemish. Nabopolassar, by now an old man, handed over command of the Babylonian army to his oldest son, Nebuchadnezzar. In 605 BC the new commander boldly crossed the Euphrates and attacked the Egyptian army head on. Jeremiah 46:12 reports heavy slaughter on both sides, but it was the Egyptians whose morale broke, and according to Jeremiah 46:5 they suffered a rout: 'their mighty ones are beaten down, and are fled apace, and look not back: for fear was round about'. We hear nothing about Assyrian survivors, and the empire was at an end. Nebuchadnezzar pursued the fleeing Egyptians to the Egyptian border, seizing Syria and Palestine on the way. At this point came news of the death of Nabopolassar, requiring Nebuchadnezzar to return to Babylon immediately. His succession followed without problem, and he became king of the Neo-Babylonian empire.

King Nebuchadnezzar

Jeremiah recognised Nebuchadnezzar as the new world power with an empire destined to endure for three generations (Jeremiah 27:7). He was a bold and successful general, and displayed statesman-like qualities in maintaining good relations with the Medes, who had annexed the northern parts of the former Assyrian empire. He was also largely responsible for the rebuilding of Babylon as a city of such splendour that, in the view of some classical writers, its 'Hanging Gardens' and its walls were two of the seven wonders of the world.

The Bible recounts some of Nebuchadnezzar's campaigns. Jehoiakim of Judah was less far-seeing than Jeremiah, so that although he made submission to Nebuchadnezzar in 605 BC, he afterwards succumbed to Egyptian blandishments, bringing down an attack upon Jerusalem in 597 BC which ended with the deportation to Babylon of the cream of the land (2 Kings 24:10–16). Subsequently Egypt invaded Palestine, leading Judah and other minor states to change their allegiance, but on the arrival of a powerful Babylonian army, Egypt abandoned its vassals and withdrew. Jerusalem was again besieged and after eighteen months taken and sacked, with further deportations (2 Kings 25:8–12). The city was left under a native governor, who was later murdered by pro-Egyptian assassins (2 Kings 25:22–6). Nebuchadnezzar also attacked Tyre, and took it after a long siege in 571 BC (Ezekiel 26:1–28:19). Nebuchadnezzar clearly intended to hold Palestine at least as far as the Egyptian border, and Ezekiel 29:19–21, supported by a fragment of cuneiform tablet, hints that he began an invasion of Egypt, but further details are lacking.

Nebuchadnezzar's own inscriptions describe his building operations, and German excavations provide some further details. He devoted considerable effort to strengthening the walls of Babylon. In Nebuchadnezzar's time the Euphrates ran through the middle of Babylon, with the oldest part of the city, some 220 ha (550 acres), on the

79 *A scale model of the centre of Babylon at the time of Nebuchadnezzar II, showing the great temple Esagila and the ziggurat Etemenanki.*

80 Above left *The ruins of the Processional Way in situ in 1956 (see also pl. XI).*

81 Above right *A sixth-century representation of Marduk, who has here adopted the dragon form of a monster he slew in primeval times.*

east bank, and the later part, rather smaller, on the west bank. Both sides were surrounded by an inner wall and an outer wall 7 m (24 ft) apart. The inner wall was some 6.5 m (21 ft) thick, the outer 3.5 m (12 ft). Both walls were reinforced with towers at intervals of 18 m (60 ft), and at least eight great gates gave entry to the city. Round the outer wall, Nabopolassar had begun a great moat over 12 m (40 ft) wide, and Nebuchadnezzar extended this to encircle the whole city, with much higher and thicker embankments than before. On the east side of Babylon, outside the moat, Nebuchadnezzar created a further line of defence, in the form of a third great wall, also strengthened with a moat.

Nebuchadnezzar restored temples in Babylon and other cities. Inside the capital the most important buildings were Marduk's great temple of Esagila and its associated ziggurat Etemenanki nearby (see fig. 79), the latter possibly the original of the biblical Tower of Babel, although it could have been the ziggurat of Borsippa (see pl. I), 15 km (9 miles) to the south. Although wrecked by Sennacherib, neither Etemenanki nor Esagila required major work, since Esarhaddon and Ashurbanipal had undertaken extensive rebuilding programmes. Nebuchadnezzar did, however, show his piety by embellishments to the ziggurat, and by refurbishing Esagila with fine woods, gold and silver and precious stones. An ancient cuneiform text, in part confirmed by excavation, gives the dimensions of the ziggurat, a structure of six reducing stages with a shrine on top as a seventh; its base was approximately 91 × 91 m (about 300 ft square) and its total height the same.

Nebuchadnezzar had several palaces in Babylon. The original palace complex (the

'Southern Palace') was by the Euphrates at the north-western corner of the old city. Nebuchadnezzar enlarged this to include five great courtyards and quarters for the garrison, administrators, the throne room, his own private quarters, and the harem. He replaced sun-dried brick with baked brick, added cedar beams for the roofing and glazed tiles for the walls, and adorned the building with gold, silver and precious stones.

The excavators identified the northern part of this palace as the site of the celebrated 'Hanging Gardens' of classical tradition. One author, Diodorus Siculus, says that they were a tiered structure 50 cubits high – about 23 m (75 ft) – built by a king to please a Persian concubine who missed the wooded hillsides of her native land. Their base comprised massive walls with passageways between, covered by stone blocks and layers of reeds, bitumen, baked brick and lead cladding. Machinery raised water from the river to irrigate the garden on top. The excavators found a double row of seven vaulted chambers with walls thick enough to bear a massive superstructure, and proposed to see these as the base described by Diodorus. Although the dimensions would in part fit the measurements given by Diodorus, most scholars today reject this identification, largely because distance from the Euphrates would have given problems with irrigation. One scholar suggests that tradition has here confused Babylon and Nineveh, and that the real Hanging Gardens were in the latter capital.

Nebuchadnezzar built a second palace north of the southern palace, outside the double city wall. Because this housed ancient monuments and trophies, some scholars speak of it as a museum. Nebuchadnezzar had a third palace at the northern extremity of the city, by the outermost wall.

Nebuchadnezzar's most impressive restoration work was the Processional Way, a roadway nearly 21 m (70 ft) wide between walls decorated with glazed tiles and a frieze of lions (see pl. XI). This was the route along which at the New Year festival Marduk was carried from his temple Esagila through the Ishtar Gate to the Akitu temple outside the city. Near the gate itself the walls were decorated with a glazed-tile frieze of bulls and dragons (see pl. X and fig. 80), representing the gods Adad and Marduk.

Except for a case of high treason in 594/3 BC, no unrest surfaced during Nebuchadnezzar's reign. But his son Amel-Marduk (Evil-Merodach of 2 Kings 25:27–30), who succeeded in 562 BC, reigned only two years before he was killed in a revolution. The man who came to power was Nebuchadnezzar's son-in-law Nergal-shar-usur (559–556 BC), named as a Babylonian magnate in Jeremiah 39:3, and known in Greek sources as Neriglissar. His main achievement was a campaign in 557 BC to protect Babylonian interests in Cilicia. His effective successor was Nabu-na'id (Nabonidus), a person of non-royal blood, who must at this time have been at least in his late fifties.

Nabonidus

Nabonidus (see fig. 82) was an enigmatic figure. He attempted to introduce worthwhile reforms, religious, economic and imperial, but so ineptly that he alienated the establishment and caused the downfall of the Neo-Babylonian empire.

He was the only son of a lady Adad-guppi, a courtier at the Babylonian court who

82 *This stele represents King Nabonidus. In a text summarising Babylonian history since the devastation wrought by Sennacherib, Nabonidus is presented as the true pious successor of other Neo-Babylonian kings.*

lived to be over a hundred. Of his father we know only his name, Nabu-balatsu-iqbi, and the fact that he was a nobleman but not of royal blood. At the end of her life Adad-guppi, or possibly her son on her behalf, wrote an inscription with the leading theme of zeal for the cult of the Moon-god Sin of Harran in north-west Assyria. This has led some scholars to conclude that she had been a priestess in Harran, but she herself made no such claim; she may simply have been a member of a prominent Harran family. Nabonidus certainly had a family connection with that city, since a text refers to his dynasty as 'the dynasty of Harran'.

Adad-guppi tells us that she 'reverenced' the Babylonian kings from the time of Nabopolassar through the reigns of Nebuchadnezzar and Neriglissar to the beginning of her son's reign in 556 BC. Another passage puts it beyond doubt that she had considerable influence at court, for she says: 'My son Nabonidus, ... I caused to stand before Nebuchadnezzar ... and Neriglissar. Night and day he kept their watch. He constantly did what was pleasing to them.'

A date of great importance to Adad-guppi was 610 BC, when, as she records, 'Sin, king of the gods, became angry with his city [Harran] and his temple and went up to heaven. The city and the people in it went to ruin.' This was the year in which the Scythians and Babylonians took Harran, and reduced its temple Ehulhul to ruins. It could well be that it was then that Adad-guppi, a member of an important patrician family of Harran, was carried off captive to the Babylonian court. Since, on her own account, she was born in 649–8 BC, she would have been thirty-nine in 610 BC. At that date Nabonidus could have been up to twenty years old, although as he was still active seventy-one years later, in 539 BC, it is unlikely that he was as much as ten.

The main sources for the reign of Nabonidus are building inscriptions from about a dozen sites. There are also economic and administrative records, chronicles, and a literary composition known as the *Verse Account of Nabonidus*. This last was a work produced by the Babylonian religious establishment, highly critical of religious changes attempted by Nabonidus and favourable to the Persian Cyrus who overthrew him. Biblical and classical traditions and a document from Qumran are more remote sources for this reign.

Once Nabonidus had been introduced to Nebuchadnezzar, his own abilities, or his mother's influence, advanced him rapidly, so that, according to Herodotus, he was one of two diplomats who brokered a peace treaty between the Lydians and Medes in Asia Minor in 585 BC. Although he can hardly have been as old as thirty-five by that time, he must already have been a senior member of Nebuchadnezzar's entourage. Certainly he and his mother were prominent in the inner court circle, for Adad-guppi specifically says that after the death of Nebuchadnezzar and Neriglissar it was she and not their sons or other court officials who performed the appropriate funerary offerings.

When Neriglissar died, in April 556 BC, he was briefly succeeded by his son Labashi-Marduk, a minor. Within a month a palace conspiracy had dethroned this boy, and put Nabonidus on the throne in his place, although he later disclaimed any previous aspirations to kingship. If he was speaking the truth, and was not involved in the conspiracy, the driving force behind the rebellion may have been his son Belshazzar, who acted as regent in Babylon for much of his father's reign, and whom the book of Daniel thought of as the actual king (Daniel 5:1–18). A further fact implicating Belshazzar is that large estates which had formerly belonged to Neriglissar quickly came into his hands by confiscation. Some southern cities initially resisted the succession of Nabonidus, but all had submitted by July.

Nabonidus, once king, took steps to emphasise his legitimate succession to the warrior kings Nebuchadnezzar and Neriglissar, and claimed that the gods had entrusted him with their armies. He early undertook a campaign to Cilicia, with such success that he was able to dedicate nearly three thousand prisoners of war to Nabu and Nergal as temple slaves.

Otherwise the main concern of Nabonidus in his early rule was with the temples. One of his earliest objectives was the restoration of Ehulhul ('House of Great Joy'), the temple of the god Sin in Harran, which had been lying in ruins since 610 BC. In an inscription of his first regnal year he claimed that his lord Marduk had reminded him that Ehulhul had lain desolate for fifty-four years, surrounded by the Umman-manda, which here meant the Medes, who had occupied the Harran district shortly after the Scythians and Nabopolassar sacked it. Now, said Marduk, Sin intended to return to his temple, and Nabonidus was to restore it for him. The restoration did not begin immediately, but the fact that Nabonidus considered it feasible reflects his grasp of international affairs. Another inscription from perhaps ten years later shows the divine message, now elaborated, presented as the record of a dream:

> The great Lord Marduk and Sin, luminary of heaven and earth, stood together. Marduk spoke to me: 'Nabonidus, king of Babylon, take bricks with your horse and wagon, rebuild Ehulhul, and establish therein the abode of the great Lord Sin.'

With reverence I answered Marduk, the greatest of the gods: 'That temple which you tell me to rebuild, the Umman-manda is all around it and his power is very great.'

Marduk replied: 'The Umman-manda of whom you spoke, he, his land, and the kings who go at his side will cease to exist.'

When the third year arrived, (Marduk) raised against him his subject Cyrus, king of Anzan, the second of that name, who with his small army scattered the widespread forces of the Umman-manda, captured Astyages, king of the Umman-manda, and took him prisoner to his land.

Cyrus, a Persian prince and a vassal of the Medes, rebelled against his overlord Astyages early in Nabonidus' reign, and finally overthrew him in 551 BC. Possibly Nabonidus had a secret alliance with Cyrus at the beginning of his reign, and so could foresee that circumstances would shortly allow him access to Harran.

Exactly when Nabonidus did the work on Ehulhul is not clear. Texts from Harran date the restoration not earlier than his thirteenth regnal year, whereas his mother, who died in the ninth year, left an inscription specifically stating that Nabonidus had already built the temple. And Nabonidus would hardly have delayed longer than necessary to implement a divine command. The different texts surely refer to different stages of the work. Nabonidus must have begun the restoration in his third year, as soon as the revolt of Cyrus had forced the Median king to withdraw from the Harran area, and kept the work going until he could finalise the restoration towards the end of his reign.

During his first two years Nabonidus strengthened his control over the temple administrations of major cities, by replacing senior officials appointed by his predecessor, and reforming the system of temple offerings. At Ur he reintroduced the obsolete office of high priestess, and made this a personal power base by installing his daughter to it (554 BC).

In his third year Nabonidus made an astonishing break with convention. Appointing his son Belshazzar as regent, he led the major part of the army to the west of the empire over 800 km (500 miles) away. There he remained for ten years. This withdrawal, transferred from Nabonidus to his more celebrated predecessor, underlies the story in Daniel 4:28–33 of Nebuchadnezzar's seven years of madness, when he was driven from men and had his dwelling with the beasts of the field.

Why this exceptional behaviour? Nabonidus himself, in a late inscription, attributed his departure to the impiety of 'people of Babylon, Borsippa, Nippur, Uruk and Larsa' in neglecting the rites of the Moon-god. By the end of his reign his allegedly heretical religious practices had aroused considerable opposition, and the inscription may allude to an earlier attempt to promote the Moon-god in the pantheon, which met resistance. If Belshazzar was indeed the power behind the throne, it would have been sound statesmanship for the controversial Nabonidus to withdraw to the west, leaving Belshazzar – with orthodox religious views – in charge in Babylonia.

Yet, in view of the energy Nabonidus displayed when he reached the west, there may have been other factors. After dealing with revolts in Syria and Transjordan, early in his fourth year Nabonidus moved southwards for Teima in west Arabia. From that base he extended direct control further south than any previous Mesopotamian ruler, conquering all major Arabian settlements as far south as Yathrib (Medina). The principal factor behind this may have been economic. South-west Arabia and regions opposite in Africa were the sole source of frankincense and other spices, and the caravan trade in these through Medina to Transjordan, Egypt and Mesopotamia had made the whole area very rich. Nabonidus' main motive was probably to gain control of these lucrative trade routes. Certainly international trade prospered during his reign, for texts mention such imports as copper and iron from Yamana (the western coast or islands of Asia Minor), iron from Lebanon, alum and papyrus (for writing Aramaic) from Egypt, and lapis lazuli from Afghanistan.

Back in Babylonia, Belshazzar as regent performed most of the royal duties, although the absence of the real king meant that the New Year festival could not take place, a ground for complaint by the religious establishment. Meanwhile, adverse international circumstances were developing. To the north and east of Babylonia, Cyrus the Persian was tightening his grasp on the former Median empire and moving westwards. This led Belshazzar, by early 547 BC at latest, to lead his army to his northern frontiers as a defensive measure. But the current objective of the Persian leader proved to be Lydia in south Asia Minor, which he took in 546 BC.

Nabonidus returned to Babylonia in 543 BC, possibly because of the rising power of Cyrus. There may also have been economic problems, for a document from Uruk in 545 BC refers to famine. His return was followed by uncompromising attempts at religious reform. Whereas earlier, although Nabonidus favoured the Moon-god he had still accorded other gods their traditional functions, now, according to the hostile *Verse Account of Nabonidus*, he was attempting to promote the Moon-god, called Sin at Harran and Ur and Ilteri in north Syria, to the headship of the pantheon. The *Verse Account* alleges that he set up at Ehulhul a divine image in unprecedented and abominable form. Late inscriptions of Nabonidus himself show him replacing other gods with Sin, crediting to Sin even Marduk's great temple of Esagila in Babylon and Nabu's temple Ezida in Borsippa. Other gods are spoken of as acting at the command of Sin. And whereas in an early inscription it was Marduk, traditional head of the pantheon, who commanded Nabonidus to restore Ehulhul, now the order came from Sin. Moreover, Nabonidus was now addressing Sin as 'king of the gods', even 'god of gods', and referring to him as 'father and creator' of other gods. It was Sin who had called him to the kingship, and he even attributed to Sin the earlier world-wide dominion of the Assyrian kings Esarhaddon and Ashurbanipal.

By the beginning of 539 BC it was apparent that an attack by Cyrus the Persian was imminent, and divine statues of major temples were brought to the capital, to prevent their falling into enemy hands. But Nabonidus had forfeited the support of the religious establishment, and when the Persian army, accompanied by a defecting Babylonian governor, crossed the Tigris it captured first Sippar and then Babylon without a battle. Cyrus – a brilliant propagandist, 'Yahweh's anointed' of Isaiah 45:1 – claimed that Marduk himself had ordered him to take Babylon, and the power changeover passed off so smoothly that temple rites continued undisturbed. Nabonidus was captured, but there is doubt as to his fate. One Greek tradition holds that he was executed, but another, supported by a cuneiform text, says that Cyrus settled him elsewhere in his domains, possibly as a governor.

This marked the end of Babylon as a world capital; that role had passed to Susa in south-west Iran. But Babylon remained the administrative hub for Mesopotamia and the administration was undisturbed. Religious rituals went on in their accustomed way, and the Crown Prince Cambyses participated in person in the New Year ritual to legitimate his father's rule.

Cambyses succeeded in 528 BC, and gave Babylonia a brief period of peace while he subjugated Egypt. A disputed succession followed his death in 522 BC, and in the ensuing strife two successive Babylonians, posing as descendants of Nabonidus, briefly installed themselves on the throne of Babylon, only to be captured and executed by Darius, the successful contender for the throne of the Persian empire.

Despite a nationalist revolt in 482 BC against Darius' successor Xerxes, Babylon remained under Persian control, with Persians increasingly administering the country, until 331 BC. Then, at a battle near Erbil, Alexander the Great finally defeated the Persians and gained control of their whole empire. After a further expedition to north-west India, Alexander returned with the project of making Babylon his world capital, but before he could put this into effect he died. His empire then split up between his generals, one of whom, Seleucus, finally gained Babylonia in 312 BC, adding Syria and eastern Asia Minor subsequently.

The final demise of Babylon came when Seleucus founded Seleucia on the Tigris as his new capital. With a drain of population to the new city, and increasing hellenisation everywhere, the Babylonian way of life was virtually at an end, although in some cities regular offerings continued to be made to Babylonian gods for another century.

Babylon in the Bible and classical literature

Before the First World War there was a group of scholars, mainly in Germany, who saw ancient Babylonia as the supreme well-head of spiritual values, with Babylonian antecedents for much of the Old Testament and some of the New. This was excessive, but parts of the Bible have an obvious Babylonian connection. The clearest instance is the Flood story in Genesis 6:13–8:22, which shows close parallels to the account of the Flood in the *Epic of Gilgamesh*. Parallels cover not only the main theme but also details; in both the divine power instructs the hero to build a ship, in both the hero loads in animals and later sends out birds, in both he makes a sacrifice on disembarking, and both end with the divine being announcing a decision never again to bring a universal Flood. The main difference – an important one – is that Israelites reinterpreted the ancient story in a monotheistic sense.

The Genesis creation stories have no clear links with Babylonia, but elsewhere there are hints of Babylonian creation concepts, perhaps transmitted indirectly through the Canaanites. For example, Isaiah 27:1 speaks of Yahweh slaying the serpent Leviathan, the dragon in the sea, and Isaiah 51:9 refers to Yahweh's destruction of the dragon Rahab; these are allusions to a combat myth of the Marduk-Tiamat type, reinterpreted in a monotheistic sense. Other passages mention Babylonian cults which came in late in the Monarchy period; thus Ezekiel 8:14–16 condemns a Tammuz cult and a sun-cult which had been introduced from Mesopotamia into Jerusalem. But often Israelites were familiar with Babylonian history and institutions without this affecting Israelite religion. Ezekiel 21:21, for example, shows that the prophet had witnessed Babylonian divination techniques, Jeremiah knew about the Babylonian gods (50:2), Isaiah had an acute perception of the dangers of meddling in Babylonian politics (39:1–7), and Deutero-Isaiah was well informed on current affairs in Babylonia (Isaiah 45:1) and on details of the cult (Isaiah 44:9–20). Much later the Talmud retained a memory of the temple of Bel in Babel and of Nebo in a place called Kursi, probably meaning Borsippa.[9]

Later religious teachers and moralists did not deal kindly with Babylon, once the most splendid city in the world. Daniel used it as his *mise-en-scène* for a number of stories to contrast pagan polytheism with true religion (2–7), and the Apocrypha's *Bel and the Dragon*, a humorous short story about dishonest priests of Bel, is set in Babylon. By the beginning of the Christian period the name of Babylon had become a synonym for depravity, so that the author of the biblical Book of Revelation used it in a coded attack upon the iniquities of imperial Rome, calling it (17:5) 'Babylon the Great, the mother of harlots and abominations of the earth'.

Babylon's ill repute went beyond Jewish and early Christian writers. Herodotus, who wrote a largely reliable account of Babylon in the fifth century BC, says that every Babylonian woman was once in her life compelled to prostitute herself to a stranger at the temple. This was a libel, but an element of fact may lie behind it. The third-millennium royal ritual concerning sacred marriage of a god and goddess had by the first millennium degenerated into the practice of lower grades of priestess offering themselves to strangers, and Herodotus may have encountered and misunderstood some form of this. Herodotus cast another slur upon Babylonia when he reported that there were no physicians. He was certainly misinformed, since physicians are well attested in cuneiform texts of most periods. Later classical writers who transmitted interesting, if not always reliable, traditions about Babylon included Diodorus Siculus (in the final century before the Christian era) and Strabo (shortly after); both gave an account of the Hanging Gardens (see p. 167). Quintus Curtius Rufus in the first century AD wrote a history of Alexander the Great which included his exploits in Babylon and his grandiose intentions for the city, which were never fulfilled.

Legacy

To deal adequately with the legacy from ancient Babylonia would require a complete book, and these remaining paragraphs can offer no more than a brief summary. The

83 *The cross in some of its forms goes far back in Mesopotamian iconography. This cylinder seal impression, from the beginning of the third millennium, shows a Maltese cross.*

most important cereals in much of the Western world are wheat for bread and barley as the basis of beer; this is because their wild ancestors grew in the Near East, where they were cultivated in prehistoric times, and then transmitted to the rest of the world through Babylonia. Similarly, our predominant meat foods are mutton, beef and pork because, despite the abundance of possible meat animals, the sheep, cow and pig were three of the four principal animals domesticated for food in the prehistoric Near East and taken over in Babylonia (the fourth was the goat, which has largely gone off the menu in recent centuries).

Technological survivals include the plough and the potter's wheel, and possibly the wheel used for transport, which have come down to us from earliest Babylonia. The concept of writing is another vital survival, even though the original technique, cuneiform on clay, fell into disuse two thousand years ago. Ancient Babylonia also gave us the place-value notation system for writing of numerals, so much more convenient than the Roman system (e.g. 78 rather than LXXVIII). We still count in sixties for some purposes, such as geometry (360 degrees in a circle) and time (division of hours into minutes and minutes into seconds), and this system originated in third-millennium Babylonia. The religious calendar still used in Christianity and Islam has affinities with the lunar calendar of ancient Babylonia. The twenty-four-hour day, although not wholly of Babylonian origin, combines Babylonian and

Egyptian elements. Astronomy, and even the names of some constellations, have their origin in Babylonian observations of the stars and planets.

These observations later developed into astrological concepts, which were handed down to us via the classical world, Byzantium and the Arabs. Some classical authors came to think of Babylonians, designated 'Chaldeans', as astrologers par excellence. In Christian art and folklore, representations of St Michael and the Dragon, and the story of St George and the Dragon, incorporate a distant memory of the myth of Marduk and Tiamat.[10] There are also symbols from Babylonia which survive in religion today. Prominent instances are the Tree of Life symbol (see pl. XII), which goes back to the beginning of the third millennium; the crescent in Islam, earlier the symbol of the Babylonian Moon-god; and the Maltese cross (see fig. 83).

Thus, although our modern life is separated from Babylonia by more than two thousand years, we remain linked by many fine strands of tradition, transmitted through Greece and Rome and the Arabs, without which our own world would be a very different place indeed.

Notes

Chapter 1

1 In antiquity the term 'Mesopotamia' was restricted to the northern part of this area.
2 Some scholars claim Herodotus obtained his data from informants.
3 For the original users, early 'alphabets' were simplified syllabic systems, in which each sign represented not a consonant alone but a consonant followed by one of several possible vowels.
4 It was also used to write Sumerian, Hittite, Hurrian, Urartian and occasionally other languages.
5 Rawlinson may not have been entirely wrong; see H. W. F. Saggs (ed.), *Nineveh and its Remains, by Henry Austen Layard* (London 1970), p. 41, n. 2.
6 J. Ross (ed.), *Letters from the East by Henry James Ross* (London 1902), p. 23.
7 Layard, *Early Adventures in Persia, Susiana, and Babylonia* II (London 1887), p. 368.
8 Layard, *Discoveries in the ruins of Nineveh and Babylon* (London 1853), p. 347.

Chapter 2

1 C. E. Larsen, 'The Mesopotamian Delta Region: A reconsideration of Lees and Falcon', *Journal of the American Oriental Society* 95 (1975), pp. 43–57.
2 The Museum of Prehistory, Schloss Charlottenburg, Berlin, has a figurine of fired clay of this date from Dolńi Vestonice, Moravia.
3 Some propose a date nearer to 5000 BC.
4 J. Oates, *Iraq* 31 (1969), p. 141.
5 A limestone tablet from Kish may be as early or earlier.
6 An heliacal rising of a planet is its first rising after it was invisible because of its position relative to the sun, and an heliacal setting is its last setting before it becomes invisible.
7 P. J. Huber, 'Astronomical Evidence for the Long and against the Middle and Short Chronologies', pp. 5–17 in P. Åström (ed.), *High, Middle or Low* (Gothenburg 1987).
8 W. Heimpel, L. Gorelick and A. J. Gwinnett, *Journal of Cuneiform Studies* 40 (1988), pp. 195–210. After the Agade period difficulties with supplies brought a decreasing use of hard stones for cylinder seals; see M. Sax, D. Collon, M. N. Leese, *Iraq* 55 (1993), pp. 77–90.
9 J. D. Muhly, *American Journal of Archaeology* 89 (1985), pp. 275–91.

Chapter 3

1 A. A. Vaiman, p. 24 in J. Harmatta and G. Komoróczy, *Wirtschaft und Gesellschaft im Alten Vorderasien* (Budapest 1974).

2 G. R. Driver and J. C. Miles, *The Babylonian Laws* II (Oxford 1955), pp. 64, 66, col. xiib, lines 37–77.

3 Driver and Miles, op. cit., p. 68, col. xiiib, lines 57–68.

4 Driver and Miles, op. cit., pp. 54, 56, col. viib, lines 33–59.

5 E. Sollberger and J.-R. Kupper, *Inscriptions Royales Sumériennes et Akkadiennes* (Paris 1971), p. 39, 1A2a. For the siting of Hamazi, see *Reallexikon der Assyriologie* 4 (Berlin 1972), pp. 70f.

6 See J. S. Cooper, *Reconstructing History from Ancient Inscriptions: The Lagash-Umma conflict* (Malibu 1983).

7 Some scholars see the Hebrew term ᶜeden as derived from this.

8 This was an abbreviated form of his full name; see Cooper, op. cit., p. 47, n. 1.

Chapter 4

1 M. C. Astour, *Eblaitica* 3 (1992), pp. 51ff., argues for an earlier empire based on Ebla.

2 C. Meyer, J. M. Todd, C. W. Beck, *Journal of Near Eastern Studies* 50 (1991), pp. 289–98.

3 B. R. Foster, *Umma in the Sargonic Period* (New Haven 1982), pp. 49–51. Labour camps may have played a larger part in early Sumer than commonly recognised. Th. Jacobsen, *Journal of Cuneiform Studies* 21 (1967), p. 100, argues that the place name Girsu, in the city-state of Lagash, meant 'naked captive(s)', so called because it was founded as a prisoner-of-war settlement.

4 See W. W. Hallo and J. Van Dijk, *The Exaltation of Inanna* (New Haven 1968), p. 3.

5 For a full list of these traditions see J. S. Cooper, *The Curse of Agade* (Baltimore 1983), p. 16.

6 I. M. Diakonoff, *Assyriological Studies* 20, pp. 104, 113ff.

7 I. M. Diakonoff, op. cit., pp. 113ff.

Chapter 5

1 Variants: 26 or 47 years.

2 Variant: 125 years.

3 S. N. Kramer, *Orientalia* 52 (1983), pp. 453–6.

4 S. N. Kramer, *Journal of Cuneiform Studies* 21 (1967), pp. 104–22.

5 A date formula makes it a one-way journey.

6 The exact number is uncertain, since some fragments could be lost pieces of other hymns.

7 P. Steinkeller, *Studies in Ancient Oriental Civilization* 46, pp. 36ff.

8 Some see a connection with the Old Testament tribal name Dedan or Dedanites of Isaiah 21:13, Jeremiah 25:23, Ezekiel 27:20, etc.

9 See S. N. Kramer, 'The marriage of Martu', pp. 11–27 in J. Klein and A. Skaist, *Bar-Ilan Studies in Assyriology dedicated to Pinhas Artzi* (Tel Aviv 1990).

Chapter 6

1 Steinkeller, op. cit., p. 22.
2 A. L. Oppenheim, 'The seafaring merchants of Ur', *Journal of the American Oriental Society* 74 (1954), pp. 6–17; W. F. Leemans, *Foreign Trade in the Old Babylonian Period* (Leiden 1960), pp. 18–56.
3 For a contemporary dynasty at Uruk, see R. D. Biggs and J. A. Brinkman (eds), *Studies presented to A. Leo Oppenheim* (Chicago 1964), p. 1.
4 F. R. Kraus, *Ein Edikt des Königs Ammi-saduqa von Babylon* (Leiden 1954).
5 More accurately Hammurapi^c.
6 I. J. Gelb, *Journal of the Institute of Asian Studies* 1 (1955), pp. 1–4.
7 J. M. Sasson, p. 252 in J.-M. Durand and J.-R. Kupper (eds), *Miscellanea Babylonica: Mélanges offerts à Maurice Birot* (Paris 1985).
8 For edition see G. R. Driver and J. C. Miles, *The Babylonian Laws* II (Oxford 1955).
9 Leemans, op. cit., p. 94.
10 Leemans, op. cit., p. 141.
11 Driver and Miles, op. cit., p. 6, col. ia, lines 1–49.
12 Cf. the reference in Ezekiel 8:14 to 'women weeping for Tammuz' (= Dumuzi).

Chapter 7

1 J. Zarins, *Journal of Cuneiform Studies* 30 (1978), pp. 4–10.
2 J. A. Brinkman, *Materials and Studies for Kassite History*, vol. 1 (Chicago 1976), p. 155, L. 2.12; p. 163, L. 3.2; p. 135, J. 2.17.
3 A. K. Grayson, *Assyrian and Babylonian Chronicles* (New York 1975), p. 176, lines 9–11.
4 A. Falkenstein and W. von Soden, *Sumerische und Akkadische Hymnen und Gebete* (Zürich/Stuttgart 1953), pp. 258f., no. 10.
5 L. W. King, *Babylonian Boundary-stones* (London 1912), p. 32, col. 1, lines 18–23, 28.
6 Farouk al-Rawi, *Revue d'Assyriologie* 86 (1992), p. 79, line 9.

Chapter 8

1 H. F. Lutz, *Selected Sumerian and Babylonian Texts* (Philadelphia 1919), no. 51, line 22.
2 J. Neumann and S. Parpola, *Journal of Near Eastern Studies* 46 (1987), pp. 161–82; P. Albert and J. Neumann, *Journal of Near Eastern Studies* 48 (1989), pp. 313–14.
3 See A. K. Grayson, *Assyrian Royal Inscriptions* 2 (Wiesbaden 1976), p. 53, n. 226.
4 H. W. F. Saggs, *Iraq* 17 (1955), p. 27, rev. 3'–5'.
5 W. G. Lambert, *Babylonian Wisdom Literature* (Oxford 1960), pp. 112, 114, lines 2–5, 11–13, 23–7, 31–4, 36–7. See also M. Dandamayer et al. (eds), *Studies . . . I. M. Diakonoff* (Warminster 1982), pp. 324–6.
6 F. Thureau-Dangin, *Rituels Accadiens* (Paris 1921), p. 144, lines 423–6. The extant text, though known only from the first millennium, reflects older practice and beliefs.

Chapter 9

1 L. Waterman, *Royal Correspondence of the Assyrian Empire* IV (Ann Arbor 1936), pp. 275ff.
2 A. L. Oppenheim, *Ancient Mesopotamia* (Chicago 1964), pp. 16f.
3 *Cuneiform Text from Babylonian Tablets in the British Museum* XXII (London 1906), pl. 1, no. 1.
4 *Catalogue of the Cuneiform Tablets in the Kouyunjik Collection of the British Museum* V (London 1899), p. xxii.

Chapter 10

1 Grayson, *Chronicles*, pp. 73–4, lines 33–7.
2 H. W. F. Saggs, *Iraq* 17 (1955), p. 23, I, lines 16f.
3 For variant traditions about this see J. Lewy, 'The chronology of Sennacherib's accession', *Archiv Orientálni* 12, pp. 225–31.
4 Waterman, op. cit. I, letter 238, rev. 6, 'there are many language groups in Nippur under the protection of the king my lord'.
5 For Assyrian references to this, see S. Parpola, pp. 171–82 in B. Alster (ed.), *Death in Mesopotamia* (Copenhagen 1980).
6 An Elamite raid on Sippar which a chronicle (Grayson, *Chronicles*, p. 83, iv, line 9) reports for Esarhaddon's sixth year was probably misplaced from twenty years earlier.
7 R. Borger, *Die Inschriften Asarhaddons* (Osnabrück 1967), pp. 25f., Episode 37.
8 See, e.g., J. A. Brinkman, *Prelude to Empire* (Philadelphia 1984), pp. 105f.; G. Frame, *Babylonia 689–627 B.C.* (Den Haag 1992), pp. 296–306.
9 *Abodah Zarah*, §11b.
10 S. N. Kramer, *Sumerian Mythology* (New York 1961), p. 77.

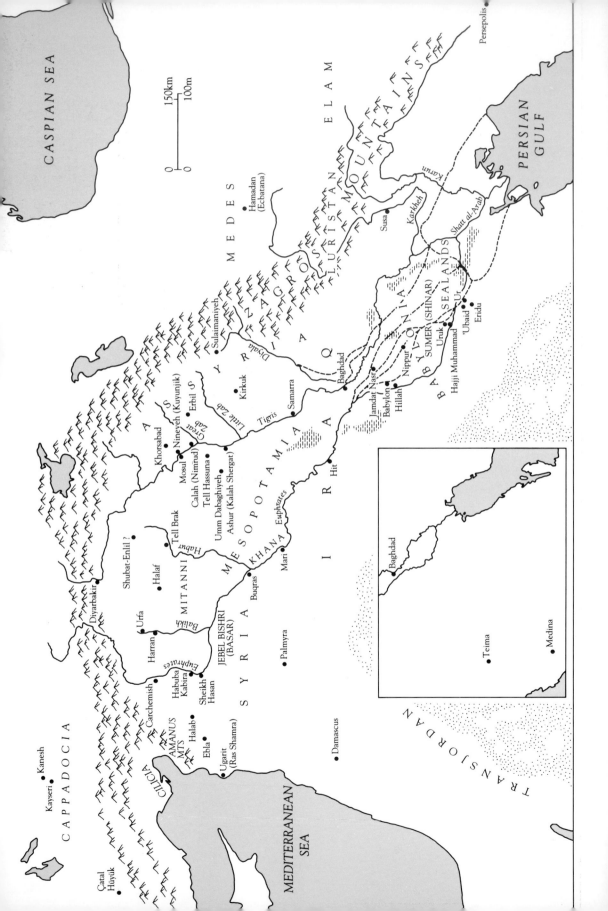

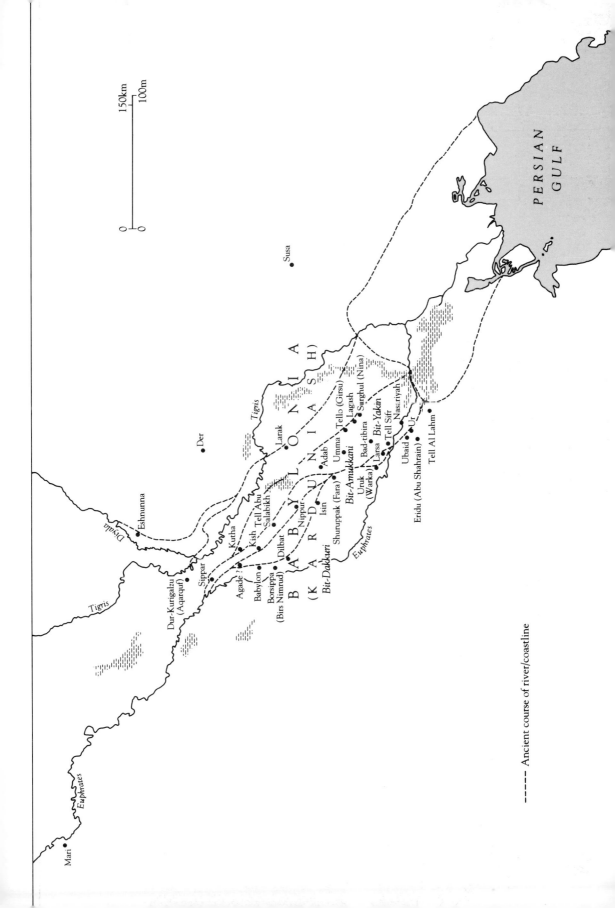

PERSIAN GULF

Susa

Der

Tigris

Eshnunna

Dur-Kurigalzu
(Aqarquf)

Sippar

Tigris

Mari

Euphrates

Agade ?

Babylon

Borsippa
(Birs Nimrud)

Kutha

Dilbat

Kish Tell Abu
Salabikh

Larak

Nippur

Isin

Shuruppak (Fara)

Adab

Umma Tello (Girsu)

Lagash

Surghul (Nina)

Bad-tibira

Bit-Amukkani

Uruk
(Warka)

Bit-Yakin

Larsa

Tell Sifr

Nasiriyah

Ubaid

Ur

Eridu (Abu Shahrain)

Tell Al Lahm

B A B Y L O N I A
(K A R - D U N I A S H)

Bit-Dakkuri

Euphrates

150km

100m

0

0

----- Ancient course of river/coastline

Chronological Chart

This outline gives only the main periods and the most important rulers and developments from the Late Uruk period onwards (all dates are BC). There is uncertainty in dating of about two centuries before 3000 BC, reducing to about half a century by 2000 BC and to less than a decade by 1000 BC.

3500   **Late Uruk (3500–3000)**
        Beginning of urbanisation,
        specialisation,
        writing,
3400   use of cylinder seals.
        Predominant language uncertain.
        Advances in irrigation.
        Uruk becomes first
3300   large urban
        complex (120–200 ha).
        Potter's wheel
        and plough invented.
3200   Monumental building;
        temples.
        Much use of copper.
        Deities increasingly
3100   anthropomorphic.

3000   **Jamdat Nasr (3000–2900)**
        Writing system now certainly represents Sumerian.
        Temple on platform as prototype of ziggurat.
        Further urban complexes developing.
2900   **Early Dynastic I (2900–2750)**
        Possible major Flood (Deluge traditions?).
        Technological advances
        in stone-working and building.
2800   More cities develop. Semitic speakers present
        in south Mesopotamia (perhaps much sooner).
      Early Dynastic II (2750–2600)
        Development of city-states. First Dynasty of Kish.
2700   Gilgamesh.
        Beginning of inter-city warfare.

Building of city defence walls.

Growth of temple estates.

2600 **Early Dynastic IIIa (2600–2500)**

Royal Tombs of Ur.

Earliest literary tablets from Abu Salabikh and Fara.

Growth of temple and royal estates.

2500 **Early Dynastic IIIb (2500–2371)**

Growing social stratification.

Increase in royal power. Sumerian writing and

institutions spread abroad.

2400

Agade period (*perhaps* **2371–c. 2200,** *but dates disputable*)

First empire founded by Sargon (2371–2316),

maintained by descendants until Naram-Sin (2291–2255).

2300 Trade links by sea with India.

Beginning of Amorite immigration.

Rebellion, invasion, imperial collapse.

Recovery of city-states.

2200 **Gutian period** (*date disputable*)

Some city-states

in south Babylonia

flourish.

2100 **Third Dynasty of Ur** (*commonly given as* **2113–2006,** *but perhaps earlier*)

Centralisation. Law-giving. Scribal schools. King controls temple estates.

International trade. Increasing Amorite immigration.

Demise of Sumerian as spoken language.

2000 **Isin-Larsa** (*or* **Old Babylonian Period,** *to include First Dynasty of Babylon*)

Breakdown of centralised government.

Growth of economy outside state sector.

Emergence of dynasties of Amorite origin.

1900 **First Dynasty of Babylon** (*commonly given as* **1894–1595,** *but perhaps earlier*)

Rise of Babylon from minor city

to become one of the major powers

in north Babylonia.

1800

Hammurabi (1792–1750) makes Babylon supreme.

'Code' of laws. Rigid social stratification.

Development of irrigation and agriculture.

1700 Distribution of land by grants to royal officers.

Flowering of literature and mathematics.

Rise of Kassites from Zagros, and Sealands dynasty in south.

Decline of dynasty of Babylon.

1600	Hittite raid on Babylon brings collapse (1595).

Kassite dynasty (c. 1570–1157)

Rise of Hurrians in north-west Mesopotamia and Syria.
Spread of Babylonian cultural influence.

1500	Beginning of use of horse for military purposes.

Assyria briefly a vassal of Hurrians.

1400	Babylonia enters into trading relations with Egypt.

Beginning of Aramaean migrations.
Considerable scribal activity in editing ancient texts.
Much building work.

1300	Assyria begins to dominate

Babylonia.
Tukulti-Ninurta I of Assyria takes Babylon and rules
for seven years. Subsequent Kassite recovery.

1200	Invasion by Elamites. Collapse of Kassite dynasty.

Second Dynasty of Isin (1156–1025)

Nebuchadnezzar I (1124–1103) inaugurates

1100	brief period of

expansion eastwards.
Babylonian
decline

1000	under pressure

from immigrant Aramaeans.
Weak native kings
in Babylonia.

900	

Assyrian intervention in Babylonian affairs.
Appearance of Chaldeans
in south Babylonia.

800	

Chaldean rulers briefly seize throne of Babylonia.

Assyrian hegemony

Merodach-baladan rebels and becomes king (721–710).

700	Sennacherib sacks Babylon (689).

Civil war (652–648); Assyrian victory.

Neo-Babylonian dynasty (626–539)

600	Nabopolassar (626–605). Attack on Assyrian empire jointly

with Medes. Nineveh taken (612).
Nebuchadnezzar II (604–562); major rebuilding of Babylon.
Nabonidus (555–539); economic and religious problems.

500	Cyrus the Persian conquers Babylonia (539).

Further Reading

THERE IS A considerable and growing literature on ancient Mesopotamian civilisation, but most of it is directed to those with a specialist background in the subject. The following is a selection of reliable works in English which do not require the reader to be a professional scholar.

The most fascinating works on Mesopotamian archaeology are still those of the first major British archaeologist of Mesopotamia, Austen Henry (christened Henry Austen) Layard, *Nineveh and its remains*, 2 vols (London, 1849 and later editions), and *Discoveries in the ruins of Nineveh and Babylon* (London, 1853). Despite its title, the first of these was not primarily about Nineveh. Both these works are in part books of travel, a device attempted by some other archaeologists of the nineteenth and twentieth centuries with less success.

David and Joan Oates, *The Rise of Civilization* (Elsevier-Phaidon, Oxford, 1976) is a well-written and authoritative account of Mesopotamian archaeology up to its publication date. Also both authoritative and readable is Seton Lloyd, *The Archaeology of Mesopotamia* (Thames & Hudson, London, 1978). Sir Leonard Woolley's own account of his important excavations at Ur is presented in an updated form in P.R.S. Moorey, *Ur 'of the Chaldees': A revised and updated edition of Sir Leonard Woolley's Excavations at Ur* (New York, 1982). J. Curtis (ed.), *Fifty Years of Mesopotamian Discovery* (British School of Archaeology in Iraq, 1982) gives a good outline of British excavations in Mesopotamia during the period indicated. For a reliable account of factors underlying the development of Mesopotamian civilisation see R. McC. Adams, *Heartland of Cities* (University of Chicago Press, 1981).

There is a useful brief introduction to ancient Mesopotamian history and culture in H.W.F. Saggs, *Everyday Life in Babylonia and Assyria* (Batsford, London, 1965 and Dorset Press, New York, 1987). Two readable books which give a fuller account are H.W.F. Saggs, *The Greatness that was Babylon* (Sidgwick & Jackson, London, 1962 and 1988) and G. Roux, *Ancient Iraq* (Penguin, Harmondsworth, 1964 and 1992). Also useful is J. Oates, *Babylon* (Thames & Hudson, London, 1979 and 1990). A. L. Oppenheim, *Ancient Mesopotamia* (University of Chicago Press, 1964, revised edition 1977) concentrates mainly upon the scribal achievement and in that area is unsurpassed. Putting the Mesopotamian achievement in the wider context of ancient civilisation as a whole is H.W.F. Saggs, *Civilisation before Greece and Rome* (Batsford, London, and Yale University Press, New Haven, 1989).

The late Th. Jacobsen of Harvard University made many important contributions to the understanding of the earlier phases of ancient Mesopotamian civilisation, and his contribution in H. Frankfort et al., *Before Philosophy* (Penguin, London and New York, 1949) is still worth reading; this work was also published by the University of Chicago Press as *The Intellectual Adventure of Ancient Man* (1946). Some of Jacobsen's best work is collected in *Towards the Image of Tammuz and Other Essays on Meso-potamian History and Culture*, edited by W. L. Moran (Harvard University Press, Cambridge, 1970), and *The Treasures of Darkness: A History of Mesopotamian Religion* (Yale University Press, New Haven, 1976). Another important book in the same area is S. N. Kramer, *The Sumerians* (University of Chicago Press, 1963). A useful companion to the latter is S. N. Kramer, *Sumerian Mythology* (Harper & Row, New York, 1961).

There is a good selection of translated texts from Mesopotamia and other parts of the ancient Near East in J. B. Pritchard (ed.), *Ancient Near Eastern Texts* (Princeton University Press, 1955 and later editions). A good up-to-date book on an important facet of ancient Mesopotamian literature is Stephanie Dalley, *Myths from Meso-potamia* (Oxford University Press, 1991). The best work on Wisdom literature, both readable and authoritative, is W. G. Lambert, *Babylonian Wisdom Literature* (Clar-endon Press, Oxford, 1960). A. L. Oppenheim's *Letters from Mesopotamia* (University of Chicago Press, 1967) gives the flavour of ancient Mesopotamian correspondence. For Babylonian mathematics and astronomy there are good sections in O. Neuge-bauer, *The Exact Sciences in Antiquities* (Princeton University Press, 1952; Harper & Row, New York, 1962). A. Moortgat, *The Art of Ancient Mesopotamia* (Phaidon, Oxford, 1969), an English translation of a German publication, gives an excellent account of its subject. There is a good introduction to cylinder seals in D. Collon, *First Impressions* (British Museum Publications, London, 1987 and 1993).

The most recent research usually appears first in articles in periodicals, of which the most important in English are *Iraq* (London), *Journal of Cuneiform Studies* (New Haven), *Journal of Near Eastern Studies* (Chicago), *Journal of the American Oriental Society* (Boston) and *American Journal of Archaeology* (Princeton). *Orientalia* (Rome) also frequently contains important relevant articles in English, as do sometimes *Journal of the Economic and Social History of the Orient* (Leiden) and *Sumer* (Baghdad).

Illustration Acknowledgements

Objects in the British Museum (Department of Western Asiatic Antiquities) are identified as WAA followed by their accession number.

COLOUR PLATES
(*between pages 64 and 65*)
I   Photo courtesy of the author
II WAA 127582 (left) and 127585 (right)
III Staatliche Museen zu Berlin–Preussischer Kulturbesitz, Vorderasiatisches Museum, VA 7248
IV Photo courtesy of the author
V   Staatliche Museen zu Berlin–Preussischer Kulturbesitz, Vorderasiatisches Museum, VA 10996
VI WAA 119296 (replica of original in the Iraq Museum, Baghdad, 4307)
VII WAA 121198A
VIII WAA ACa.55 (replica of original in the Iraq Museum, Baghdad, 8269)
IX Photo courtesy of the author
X   Staatliche Museen zu Berlin–Preussischer Kulturbesitz, Vorderasiatisches Museum, VAM F 297
XI Staatliche Museen zu Berlin–Preussischer Kulturbesitz, Vorderasiatisches Museum
XII WAA 122200

BLACK AND WHITE FIGURES
Frontispiece WAA 102485
1   WAA 89359, C. J. Rich Collection
2   National Portrait Gallery, London, 1797
3   Photograph courtesy of the author
4   WAA 114207
5   WAA 51.1–1.217
6   WAA 121201
7   WAA 91667
8   WAA 125380
9   Staatliche Museen zu Berlin–Preussischer Kulturbesitz, Vorderasiatisches Museum, VA 11965, VAN 6663
10 WAA 89769
11 WAA 114308
12 WAA 89110
13 Staatliche Museen zu Berlin–Preussischer Kulturbesitz, Vorderasiatisches Museum, VAN 8826
14 Staatliche Museen zu Berlin–Preussischer Kulturbesitz,

Vorderasiatisches Museum, VAN 72
15 Iraq Museum, Baghdad; Photo Hirmer Verlag, Munich
16 WAA 116721
17 Ashmolean Museum, Oxford, Department of Antiquities 1949.873
18 Iraq Museum, Baghdad; Photo Hirmer Verlag, Munich
19 WAA 120000
20 Photo courtesy of the author
21 WAA 134300
22 Ashmolean Museum, Oxford, Department of Antiquities 1926.564
23 Staatliche Museen zu Berlin–Preussischer Kulturbesitz, Vorderasiatisches Museum, VAN 11257
24 WAA 140853
25 WAA 140855
26 WAA 140852
27 WAA 140854
28 WAA 89769 (and others)
29 Ashmolean Museum, Oxford, Department of Antiquities 1964.744
30 WAA 91027
31 WAA 121545
32 Iraq Museum, Baghdad; Photo Hirmer Verlag, Munich
33 WAA 116754 (replica of original in the Iraq Museum, Baghdad)
34 WAA 121201
35 Musée du Louvre, Paris, Département des Antiquités Orientales, AO 2346
36 Musée du Louvre, Paris, Département des Antiquités Orientales, AO 2344
37 WAA 121201
38 WAA 120834, 1828.10–9.379a–n
39 Iraq Museum, Baghdad, 55639; Photo Hirmer Verlag, Munich
40 WAA 92687
41 WAA 133043
42 University of Pennsylvania Museum, Philadelphia (negative number S4–139330), CBS 16665
43 WAA 125929
44 Musée du Louvre, Paris, Département des Antiquités Orientales, SB4
45 WAA L1168 (on loan from the Musée du Louvre, Paris)
46 WAA 90852
47 WAA 102613
48 WAA 122910

49 Staatliche Museen zu Berlin–Preussischer Kulturbesitz, Vorderasiatisches Museum, VA 8790, VAN 7558
50 University of Pennsylvania Museum, Philadelphia (negative number S4–140070)
51 WAA Photo E3592
52 Iraq Museum, Baghdad, 23477; Photo Hirmer Verlag, Munich
53 WAA 113896
54 WAA 118560
55 WAA 91144
56 WAA 22454
57 WAA 102462
58 WAA 98493 (replica of original in the Musée du Louvre, Paris)
59 WAA 15285
60 WAA 116624
61 WAA 29785
62 WAA 102485
63 Staatliche Museen zu Berlin–Preussischer Kulturbesitz, Vorderasiatisches Museum, VA 10983
64 WAA 90858
65 Staatliche Museen zu Berlin–Preussischer Kulturbesitz, Vorderasiatisches Museum, VA 8384, VAN 761
66 WAA 118882
67 WAA 33238
68 Photo courtesy of Professor Farouk al-Rawi
69 WAA 92668
70 WAA 117759
71 WAA 86263
72 WAA 129480
73 WAA 91000
74 WAA 90922
75 Staatliche Museen zu Berlin–Preussischer Kulturbesitz, Vorderasiatisches Museum, VA 2663, VAN 8983
76 WAA 124774b
77 WAA 124931
78 WAA 124925–6
79 Staatliche Museen zu Berlin–Preussischer Kulturbesitz, Vorderasiatisches Museum, VAN 3600
80 Photo courtesy of the author
81 Musée du Louvre, Paris, Département des Antiquités Orientales, AO 4106
82 WAA 40837
83 WAA 119307

Index of Biblical References

General Index

Page entries in italics indicate figures.

Abieshu 114
Abraham 101
Abu Salabikh 78, 145
Abu Shahrain 16, 25
abzu 34, 37
Achaemenid empire 10, 21 48, 142
Adab 18
Adad 122, 167
Adad-guppi 167–9
Adad-narari I 119
Adad-shuma-usur 120
adultery 103, 105, 107
Afghanistan 38, 121, 132, 171
Agade (city) 29, 84, 102; dynasty and
     empire 29, 66, 68–75, 89–91, 128
Agga 60–1
agriculture 20, 98
Agum I 116
Agum II (Agum-kakrime) 116
Ahlamu 129, 132
Akhenaton 116
Akitu (festival and temple) 131, 136,
     167
Akkad, Akkadê *see* Agade
Akkadian language 11, 17, 29–30, 32,
     67, 78 9, 102, 108, 116, 140
Akurgal 62
Alexander the Great 9, 142, 172
alphabet: Canaanite-Phoenician 141;
     Greek 140
Al-Hiba 18
Al-Ukhaimir 16
Amanus 33, 101
Amar-Sin 90
ambassadors 98, 117–18; *see also*
     diplomacy
Amel-Marduk 167
Amenophis III and IV 116, *118*
Ammiditana 114
Ammisaduqa 28, 97, 114
'Amori (Amorites in Bible) 91
Amorites 31, 90, 92 4, 97, 99, 126, 128
Amraphel, king of Shinar 101
amulets 146, 150
Amurru *see* Amorites
Amurru (a god) 93
An, Anu 37, 102, 111, 122, 126, 152
Anatolia 101
Andrae, W. 18
Antu 122
Anzu 108, 151
Apsu 126
Arabs 158–9, 161, *162*, 163
Aramaeans 117, 127–35, 136, 138,
     140–1, 153, 156, 158–9, 161
Aramaic language and inscriptions 134,
     140, *141*, 141–3
Aratta 32, 38
archaeological terminology 23–4
architecture 40, 60, *124*, pl. V
archives 15, 71, 76, 101, 105, 145–6
art, religious 34, 38, 40
Asag 34
Asaluhi *see* Marduk
Ashur 89, 98, 101, 119–20, 131, 144–5,
     164
Ashurbanipal 15, 144–8, 160–3, 166,
     171

Ashur-bel-kala 129, 132, 139
Ashur-bel-nisheshu 116
Ashur-dan I 121
Ashur-dan II 130, 139
Ashur-etil-ilani 163
Ashur-nadin-shumi 157
Ashur-nasir-pal 120
Ashur-nasir-pal II 132, 153
Ashur-resh-ishi 129
Ashur-uballit I 118–19, 122
Ashur-uballit II 164
Asmar *see* Eshnunna
assembly 33, 51–2, 54, 87, 104
Assyria 98, 101, 115–16, 118–19, 125,
     138
astrology 175
astronomical texts 142, 149;
     observations of Venus 27–8, 114
Astyages 170
Azupiranu 67

Babil, Babila 7, 9, 97
Babylon 7, 9, 15, 18, 20–1, 68, 80, 90,
     100–102, 107, 114, 119, 131–3, 135,
     137–8 et passim; Alexander's
     intended capital 172; capture by
     Cyrus 171–2; capture by Tukulti-
     Ninurta I 119–20; First Dynasty 94,
     97, 114; Hanging Gardens 20, 165,
     167; in the Bible and classics 172;
     legacy and traditions 172–5, *174*;
     origin 97; palaces 166–7; rebuilding
     by Nebuchadnezzar 165
Babylonia: building 122; Chaldean
     kings 153; civil war 161; under
     Esarhaddon 159–60; religious
     influence 120
Bad-tibira 60
Basar 92
Belshazzar 20, 169–71
Bel-ibni 157
Bel-iqisha 159
Benjamin of Tudela 9
Benjaminites 92
Berossus 163
Beth-eden *see* Bit-Adini
Bible 17, 103, 130
Birs Nimrud 9, 16, pl. I
Bisitun 10, 142
Bismaya 18
Bit-Adini 131–2
Bit-Amukkani 134, 154, 157
Bit-Bakhiani 130
Bit-Bazi 131
Bit-Dakkuri 134, 157, 159
Bit-Khalupe 130
Bit-Sha'alli 134, 157
Bit-Shilani 134
Bit-Yakin 134, 154, 157
Bit-Zamani 130
boats *41*, 68, 97, 152; *see also* shipping
Borsippa 9, 16, 102, 131–2, 135,
     146–7, 155–6, 159, 166, 171, pl. I
Botta, Paul-Emile 12
bricks, types of 43
bride-price 106–7
British Museum 12–13, 15, 18

bronze 38
Bull of Heaven 111
Buqras 26
Burna-Buriash I 116
Burna-Buriash II 117–18, *118*

Calah 45, 142, 146; *see also* Nimrud
calendar 37, 88, 174
Cambyses 172
Canaan 129; Canaanites 92, 173
cannibalism 151, 161
Canning, Sir Stratford 13
Cappadocia 70
Carchemish 101, 129–31, 164
carnelian 38, 89, 121
Çatal Hüyük 23
Chaldeans 133–5, 138, 153–4, *156*,
     157, 161
Choga Mami 24–5
chronicles 67, 75, 80, 98, 116–17,
     119–20, 131–2, 135, 144, 155, 157,
     160, 163–4, 168
chronology 26, 60, 66, 83, 114, 139
Cilicia 101
cities, early 7–9, 20–1, 23, 26, 30, 34–7,
     40–6
civilisation, beginning of 8 9, 17, 23,
     30–2
clay tablets 46, 48, 115, *143*
clay tokens 46, 47
climatic change 22, 81, 91, 129–30
colophons 143–6
conservation 87
copper 26, 38, 101
corvée service 55, 133
creation: Babylonian concepts 173;
     cosmic 37; of man 151
crescent (in Islam) 175
Crete 100–1, 140
cuneiform 10, 76–7, 116, 125, 140;
     alphabetic script 145; inscriptions
     15 16, 18–19, 92, 130; lists of signs
     144
Cyaxares 163–4
cylinder seals 26, 33, 34, 38, *38*, 40, *42*,
     46, 48–51, *49*, *50*, 60, 64, 100, 104,
     121, 143, *152*, *174*
Cyrus the Persian 142, 169–72

Damascus 130, 133, 143
Darius 142, 172
date formulae 96, 99, 113
David 130
debts, royal decrees cancelling 97
defence walls 33, 61, 91, 93, 96, 165–7
deities, anthropomorphic 35; *see also*
     individual names
demons 149–50
deportation 154, 161
Der 96, 98, 153, 155
Didanum, Didnum 91
Dilbat 102
Dilmun 32, 67
Diodorus Siculus 167
diplomacy 115, 121, 125, 141
disease 37, 107
divination 20, 87, 147, *148*, 173

M7100 –IL
4 ⊗